ABOUT THIS PUBLICATION

FOR SERVICE ASSISTANCE

Customer Service Department
704.898.0770

North Carolina General Statues is published by The Muliti-Media Group of Greater Charlotte in Charlotte, North Carolina. Copyright 2015 by the Multi-Media Group of Greater Charlotte. This book or parts thereof may not be reproduced in any form, stored in a retrieval system, or transmitted in any form by any means—electronic, mechanical, photocopy, recording or otherwise—without prior written permission of the publisher, except as provided by United States of America copyright law.

The records required by U.S. Code 2257(a) through (c) and the pertinent regulations 28 C.F.R. Cli. 1, Part 75 with respect to this publication and all materials associated with such records are maintained by The Multi-Media Group of Greater Charlotte, Publisher and available for review by Attorney General.

www.visionbooks.org

Copyright © 2015 by MMGGC
All rights reserved!

TID: 4994007
ISBN (10) digit: 150233674X
ISBN (13) digit: 978-1502336743

123-4-56789-01234-Paperback
123-4-56789-01234-Hardback

First Edition

090520140547

Printed in the United States of America

2015 EDITION

North Carolina Criminal Law And Procedure-Pamphlet # 13

Printed In conjunction with the Administration of the Courts

North Carolina Criminal Law and Procedure
Pamphlet Reference Guide

Chapters	Pamphlet
Chapter 1 Civil Procedure	1
Chapter 1 Civil Procedure (Continue)	2
Chapter 1A Rules of Civil Procedure	2
Chapter 1B Contribution.	2
Chapter 1C Enforcement of Judgments.	2
Chapter 1D Punitive Damages.	2
Chapter 1E Eastern Band of Cherokee Indians.	2
Chapter 1F North Carolina Uniform Interstate Depositions and Discovery Act.	2
Chapter 2 - Clerk of Superior Court [Repealed and Transferred.]	3
Chapter 3 - Commissioners of Affidavits and Deeds [Repealed.]	3
Chapter 4 - Common Law	3
Chapter 5 - Contempt [Repealed.]	3
Chapter 5A - Contempt	3
Chapter 6 - Liability for Court Costs	3
Chapter 7 - Courts [Repealed and Transferred.]	3
Chapter 7A – Judicial Department	3
Chapter 7A – Continuation (Judicial Department)	4
Chapter 7A – Continuation (Judicial Department)	5
Chapter 7B - Juvenile Code	5
Chapter 8 - Evidence	6
Chapter 8A - Interpreters for Deaf Persons [Recodified.]	6
Chapter 8B - Interpreters for Deaf Persons	6
Chapter 8C - Evidence Code	6
Chapter 9 - Jurors	6
Chapter 10 - Notaries [Repealed.]	6
Chapter 10A - Notaries [Recodified.]	6
Chapter 10B - Notaries	6
Chapter 11 - Oaths	6
Chapter 12 - Statutory Construction	6
Chapter 13 - Citizenship Restored	6
Chapter 14 - Criminal Law	7
Chapter 14 –Criminal Law (Continuation)	8
Chapter 15 - Criminal Procedure	9
Chapter 15A - Criminal Procedure Act (Continuation)	10
Chapter 15A - Criminal Procedure Act (Continuation)	11
Chapter 15B - Victims Compensation	11
Chapter 15C - Address Confidentiality Program	11
Chapter 16 - Gaming Contracts and Futures	11
Chapter 17 - Habeas Corpus	11

Chapter 17A - Law-Enforcement Officers [Recodified.] 11
Chapter 17B - North Carolina Criminal Justice 11
Education and Training System [Recodified.] Chapter 17C - North Carolina
Criminal Justice Education and Training Standards Commission 11
Chapter 17D - North Carolina Justice Academy 11
Chapter 17E - North Carolina Sheriffs' Education and
Training Standards Commission 11
Chapter 18 - Regulation of Intoxicating Liquors [Repealed.] 12
Chapter 18A - Regulation of Intoxicating Liquors [Repealed.] 12
Chapter 18B - Regulation of Alcoholic Beverages 12
Chapter 18C - North Carolina State Lottery 12
Chapter 19 - Offenses against Public Morals 12
Chapter 19A - Protection of Animals 12
Chapter 20 - Motor Vehicles 13
Chapter 20 - Motor Vehicles (Continuation) 14
Chapter 20 - Motor Vehicles (Continuation) 15
Chapter 20 - Motor Vehicles (Continuation) 16
Chapter 21 - Bills of Lading 17
Chapter 22 - Contracts Requiring Writing 17
Chapter 22A - Signatures 17
Chapter 22B - Contracts Against Public Policy 17
Chapter 22C - Payments to Subcontractors 17
Chapter 23 - Debtor and Creditor 17
Chapter 24 – Interest 17
Chapter 25 – Uniform Commercial Code 18
Chapter 25 – Uniform Commercial Code (Continuation) 19
Chapter 25A – Retail Installment Sales Act 20
Chapter 25B - Credit 20
Chapter 25C - Sales of Artwork 20
Chapter 26 - Suretyship 20
Chapter 27 - Warehouse Receipts [Repealed.] 20
Chapter 28 - Administration [Repealed.] 20
Chapter 28A - Administration of Decedents' Estates 20
Chapter 28B - Estates of Absentees in Military Service 20
Chapter 28C - Estates of Missing Persons 20
Chapter 29 - Intestate Succession 21
Chapter 30 - Surviving Spouses 21
Chapter 31 - Wills 21
Chapter 31A - Acts Barring Property Rights 21
Chapter 31B - Renunciation of Property and Renunciation of
Fiduciary Powers Act 21
Chapter 31C - Uniform Disposition of Community Property
Rights at Death Act 21
Chapter 32 - Fiduciaries 21
Chapter 32A - Powers of Attorney 21
Chapter 33 - Guardian and Ward [Repealed and Recodified.] 21

Chapter 33A - North Carolina Uniform Transfers to Minors Act	21
Chapter 33B - North Carolina Uniform Custodial Trust Act	21
Chapter 34 - Veterans' Guardianship Act	22
Chapter 35 - Sterilization Procedures	22
Chapter 35A - Incompetency and Guardianship	22
Chapter 36 - Trusts and Trustees [Repealed.]	22
Chapter 36A - Trusts and Trustees	22
Chapter 36B - Uniform Management of Institutional Funds Act [Repealed.]	22
Chapter 36C - North Carolina Uniform Trust Code	22
Chapter 36D - North Carolina Community Third Party Trusts, Pooled Trusts	23
Chapter 36E - Uniform Prudent Management of Institutional Funds Act	23
Chapter 37 - Allocation of Principal and Income [Repealed.]	23
Chapter 37A - Uniform Principal and Income Act	23
Chapter 38 - Boundaries	23
Chapter 38A - Landowner Liability	23
Chapter 39 - Conveyances	23
Chapter 39A - Transfer Fee Covenants Prohibited	23
Chapter 40 - Eminent Domain [Repealed.]	23
Chapter 40A - Eminent Domain	23
Chapter 41 - Estates	23
Chapter 41A - State Fair Housing Act	23
Chapter 42 - Landlord and Tenant	23
Chapter 42A - Vacation Rental Act	23
Chapter 43 - Land Registration	23
Chapter 44 - Liens	24
Chapter 44A - Statutory Liens and Charges	24
Chapter 45 - Mortgages and Deeds of Trust	24
Chapter 45A - Good Funds Settlement Act	24
Chapter 46 - Partition	24
Chapter 47 - Probate and Registration	25
Chapter 47A - Unit Ownership	25
Chapter 47B - Real Property Marketable Title Act	25
Chapter 47C - North Carolina Condominium Act	25
Chapter 47D - Notice of Settlement Act [Expired.]	25
Chapter 47E - Residential Property Disclosure Act	25
Chapter 47F - North Carolina Planned Community Act	25
Chapter 47G - Option to Purchase Contracts	25
Chapter 47H - Contracts for Deed	25
Chapter 48 - Adoptions +	26
Chapter 48A - Minors	26
Chapter 49 - Bastardy	26
Chapter 49A - Rights of Children	26
Chapter 50 - Divorce and Alimony	26
Chapter 50A - Uniform Child-Custody Jurisdiction and	

Enforcement Act	26
Chapter 50B - Domestic Violence	26
Chapter 50C - Civil No-Contact Orders	26
Chapter 51 - Marriage	26
Chapter 52 - Powers and Liabilities of Married Persons	27
Chapter 52A - Uniform Reciprocal Enforcement of Support Act [Repealed.]	27
Chapter 52B - Uniform Premarital Agreement Act	27
Chapter 52C - Uniform Interstate Family Support Act	27
Chapter 53 - Banks	27
Chapter 53A - Business Development Corporations and North Carolina Capital Resource Corporations	28
Chapter 53B - Financial Privacy Act	28
Chapter 54 - Cooperative Organizations	28
Chapter 54A - Capital Stock Savings and Loan Associations [Repealed.]	28
Chapter 54B - Savings and Loan Associations	29
Chapter 54C - Savings Banks	29
Chapter 55 - North Carolina Business Corporation Act	30
Chapter 55A - North Carolina Nonprofit Corporation Act	31
Chapter 55B - Professional Corporation Act	31
Chapter 55C - Foreign Trade Zones	31
Chapter 55D - Filings, Names, and Registered Agents for Corporations, Nonprofit Corporations, and Partnerships	31
Chapter 56 - Electric, Telegraph and Power Companies [Repealed.]	31
Chapter 57 - Hospital, Medical and Dental Service Corporations [Recodified.]	31
Chapter 57A - Health Maintenance Organization Act [Recodified.]	31
Chapter 57B - Health Maintenance Organization Act [Recodified.]	31
Chapter 57C - North Carolina Limited Liability Company Act.	31
Chapter 58 - Insurance.	32
Chapter 58 - Insurance (Continuation)	33
Chapter 58 - Insurance (Continuation)	34
Chapter 58 - Insurance (Continuation)	35
Chapter 58 - Insurance (Continuation)	36
Chapter 58 - Insurance (Continuation)	37
Chapter 58 - Insurance (Continuation)	38
Chapter 58A - North Carolina Health Insurance Trust Commission [Recodified.]	38
Chapter 59 - Partnership.	39
Chapter 59B - Uniform Unincorporated Nonprofit Association Act.	39
Chapter 60 - Railroads and Other Carriers [Repealed and Transferred.]	39
Chapter 61 - Religious Societies	39
Chapter 62 - Public Utilities	39

Chapter 62 - Public Utilities (Continuation)	40
Chapter 62A - Public Safety Telephone Service And Wireless Telephone Service	40
Chapter 63 - Aeronautics	40
Chapter 63A - North Carolina Global TransPark Authority	40
Chapter 64 - Aliens	40
Chapter 65 – Cemeteries	40
Chapter 66 - Commerce and Business	41
Chapter 67 - Dogs	41
Chapter 68 - Fences and Stock Law	41
Chapter 69 - Fire Protection	41
Chapter 70 - Indian Antiquities, Archaeological Resources and Unmarked Human Skeletal Remains Protection	42
Chapter 71 - Indians [Repealed.]	42
Chapter 71A - Indians	42
Chapter 72 - Inns, Hotels and Restaurants	42
Chapter 73 - Mills	42
Chapter 74 - Mines and Quarries	42
Chapter 74A - Company Police [Repealed.]	42
Chapter 74B - Private Protective Services Act [Repealed.]	42
Chapter 74C - Private Protective Services	42
Chapter 74D - Alarm Systems	42
Chapter 74E - Company Police Act	42
Chapter 74F - Locksmith Licensing Act	42
Chapter 74G - Campus Police Act	42
Chapter 75 - Monopolies, Trusts and Consumer Protection	42
Chapter 75A - Boating and Water Safety	43
Chapter 75B - Discrimination in Business	43
Chapter 75C - Motion Picture Fair Competition Act	43
Chapter 75D - Racketeer Influenced and Corrupt Organizations	43
Chapter 75E - Unlawful Activities in Connection With Certain Corporate Transactions	43
Chapter 76 - Navigation	43
Chapter 76A - Navigation and Pilotage Commissions	43
Chapter 77 - Rivers, Creeks, and Coastal Waters	43
Chapter 78 - Securities Law [Repealed.]	43
Chapter 78A - North Carolina Securities Act	43
Chapter 78B - Tender Offer Disclosure Act [Repealed.]	43
Chapter 78C - Investment Advisers	43
Chapter 78D - Commodities Act	43
Chapter 79 - Strays [Repealed.]	43
Chapter 80 - Trademarks, Brands, etc.	44
Chapter 81 - Weights and Measures [Recodified.]	44
Chapter 81A - Weights and Measures Act of 1975.	44
Chapter 82 - Wrecks [Repealed.]	44
Chapter 83 - Architects [Recodified.]	44

Chapter 83A - Architects	44
Chapter 84 - Attorneys-at-Law	44
Chapter 84A - Foreign Legal Consultants	44
Chapter 85 - Auctions and Auctioneers [Repealed.]	44
Chapter 85A - Bail Bondsmen and Runners [Recodified.]	44
Chapter 85B - Auctions and Auctioneers	44
Chapter 85C - Bail Bondsmen and Runners [Recodified.]	44
Chapter 86 - Barbers [Recodified.]	44
Chapter 86A - Barbers	44
Chapter 87 - Contractors	44
Chapter 88 - Cosmetic Art [Repealed.]	44
Chapter 88A - Electrolysis Practice Act	44
Chapter 88B - Cosmetic Art	45
Chapter 89 - Engineering and Land Surveying [Recodified.]	45
Chapter 89A - Landscape Architects	45
Chapter 89B - Foresters	45
Chapter 89C - Engineering and Land Surveying	45
Chapter 89D - Landscape Contractors	45
Chapter 89E - Geologists Licensing Act	45
Chapter 89F - North Carolina Soil Scientist Licensing Act	45
Chapter 89G - Irrigation Contractors	45
Chapter 90 - Medicine and Allied Occupations	45
Chapter 90 - Medicine and Allied Occupations (Continuation)	46
Chapter 90 - Medicine and Allied Occupations (Continuation)	47
Chapter 90 - Medicine and Allied Occupations (Continuation)	48
Chapter 90A - Sanitarians and Water and Wastewater Treatment Facility Operators	48
Chapter 90B - Social Worker Certification and Licensure Act	48
Chapter 90C - North Carolina Recreational Therapy Licensure Act	48
Chapter 90D - Interpreters and Transliterators	48
Chapter 91 - Pawnbrokers [Repealed.]	48
Chapter 91A - Pawnbrokers Modernization Act of 1989	48
Chapter 92 - Photographers [Deleted.]	48
Chapter 93 - Certified Public Accountants	48
Chapter 93A - Real Estate License Law	49
Chapter 93B - Occupational Licensing Boards	49
Chapter 93C - Watchmakers [Repealed.]	49
Chapter 93D - North Carolina State Hearing Aid Dealers and Fitters Board.	49
Chapter 93E - North Carolina Appraisers Act	49
Chapter 94 - Apprenticeship	49
Chapter 95 - Department of Labor and Labor Regulations	49
Chapter 95 - Department of Labor and Labor Regulations (Continuation)	50
Chapter 96 - Employment Security	50
Chapter 97 - Workers' Compensation Act	50
Chapter 97 - Workers' Compensation Act (Continuation)	51

Chapter 98 - Burnt and Lost Records	51
Chapter 99 - Libel and Slander	51
Chapter 99A - Civil Remedies for Criminal Actions	51
Chapter 99B - Products Liability	51
Chapter 99C - Actions Relating to Winter Sports Safety and Accidents	51
Chapter 99D - Civil Rights	51
Chapter 99E - Special Liability Provisions	51
Chapter 100 - Monuments, Memorials and Parks	51
Chapter 101 - Names of Persons	51
Chapter 102 - Official Survey Base	51
Chapter 103 - Sundays, Holidays and Special Days	51
Chapter 104 - United States Lands	51
Chapter 104A - Degrees of Kinship	51
Chapter 104B - Hurricanes or Other Acts of Nature	51
Chapter 104C - Atomic Energy, Radioactivity and Ionizing Radiation [Repealed and Recodified.]	51
Chapter 104D - Southern States Energy Compact	51
Chapter 104E - North Carolina Radiation Protection Act	51
Chapter 104F - Southeast Interstate Low-Level Radioactive Waste Management Compact [Repealed]	51
Chapter 104G - North Carolina Low-Level Radioactive Waste Management Authority Act of 1987 [Repealed]	51
Chapter 105 - Taxation	51
Chapter 105 - Taxation (Continuation)	52
Chapter 105 - Taxation (Continuation)	53
Chapter 105 - Taxation (Continuation)	54
Chapter 105A - Setoff Debt Collection Act	55
Chapter 105B - Defaulted Student Loan Recovery Act	55
Chapter 106 - Agriculture	55
Chapter 106 - Agriculture (Continue)	56
Chapter 106 - Agriculture (Continue)	57
Chapter 107 - Agricultural Development Districts [Repealed.]	57
Chapter 108 - Social Services [Repealed and Recodified.]	57
Chapter 108A - Social Services	57
Chapter 108B - Community Action Programs	58
Chapter 108C Medicaid and Health Choice Provider Requirements.	58
Chapter 108D Medicaid Managed Care for Behavioral Health Services.	58
Chapter 109 - Bonds [Recodified.]	58
Chapter 110 - Child Welfare	58
Chapter 111 - Aid to the Blind	58
Chapter 112 - Confederate Homes and Pensions [Repealed.]	58
Chapter 113 - Conservation and Development	58
Chapter 113 - Conservation and Development (Continuation)	59

Chapter 113A - Pollution Control and Environment	59
Chapter 113A - Pollution Control and Environment (Continuation)	60
Chapter 113B - North Carolina Energy Policy Act of 1975	60
Chapter 114 - Department of Justice	60
Chapter 115 - Elementary and Secondary Education [Repealed.]	60
Chapter 115A - Community Colleges, Technical Institutes, and Industrial Education Centers [Repealed.]	60
Chapter 115B - Tuition and Fee Waivers	60
Chapter 115C - Elementary and Secondary Education	60
Chapter 115C - Elementary and Secondary Education (Continuation)	61
Chapter 115C - Elementary and Secondary Education (Continuation)	62
Chapter 115C - Elementary and Secondary Education (Continuation)	63
Chapter 115D - Community Colleges	63
Chapter 115E - Private Educational Facilities Finance Act [Recodified]	63
Chapter 116 - Higher Education	63
Chapter 116 - Higher Education (Continuation)	63
Chapter 116A - Escheats and Abandoned Property [Repealed.]	64
Chapter 116B - Escheats and Abandoned Property	64
Chapter 116C - Continuum of Education Programs	64
Chapter 116D - Higher Education Bonds	64
Chapter 117 - Electrification	64
Chapter 118 - Firemen's and Rescue Squad Workers' Relief and Pension Funds [Recodified.]	64
Chapter 118A - Firemen's Death Benefit Act [Repealed.]	64
Chapter 118B - Members of a Rescue Squad Death Benefit Act [Repealed.]	64
Chapter 119 - Gasoline and Oil Inspection and Regulation	64
Chapter 120 - General Assembly	65
Chapter 120 - General Assembly (Continuation)	66
Chapter 120 - General Assembly (Continuation)	67
Chapter 120C - Lobbying	67
Chapter 121 - Archives and History	67
Chapter 122 - Hospitals for the Mentally Disordered [Repealed.]	67
Chapter 122A - North Carolina Housing Finance Agency	67
Chapter 122B - North Carolina Agricultural Facilities Finance Act [Repealed.]	67
Chapter 122C - Mental Health, Developmental Disabilities, and Substance Abuse Act of 1985	67
Chapter 122C - Mental Health, Developmental Disabilities, and Substance Abuse Act of 1985 (Continuation)	68
Chapter 122D - North Carolina Agricultural Finance Act	68

Chapter 122E - North Carolina Housing Trust and Oil Overcharge Act	68
Chapter 123 - Impeachment	69
Chapter 123A - Industrial Development [Repealed.]	69
Chapter 124 - Internal Improvements	69
Chapter 125 - Libraries	69
Chapter 126 - State Personnel System	69
Chapter 127 - Militia [Repealed.]	69
Chapter 127A - Militia	69
Chapter 127B - Military Affairs	69
Chapter 127C - Advisory Commission on Military Affairs	69
Chapter 128 - Offices and Public Officers	69
Chapter 128 - Offices and Public Officers (Continuation)	70
Chapter 129 - Public Buildings and Grounds	70
Chapter 130 - Public Health [Repealed.]	70
Chapter 130A - Public Health	70
Chapter 130A - Public Health (Continuation)	71
Chapter 130A - Public Health (Continuation)	72
Chapter 130B - Hazardous Waste Management Commission [Repealed.]	72
Chapter 131 - Public Hospitals [Repealed.]	72
Chapter 131A - Health Care Facilities Finance Act	72
Chapter 131B - Licensing of Ambulatory Surgical Facilities [Repealed.]	72
Chapter 131C - Charitable Solicitation Licensure Act [Repealed.]	72
Chapter 131D - Inspection and Licensing of Facilities	72
Chapter 131E - Health Care Facilities and Services	72
Chapter 131E - Health Care Facilities and Services (Continuation)	73
Chapter 131F - Solicitation of Contributions	73
Chapter 132 - Public Records	73
Chapter 133 - Public Works	74
Chapter 134 - Youth Development [Recodified.]	74
Chapter 134A - Youth Services [Repealed.]	74
Chapter 135 - Retirement System for Teachers and State Employees; Social Security; Health Insurance Program for Children	74
Chapter 135 - Retirement System for Teachers and State Employees; Social Security; Health Insurance Program for Children	75
Chapter 136 - Transportation	75
Chapter 136 - Transportation (Continuation)	76
Chapter 137 - Rural Rehabilitation [Repealed.]	76
Chapter 138 - Salaries, Fees and Allowances	76
Chapter 138A - State Government Ethics Act	76
Chapter 139 - Soil and Water Conservation Districts	76

Chapter 140 - State Art Museum; Symphony and Art Societies	76
Chapter 140A - State Awards System	76
Chapter 141 - State Boundaries	76
Chapter 142 - State Debt	76
Chapter 143 - State Departments, Institutions, and Commissions	77
Chapter 143 - State Departments, Institutions, and Commissions (Continuation)	78
Chapter 143 - State Departments, Institutions, and Commissions (Continuation)	79
Chapter 143 - State Departments, Institutions, and Commissions (Continuation)	80
Chapter 143A - State Government Reorganization	80
Chapter 143B - Executive Organization Act of 1973	80
Chapter 143B - Executive Organization Act of 1973 (Continuation)	81
Chapter 143B - Executive Organization Act of 1973 (Continuation)	82
Chapter 143C - State Budget Act	83
Chapter 143D - The State Governmental Accountability and Internal Control Act	83
Chapter 144 - State Flag, Official Governmental Flags, Motto, and Colors	83
Chapter 145 - State Symbols and Other Official Adoptions.	83
Chapter 146 - State Lands	83
Chapter 147 - State Officers	83
Chapter 148 - State Prison System	84
Chapter 149 - State Song and Toast	84
Chapter 150 - Uniform Revocation of Licenses [Repealed.]	84
Chapter 150A - Administrative Procedure Act [Recodified.]	84
Chapter 150B - Administrative Procedure Act	84
Chapter 151 - Constables [Repealed.]	84
Chapter 152 - Coroners	84
Chapter 152A - County Medical Examiner [Repealed.]	84
Chapter 152A - County Medical Examiner [Repealed.] (Continuation)	85
Chapter 153 - Counties and County Commissioners [Repealed.]	85
Chapter 153A - Counties	85
Chapter 153B - Mountain Resources Planning Act	85
Chapter 153C - Uwharrie Regional Resources Act	85
Chapter 154 - County Surveyor [Repealed.]	85
Chapter 155 - County Treasurer [Repealed.]	85
Chapter 156 - Drainage	85
Chapter 156 – Drainage (Continuation)	86

Chapter 157 - Housing Authorities and Projects	86
Chapter 157A - Historic Properties Commissions [Transferred.]	86
Chapter 158 - Local Development	86
Chapter 159 - Local Government Finance	86
Chapter 159 - Local Government Finance (Continuation)	87
Chapter 159A - Pollution Abatement and Industrial Facilities Financing Act [Unconstitutional.]	87
Chapter 159B - Joint Municipal Electric Power and Energy Act	87
Chapter 159C - Industrial and Pollution Control Facilities Financing Act	87
Chapter 159D - The North Carolina Capital Facilities Financing Act	87
Chapter 159E - Registered Public Obligations Act	87
Chapter 159F - North Carolina Energy Development Authority [Repealed.]	87
Chapter 159G - Water Infrastructure	87
Chapter 159H - [Reserved.]	87
Chapter 159I - Solid Waste Management Loan Program and Local Government Special Obligation Bonds	87
Chapter 160 - Municipal Corporations [Repealed And Transferred.]	87
Chapter 160A - Cities and Towns	88
Chapter 160A - Cities and Towns (Continuation)	89
Chapter 160B - Consolidated City-County Act	89
Chapter 160C - Baseball Park Districts [Repealed.]	90
Chapter 161 - Register of Deeds	90
Chapter 162 - Sheriff	90
Chapter 162A - Water and Sewer Systems	90
Chapter 162B Continuity of Local Government in Emergency.	90
Chapter 163 Elections and Election Laws.	90
Chapter 163 Elections and Election Laws. (Continuation)	91
Chapter 164 Concerning the General Statutes of North Carolina.	92
Chapter 165 Veterans.	92
Chapter 166 Civil Preparedness Agencies [Repealed.]	92
Chapter 166A North Carolina Emergency Management Act.	92
Chapter 167 State Civil Air Patrol [Repealed.]	92
Chapter 168 Persons with Disabilities.	92
Chapter 168A Persons With Disabilities Protection Act.	92

Chapter 20.

Motor Vehicles.

Article 1.

Division of Motor Vehicles.

§ 20-1. Division of Motor Vehicles established.

The Division of Motor Vehicles of the Department of Transportation is established. This Chapter sets out the powers and duties of the Division. (1941, c. 36, s. 1; 1949, c. 1167; 1973, c. 476, s. 193; 1975, c. 716, s. 5; c. 863; 1987, c. 827, s. 2; c. 847, s. 1; 1995 (Reg. Sess., 1996), c. 756, s. 1.)

§ 20-2. Commissioner of Motor Vehicles; rules.

(a)   Commissioner and Assistants. - The Division of Motor Vehicles shall be administered by the Commissioner of Motor Vehicles, who shall be appointed by and serve at the pleasure of the Secretary of the Department of Transportation. The Commissioner shall be paid an annual salary to be fixed by the Governor and allowed traveling expenses as allowed by law.

In any action, proceeding, or matter of any kind, to which the Commissioner of Motor Vehicles is a party or in which he may have an interest, all pleadings, legal notices, proof of claim, warrants for collection, certificates of tax liability, executions, and other legal documents, may be signed and verified on behalf of the Commissioner of Motor Vehicles by the Assistant Commissioner of Motor Vehicles or by any director or assistant director of any section of the Division of Motor Vehicles or by any other agent or employee of the Division so authorized by the Commissioner of Motor Vehicles.

(b)   Rules. - The Commissioner may adopt rules to implement this Chapter. Chapter 150B of the General Statutes governs the adoption of rules by the Commissioner. (1941, c. 36, s. 2; 1945, c. 527; 1955, c. 472; 1975, c. 716, s. 5; 1983, c. 717, s. 5; 1983 (Reg. Sess., 1984), c. 1034, s. 164; 1991, c. 477, s. 4; 2012-142, s. 25.1(b).)

§ 20-3. Organization of Division.

The Commissioner, subject to the approval of the Secretary of the Department of Transportation, shall organize and administer the Division in such manner as he may deem necessary to conduct the work of the Division. (1941, c. 36, s. 3; 1975, c. 716, s. 5.)

§ 20-3.1. Purchase of additional airplanes.

The Division of Motor Vehicles shall not purchase additional airplanes without the express authorization of the General Assembly. (1963, c. 911, s. 1 1/2; 1971, c. 198; 1975, c. 716, s. 5.)

§ 20-4: Repealed by Session Laws 2002-190, s. 4, effective January 1, 2003.

§ 20-4.01. Definitions.

Unless the context requires otherwise, the following definitions apply throughout this Chapter to the defined words and phrases and their cognates:

(1a)   Alcohol. - Any substance containing any form of alcohol, including ethanol, methanol, propanol, and isopropanol.

(1b)   Alcohol Concentration. - The concentration of alcohol in a person, expressed either as:

a.   Grams of alcohol per 100 milliliters of blood; or

b.   Grams of alcohol per 210 liters of breath.

The results of a defendant's alcohol concentration determined by a chemical analysis of the defendant's breath or blood shall be reported to the hundredths. Any result between hundredths shall be reported to the next lower hundredth.

(1c)   All-Terrain Vehicle or ATV. - A motorized vehicle 50 inches or less in width that is designed to travel on three or more low-pressure tires and manufactured for off-highway use. The terms "all-terrain vehicle" or "ATV" do not include a golf cart or a utility vehicle, as defined in this section, or a riding lawn mower.

(1d)   Business District. - The territory prescribed as such by ordinance of the Board of Transportation.

(2) Canceled. - As applied to drivers' licenses and permits, a declaration that a license or permit which was issued through error or fraud, or to which G.S. 20-15(a)(3) applies, is void and terminated.

(2a) Class A Motor Vehicle. - A combination of motor vehicles that meets either of the following descriptions:

a. Has a combined GVWR of at least 26,001 pounds and includes as part of the combination a towed unit that has a GVWR of at least 10,001 pounds.

b. Has a combined GVWR of less than 26,001 pounds and includes as part of the combination a towed unit that has a GVWR of at least 10,001 pounds.

(2b) Class B Motor Vehicle. - Any of the following:

a. A single motor vehicle that has a GVWR of at least 26,001 pounds.

b. A combination of motor vehicles that includes as part of the combination a towing unit that has a GVWR of at least 26,001 pounds and a towed unit that has a GVWR of less than 10,001 pounds.

(2c) Class C Motor Vehicle. - Any of the following:

a. A single motor vehicle not included in Class B.

b. A combination of motor vehicles not included in Class A or Class B.

(3) Repealed by Session Laws 1979, c. 667, s. 1.

(3a) Chemical Analysis. - A test or tests of the breath, blood, or other bodily fluid or substance of a person to determine the person's alcohol concentration or presence of an impairing substance, performed in accordance with G.S. 20-139.1, including duplicate or sequential analyses.

(3b) Chemical Analyst. - A person granted a permit by the Department of Health and Human Services under G.S. 20-139.1 to perform chemical analyses.

(3c) Commercial Drivers License (CDL). - A license issued by a state to an individual who resides in the state that authorizes the individual to drive a class of commercial motor vehicle. A "nonresident commercial drivers license

(NRCDL)" is issued by a state to an individual who resides in a foreign jurisdiction.

(3d)   Commercial Motor Vehicle. - Any of the following motor vehicles that are designed or used to transport passengers or property:

a.   A Class A motor vehicle that has a combined GVWR of at least 26,001 pounds and includes as part of the combination a towed unit that has a GVWR of at least 10,001 pounds.

b.   A Class B motor vehicle.

c.   A Class C motor vehicle that meets either of the following descriptions:

1.   Is designed to transport 16 or more passengers, including the driver.

2.   Is transporting hazardous materials and is required to be placarded in accordance with 49 C.F.R. Part 172, Subpart F.

d.   Repealed by Session Laws 1999, c. 330, s. 9, effective December 1, 1999.

(4)   Commissioner. - The Commissioner of Motor Vehicles.

(4a)   Conviction. - A conviction for an offense committed in North Carolina or another state:

a.   In-State. When referring to an offense committed in North Carolina, the term means any of the following:

1.   A final conviction of a criminal offense, including a no contest plea.

2.   A determination that a person is responsible for an infraction, including a no contest plea.

3.   An unvacated forfeiture of cash in the full amount of a bond required by Article 26 of Chapter 15A of the General Statutes.

4.   A third or subsequent prayer for judgment continued within any five-year period.

5. Any prayer for judgment continued if the offender holds a commercial drivers license or if the offense occurs in a commercial motor vehicle.

b. Out-of-State. When referring to an offense committed outside North Carolina, the term means any of the following:

1. An unvacated adjudication of guilt.

2. A determination that a person has violated or failed to comply with the law in a court of original jurisdiction or an authorized administrative tribunal.

3. An unvacated forfeiture of bail or collateral deposited to secure the person's appearance in court.

4. A violation of a condition of release without bail, regardless of whether or not the penalty is rebated, suspended, or probated.

5. A final conviction of a criminal offense, including a no contest plea.

6. Any prayer for judgment continued, including any payment of a fine or court costs, if the offender holds a commercial drivers license or if the offense occurs in a commercial motor vehicle.

(4b) Crash. - Any event that results in injury or property damage attributable directly to the motion of a motor vehicle or its load. The terms collision, accident, and crash and their cognates are synonymous.

(5) Dealer. - Every person engaged in the business of buying, selling, distributing, or exchanging motor vehicles, trailers, or semitrailers in this State, and having an established place of business in this State.

The terms "motor vehicle dealer," "new motor vehicle dealer," and "used motor vehicle dealer" as used in Article 12 of this Chapter have the meaning set forth in G.S. 20-286.

(5a) Dedicated natural gas vehicle. - A four-wheeled motor vehicle that meets each of the following requirements:

a. Is made by a manufacturer primarily for use on public streets, roads, and highways and meets National Highway Traffic Safety Administration standards included in 49 C.F.R. § 571.

b.   Has not been modified from original manufacturer specifications with regard to power train or any manner of powering the vehicle.

c.   Is powered solely by natural gas.

d.   Is rated at not more than 8,500 pounds unloaded gross vehicle weight.

e.   Has a maximum speed capability of at least 65 miles per hour.

(5b)   Disqualification. - A withdrawal of the privilege to drive a commercial motor vehicle.

(6)   Division. - The Division of Motor Vehicles acting directly or through its duly authorized officers and agents.

(7)   Driver. - The operator of a vehicle, as defined in subdivision (25). The terms "driver" and "operator" and their cognates are synonymous.

(7a)   Electric Personal Assistive Mobility Device. - A self-balancing nontandem two-wheeled device, designed to transport one person, with a propulsion system that limits the maximum speed of the device to 15 miles per hour or less.

(7b)   Employer. - Any person who owns or leases a commercial motor vehicle or assigns a person to drive a commercial motor vehicle and would be subject to the alcohol and controlled substance testing provisions of 49 C.F.R. § 382 and also includes any consortium or third-party administrator administering the alcohol and controlled substance testing program on behalf of owner-operators subject to the provisions of 49 C.F.R. § 382.

(8)   Essential Parts. - All integral and body parts of a vehicle of any type required to be registered hereunder, the removal, alteration, or substitution of which would tend to conceal the identity of the vehicle or substantially alter its appearance, model, type, or mode of operation.

(9)   Established Place of Business. - Except as provided in G.S. 20-286, the place actually occupied by a dealer or manufacturer at which a permanent business of bargaining, trading, and selling motor vehicles is or will be carried on and at which the books, records, and files necessary and incident to the

conduct of the business of automobile dealers or manufacturers shall be kept and maintained.

(10)   Explosives. - Any chemical compound or mechanical mixture that is commonly used or intended for the purpose of producing an explosion and which contains any oxidizing and combustive units or other ingredients in such proportions, quantities, or packing that an ignition by fire, by friction, by concussion, by percussion, or by detonator of any part of the compound or mixture may cause such a sudden generation of highly heated gases that the resultant gaseous pressures are capable of producing destructible effects on contiguous objects or of destroying life or limb.

(11)   Farm Tractor. - Every motor vehicle designed and used primarily as a farm implement for drawing plows, mowing machines, and other implements of husbandry.

(11a)   For-Hire Motor Carrier. - A person who transports passengers or property by motor vehicle for compensation.

(12)   Foreign Vehicle. - Every vehicle of a type required to be registered hereunder brought into this State from another state, territory, or country, other than in the ordinary course of business, by or through a manufacturer or dealer and not registered in this State.

(12a)   Fuel cell electric vehicle. - A four-wheeled motor vehicle that meets each of the following requirements:

a.   Is made by a manufacturer primarily for use on public streets, roads, and highways and meets National Highway Traffic Safety Administration standards included in 49 C.F.R. § 571.

b.   Has not been modified from original manufacturer specifications with regard to power train or any manner of powering the vehicle.

c.   Uses hydrogen and a fuel cell to produce electricity on board to power an electric motor to propel the vehicle.

d.   Is rated at not more than 8,500 pounds unloaded gross vehicle weight.

e.   Has a maximum speed capability of at least 65 miles per hour.

(12b)   Golf Cart. - A vehicle designed and manufactured for operation on a golf course for sporting or recreational purposes and that is not capable of exceeding speeds of 20 miles per hour.

(12c)   Gross Combination Weight Rating (GCWR). - Defined in 49 C.F.R. § 390.5.

(12d)   Gross Combined Weight (GCW). - The total weight of a combination (articulated) motor vehicle, including passengers, fuel, cargo, and attachments.

(12e)   Gross Vehicle Weight (GVW). - The total weight of a vehicle, including passengers, fuel, cargo, and attachments.

(12f)   Gross Vehicle Weight Rating (GVWR). - The value specified by the manufacturer as the maximum loaded weight a vehicle is capable of safely hauling. The GVWR of a combination vehicle is the GVWR of the power unit plus the GVWR of the towed unit or units. When a vehicle is determined by an enforcement officer to be structurally altered in any way from the manufacturer's original design in an attempt to increase the hauling capacity of the vehicle, the GVWR of that vehicle shall be deemed to be the greater of the license weight or the total weight of the vehicle or combination of vehicles for the purpose of enforcing this Chapter. For the purpose of classification of commercial drivers license and skills testing, the manufacturer's GVWR shall be used.

(12g)   Hazardous Materials. - Any material that has been designated as hazardous under 49 U.S.C. § 5103 and is required to be placarded under Subpart F of Part 172 of Title 49 of the Code of Federal Regulations, or any quantity of a material listed as a select agent or toxin under Part 73 of Title 42 of the Code of Federal Regulations.

(13)   Highway. - The entire width between property or right-of-way lines of every way or place of whatever nature, when any part thereof is open to the use of the public as a matter of right for the purposes of vehicular traffic. The terms "highway" and "street" and their cognates are synonymous.

(14)   House Trailer. - Any trailer or semitrailer designed and equipped to provide living or sleeping facilities and drawn by a motor vehicle.

(14a)   Impairing Substance. - Alcohol, controlled substance under Chapter 90 of the General Statutes, any other drug or psychoactive substance capable of impairing a person's physical or mental faculties, or any combination of these substances.

(15) Implement of Husbandry. - Every vehicle which is designed for agricultural purposes and used exclusively in the conduct of agricultural operations.

(15a) Inoperable Vehicle. - A motor vehicle that is substantially disassembled and for this reason is mechanically unfit or unsafe to be operated or moved upon a public street, highway, or public vehicular area.

(16) Intersection. - The area embraced within the prolongation of the lateral curblines or, if none, then the lateral edge of roadway lines of two or more highways which join one another at any angle whether or not one such highway crosses the other.

Where a highway includes two roadways 30 feet or more apart, then every crossing of each roadway of such divided highway by an intersecting highway shall be regarded as a separate intersection. In the event that such intersecting highway also includes two roadways 30 feet or more apart, then every crossing of two roadways of such highways shall be regarded as a separate intersection.

(17) License. - Any driver's license or any other license or permit to operate a motor vehicle issued under or granted by the laws of this State including:

a. Any temporary license or learner's permit;

b. The privilege of any person to drive a motor vehicle whether or not such person holds a valid license; and

c. Any nonresident's operating privilege.

(18) Local Authorities. - Every county, municipality, or other territorial district with a local board or body having authority to adopt local police regulations under the Constitution and laws of this State.

(19) Manufacturer. - Every person, resident, or nonresident of this State, who manufactures or assembles motor vehicles.

(20) Manufacturer's Certificate. - A certification on a form approved by the Division, signed by the manufacturer, indicating the name of the person or

dealer to whom the therein-described vehicle is transferred, the date of transfer and that such vehicle is the first transfer of such vehicle in ordinary trade and commerce. The description of the vehicle shall include the make, model, year, type of body, identification number or numbers, and such other information as the Division may require.

(21) Metal Tire. - Every tire the surface of which in contact with the highway is wholly or partly of metal or other hard, nonresilient material.

(21a) Moped. - A type of passenger vehicle as defined in G.S. 105-164.3.

(21b) Motor Carrier. - A for-hire motor carrier or a private motor carrier.

(22) Motorcycle. - A type of passenger vehicle as defined in G.S. 20-4.01(27).

(23) Motor Vehicle. - Every vehicle which is self-propelled and every vehicle designed to run upon the highways which is pulled by a self-propelled vehicle. This shall not include mopeds as defined in G.S. 20-4.01(27)d1.

(24) Nonresident. - Any person whose legal residence is in some state, territory, or jurisdiction other than North Carolina or in a foreign country.

(24a) Offense Involving Impaired Driving. - Any of the following offenses:

a. Impaired driving under G.S. 20-138.1.

b. Any offense set forth under G.S. 20-141.4 when conviction is based upon impaired driving or a substantially similar offense under previous law.

c. First or second degree murder under G.S. 14-17 or involuntary manslaughter under G.S. 14-18 when conviction is based upon impaired driving or a substantially similar offense under previous law.

d. An offense committed in another jurisdiction which prohibits substantially similar conduct prohibited by the offenses in this subsection.

e. A repealed or superseded offense substantially similar to impaired driving, including offenses under former G.S. 20-138 or G.S. 20-139.

f.   Impaired driving in a commercial motor vehicle under G.S. 20-138.2, except that convictions of impaired driving under G.S. 20-138.1 and G.S. 20-138.2 arising out of the same transaction shall be considered a single conviction of an offense involving impaired driving for any purpose under this Chapter.

g.   Habitual impaired driving under G.S. 20-138.5.

A conviction under former G.S. 20-140(c) is not an offense involving impaired driving.

(25)   Operator. - A person in actual physical control of a vehicle which is in motion or which has the engine running. The terms "operator" and "driver" and their cognates are synonymous.

(25a)   Out of Service Order. - A declaration that a driver, a commercial motor vehicle, or a motor carrier operation is out-of-service.

(26)   Owner. - A person holding the legal title to a vehicle, or in the event a vehicle is the subject of a chattel mortgage or an agreement for the conditional sale or lease thereof or other like agreement, with the right of purchase upon performance of the conditions stated in the agreement, and with the immediate right of possession vested in the mortgagor, conditional vendee or lessee, said mortgagor, conditional vendee or lessee shall be deemed the owner for the purpose of this Chapter. For the purposes of this Chapter, the lessee of a vehicle owned by the government of the United States shall be considered the owner of said vehicle.

(27)   Passenger Vehicles. -

a.   Excursion passenger vehicles. - Vehicles transporting persons on sight-seeing or travel tours.

b.   For hire passenger vehicles. - Vehicles transporting persons for compensation. This classification shall not include vehicles operated as ambulances; vehicles operated by the owner where the costs of operation are shared by the passengers; vehicles operated pursuant to a ridesharing arrangement as defined in G.S. 136-44.21; vehicles transporting students for the public school system under contract with the State Board of Education or vehicles leased to the United States of America or any of its agencies on a nonprofit basis; or vehicles used for human service or volunteer transportation.

c. Common carriers of passengers. - Vehicles operated under a certificate of authority issued by the Utilities Commission for operation on the highways of this State between fixed termini or over a regular route for the transportation of persons for compensation.

c1. Child care vehicles. - Vehicles under the direction and control of a child care facility, as defined in G.S. 110-86(3), and driven by an owner, employee, or agent of the child care facility for the primary purpose of transporting children to and from the child care facility, or to and from a place for participation in an event or activity in connection with the child care facility.

d. Motorcycles. - Vehicles having a saddle for the use of the rider and designed to travel on not more than three wheels in contact with the ground, including motor scooters and motor-driven bicycles, but excluding tractors and utility vehicles equipped with an additional form of device designed to transport property, three-wheeled vehicles while being used by law-enforcement agencies and mopeds as defined in subdivision d1 of this subsection.

d1. Moped. - Defined in G.S. 105-164.3.

d2. Motor home or house car. - A vehicular unit, designed to provide temporary living quarters, built into as an integral part, or permanently attached to, a self-propelled motor vehicle chassis or van. The vehicle must provide at least four of the following facilities: cooking, refrigeration or icebox, self-contained toilet, heating or air conditioning, a portable water supply system including a faucet and sink, separate 110-125 volt electrical power supply, or an LP gas supply.

d3. School activity bus. - A vehicle, generally painted a different color from a school bus, whose primary purpose is to transport school students and others to or from a place for participation in an event other than regular classroom work. The term includes a public, private, or parochial vehicle that meets this description.

d4. School bus. - A vehicle whose primary purpose is to transport school students over an established route to and from school for the regularly scheduled school day, that is equipped with alternately flashing red lights on the front and rear and a mechanical stop signal, that is painted primarily yellow below the roofline, and that bears the plainly visible words "School Bus" on the front and rear. The term includes a public, private, or parochial vehicle that meets this description.

e. U-drive-it passenger vehicles. - Passenger vehicles included in the definition of U-drive-it vehicles set forth in this section.

f. Ambulances. - Vehicles equipped for transporting wounded, injured, or sick persons.

g. Private passenger vehicles. - All other passenger vehicles not included in the above definitions.

h. Low-speed vehicle. A four-wheeled electric vehicle whose top speed is greater than 20 miles per hour but less than 25 miles per hour.

(28) Person. - Every individual, firm, partnership, association, corporation, governmental agency, or combination thereof of whatsoever form or character.

(28a) Plug-in electric vehicle. - A four-wheeled motor vehicle that meets each of the following requirements:

a. Is made by a manufacturer primarily for use on public streets, roads, and highways and meets National Highway Traffic Safety Administration standards included in 49 C.F.R. § 571.

b. Has not been modified from original manufacturer specifications with regard to power train or any manner of powering the vehicle.

c. Is rated at not more than 8,500 pounds unloaded gross vehicle weight.

d. Has a maximum speed capability of at least 65 miles per hour.

e. Draws electricity from a battery that has all of the following characteristics:

1. A capacity of not less than four kilowatt hours.

2. Capable of being recharged from an external source of electricity.

(29) Pneumatic Tire. - Every tire in which compressed air is designed to support the load.

(29a)   Private Motor Carrier. - A person who transports passengers or property by motor vehicle in interstate commerce and is not a for-hire motor carrier.

(30)   Private Road or Driveway. - Every road or driveway not open to the use of the public as a matter of right for the purpose of vehicular traffic.

(31)   Property-Hauling Vehicles. -

a.   Vehicles used for the transportation of property.

b., c.   Repealed by Session Laws 1995 (Regular Session, 1996), c. 756, s. 4.

d.   Semitrailers. - Vehicles without motive power designed for carrying property or persons and for being drawn by a motor vehicle, and so constructed that part of their weight or their load rests upon or is carried by the pulling vehicle.

e.   Trailers. - Vehicles without motive power designed for carrying property or persons wholly on their own structure and to be drawn by a motor vehicle, including "pole trailers" or a pair of wheels used primarily to balance a load rather than for purposes of transportation.

f.   Repealed by Session Laws 1995 (Regular Session, 1996), c. 756, s. 4.

(31a)   Provisional Licensee. - A person under the age of 18 years.

(32)   Public Vehicular Area. - Any area within the State of North Carolina that meets one or more of the following requirements:

a.   The area is used by the public for vehicular traffic at any time, including by way of illustration and not limitation any drive, driveway, road, roadway, street, alley, or parking lot upon the grounds and premises of any of the following:

1.   Any public or private hospital, college, university, school, orphanage, church, or any of the institutions, parks or other facilities maintained and supported by the State of North Carolina or any of its subdivisions.

2.   Any service station, drive-in theater, supermarket, store, restaurant, or office building, or any other business, residential, or municipal establishment

providing parking space whether the business or establishment is open or closed.

3. Any property owned by the United States and subject to the jurisdiction of the State of North Carolina. (The inclusion of property owned by the United States in this definition shall not limit assimilation of North Carolina law when applicable under the provisions of Title 18, United States Code, section 13).

b. The area is a beach area used by the public for vehicular traffic.

c. The area is a road used by vehicular traffic within or leading to a gated or non-gated subdivision or community, whether or not the subdivision or community roads have been offered for dedication to the public.

d. The area is a portion of private property used by vehicular traffic and designated by the private property owner as a public vehicular area in accordance with G.S. 20-219.4.

(32a) Recreational Vehicle. - A vehicular type unit primarily designed as temporary living quarters for recreational, camping, or travel use that either has its own motive power or is mounted on, or towed by, another vehicle. The basic entities are camping trailer, fifth-wheel travel trailer, motor home, travel trailer, and truck camper.

a. Motor home. - As defined in G.S. 20-4.01(27)d2.

b. Travel trailer. - A vehicular unit mounted on wheels, designed to provide temporary living quarters for recreational, camping, or travel use, and of a size or weight that does not require a special highway movement permit when towed by a motorized vehicle.

c. Fifth-wheel trailer. - A vehicular unit mounted on wheels designed to provide temporary living quarters for recreational, camping, or travel use, of a size and weight that does not require a special highway movement permit and designed to be towed by a motorized vehicle that contains a towing mechanism that is mounted above or forward of the tow vehicle's rear axle.

d. Camping trailer. - A vehicular portable unit mounted on wheels and constructed with collapsible partial side walls that fold for towing by another vehicle and unfold at the campsite to provide temporary living quarters for recreational, camping, or travel use.

e. Truck camper. - A portable unit that is constructed to provide temporary living quarters for recreational, camping, or travel use, consisting of a roof, floor, and sides and is designed to be loaded onto and unloaded from the bed of a pickup truck.

(32b) Regular Drivers License. - A license to drive a commercial motor vehicle that is exempt from the commercial drivers license requirements or a noncommercial motor vehicle.

(33) a. Flood Vehicle. - A motor vehicle that has been submerged or partially submerged in water to the extent that damage to the body, engine, transmission, or differential has occurred.

b. Non-U.S.A. Vehicle. - A motor vehicle manufactured outside of the United States and not intended by the manufacturer for sale in the United States.

c. Reconstructed Vehicle. - A motor vehicle of a type required to be registered hereunder that has been materially altered from original construction due to removal, addition or substitution of new or used essential parts; and includes glider kits and custom assembled vehicles.

d. Salvage Motor Vehicle. - Any motor vehicle damaged by collision or other occurrence to the extent that the cost of repairs to the vehicle and rendering the vehicle safe for use on the public streets and highways would exceed seventy-five percent (75%) of its fair retail market value, whether or not the motor vehicle has been declared a total loss by an insurer. Repairs shall include the cost of parts and labor. Fair market retail values shall be as found in the NADA Pricing Guide Book or other publications approved by the Commissioner.

e. Salvage Rebuilt Vehicle. - A salvage vehicle that has been rebuilt for title and registration.

f. Junk Vehicle. - A motor vehicle which is incapable of operation or use upon the highways and has no resale value except as a source of parts or scrap, and shall not be titled or registered.

(33a) Relevant Time after the Driving. - Any time after the driving in which the driver still has in his body alcohol consumed before or during the driving.

(33b) Reportable Crash. - A crash involving a motor vehicle that results in one or more of the following:

a. Death or injury of a human being.

b. Total property damage of one thousand dollars ($1,000) or more, or property damage of any amount to a vehicle seized pursuant to G. S. 20-28.3.

(33c) Reserve components of the Armed Forces of the United States. - The organizations listed in Title 10 United States Code, section 10101, which specifically includes the Army and Air National Guard.

(34) Resident. - Any person who resides within this State for other than a temporary or transitory purpose for more than six months shall be presumed to be a resident of this State; but absence from the State for more than six months shall raise no presumption that the person is not a resident of this State.

(35) Residential District. - The territory prescribed as such by ordinance of the Department of Transportation.

(36) Revocation or Suspension. - Termination of a licensee's or permittee's privilege to drive or termination of the registration of a vehicle for a period of time stated in an order of revocation or suspension. The terms "revocation" or "suspension" or a combination of both terms shall be used synonymously.

(37) Road Tractors. - Vehicles designed and used for drawing other vehicles upon the highway and not so constructed as to carry any part of the load, either independently or as a part of the weight of the vehicle so drawn.

(38) Roadway. - That portion of a highway improved, designed, or ordinarily used for vehicular travel, exclusive of the shoulder. In the event a highway includes two or more separate roadways the term "roadway" as used herein shall refer to any such roadway separately but not to all such roadways collectively.

(39) Safety Zone. - Traffic island or other space officially set aside within a highway for the exclusive use of pedestrians and which is so plainly marked or indicated by proper signs as to be plainly visible at all times while set apart as a safety zone.

(40) Security Agreement. - Written agreement which reserves or creates a security interest.

(41) Security Interest. - An interest in a vehicle reserved or created by agreement and which secures payments or performance of an obligation. The term includes but is not limited to the interest of a chattel mortgagee, the interest of a vendor under a conditional sales contract, the interest of a trustee under a chattel deed of trust, and the interest of a lessor under a lease intended as security. A security interest is "perfected" when it is valid against third parties generally.

(41a) Serious Traffic Violation. - A conviction of one of the following offenses when operating a commercial or other motor vehicle:

a. Excessive speeding, involving a single charge of any speed 15 miles per hour or more above the posted speed limit.

b. Careless and reckless driving.

c. A violation of any State or local law relating to motor vehicle traffic control, other than a parking violation, arising in connection with a fatal accident.

d. Improper or erratic lane changes.

e. Following the vehicle ahead too closely.

f. Driving a commercial motor vehicle without obtaining a commercial drivers license.

g. Driving a commercial motor vehicle without a commercial drivers license in the driver's possession.

h. Driving a commercial motor vehicle without the proper class of commercial drivers license or endorsements for the specific vehicle group being operated or for the passenger or type of cargo being transported.

(42) Solid Tire. - Every tire of rubber or other resilient material which does not depend upon compressed air for the support of the load.

(43) Specially Constructed Vehicles. - Motor vehicles required to be registered under this Chapter and that fit within one of the following categories:

a. Replica vehicle. - A vehicle, excluding motorcycles, that when assembled replicates an earlier year, make, and model vehicle.

b. Street rod vehicle. - A vehicle, excluding motorcycles, manufactured prior to 1949 that has been materially altered or has a body constructed from nonoriginal materials.

c. Custom-built vehicle. - A vehicle, including motorcycles, reconstructed or assembled by a nonmanufacturer from new or used parts that has an exterior that does not replicate or resemble any other manufactured vehicle. This category also includes any motorcycle that was originally sold unassembled and manufactured from a kit or that has been materially altered or that has a body constructed from nonoriginal materials.

(44) Special Mobile Equipment. - Defined in G.S. 105-164.3.

(44a) Specialty Vehicles. - Vehicles of a type required to be registered under this Chapter that are modified from their original construction for an educational, emergency services, or public safety use.

(45) State. - A state, territory, or possession of the United States, District of Columbia, Commonwealth of Puerto Rico, a province of Canada, or the Sovereign Nation of the Eastern Band of the Cherokee Indians with tribal lands, as defined in 18 U.S.C. § 1151, located within the boundaries of the State of North Carolina. For provisions in this Chapter that apply to commercial drivers licenses, "state" means a state of the United States and the District of Columbia.

(46) Street. - A highway, as defined in subdivision (13). The terms "highway" and "street" and their cognates are synonymous.

(47) Suspension. - Termination of a licensee's or permittee's privilege to drive or termination of the registration of a vehicle for a period of time stated in an order of revocation or suspension. The terms "revocation" or "suspension" or a combination of both terms shall be used synonymously.

(48) Truck Tractors. - Vehicles designed and used primarily for drawing other vehicles and not so constructed as to carry any load independent of the vehicle so drawn.

(48a) U-drive-it vehicles. - The following vehicles that are rented to a person, to be operated by that person:

a. A private passenger vehicle other than the following:

1. A private passenger vehicle of nine-passenger capacity or less that is rented for a term of one year or more.

2. A private passenger vehicle that is rented to public school authorities for driver-training instruction.

b. A property-hauling vehicle under 7,000 pounds that does not haul products for hire and that is rented for a term of less than one year.

c. Motorcycles.

(48b) Under the Influence of an Impairing Substance. - The state of a person having his physical or mental faculties, or both, appreciably impaired by an impairing substance.

(48c) Utility Vehicle. - A motor vehicle that is (i) designed for off-road use and (ii) used for general maintenance, security, agricultural, or horticultural purposes. "Utility vehicle" does not include an all-terrain vehicle or golf cart, as defined in this section, or a riding lawn mower.

(49) Vehicle. - Every device in, upon, or by which any person or property is or may be transported or drawn upon a highway, excepting devices moved by human power or used exclusively upon fixed rails or tracks; provided, that for the purposes of this Chapter bicycles shall be deemed vehicles and every rider of a bicycle upon a highway shall be subject to the provisions of this Chapter applicable to the driver of a vehicle except those which by their nature can have no application. This term shall not include a device which is designed for and intended to be used as a means of transportation for a person with a mobility impairment, or who uses the device for mobility enhancement, is suitable for use both inside and outside a building, including on sidewalks, and is limited by design to 15 miles per hour when the device is being operated by a person with a mobility impairment, or who uses the device for mobility enhancement. This term shall not include an electric personal assistive mobility device as defined in G.S. 20-4.01(7a).

(50) Wreckers. - Vehicles with permanently attached cranes used to move other vehicles; provided, that said wreckers shall be equipped with adequate brakes for units being towed. (1973, c. 1330, s. 1; 1975, cc. 94, 208; c. 716, s. 5; c. 743; c. 859, s. 1; 1977, c. 313; c. 464, s. 34; 1979, c. 39; c. 423, s. 1; c. 574, ss. 1-4; c. 667, s. 1; c. 680; 1981, c. 606, s. 3; c. 792, s. 2; 1983, c. 435, s. 8; 1983 (Reg. Sess., 1984), c. 1101, ss. 1-3; 1985, c. 509, s. 6; 1987, c. 607, s. 2; c. 658, s. 1; 1987 (Reg. Sess., 1988), c. 1069; c. 1105, s. 1; c. 1112, ss. 1-3; 1989, c. 455, ss. 1, 2; c. 727, s. 219(1); c. 771, ss. 1, 18; 1991, c. 449, s. 2; c. 726, ss. 1-4; 1991 (Reg. Sess., 1992), c. 1015, s. 1; 1993 (Reg. Sess., 1994), c. 761, s. 22; 1995, c. 191, s. 1; 1995 (Reg. Sess., 1996), c. 756, ss. 2-4; 1997-379, s. 5.1; 1997-443, s. 11A.8; 1997-456, s. 27; 1998-149, s. 1; 1998-182, ss. 1, 1.1, 26; 1998-217, s. 62(e); 1999-330, s. 9; 1999-337, s. 28(c)-(e); 1999-406, s. 14; 1999-452, ss. 1-5; 2000-155, s. 9; 2000-173, s. 10(c); 2001-212, s. 2; 2001-341, ss. 1, 2; 2001-356, ss. 1, 2; 2001-441, s. 1; 2001-487, ss. 50(a), 51; 2002-72, s. 19(b); 2002-98, ss. 1-3; 2003-397, s. 1; 2005-282, s. 1; 2005-349, ss. 1-3; 2006-253, s. 8; 2007-56, s. 4; 2007-382, ss. 2, 3; 2007-455, s. 1; 2007-493, s. 1; 2008-156, s. 1; 2009-274, s. 1; 2009-405, ss. 1, 4; 2009-416, ss. 1, 2; 2010-129, s. 1; 2011-95, s. 1; 2011-206, s. 1; 2013-410, s. 47.5.)

Article 1A.

Reciprocity Agreements as to Registration and Licensing.

§ 20-4.1. Declaration of policy.

It is the policy of this State to promote and encourage the fullest possible use of its highway system by authorizing the making and execution of motor vehicle reciprocal registration agreements, arrangements and declarations with other states, provinces, territories and countries with respect to vehicles registered in this and such other states, provinces, territories and countries thus contributing to the economic and social development and growth of this State. (1961, c. 642, s. 1.)

§ 20-4.2. Definitions.

As used in this Article:

(1)   "Commercial vehicle" means any vehicle which is operated in furtherance of any commercial enterprise.

(2)   "Commissioner" means the Commissioner of Motor Vehicles of North Carolina.

(3)   "Division" means the Division of Motor Vehicles of North Carolina.

(4)   "Jurisdiction" means and includes a state, district, territory or possession of the United States, a foreign country and a state or province of a foreign country.

(5)   "Properly registered," as applied to place of registration, means:

a.   The jurisdiction where the person registering the vehicle has his legal residence, or

b.   In the case of a commercial vehicle, including a leased vehicle, the jurisdiction in which it is registered if the commercial enterprise in which such vehicle is used has a place of business therein, and, if the vehicle is most frequently dispatched, garaged, serviced, maintained, operated or otherwise controlled in or from such place of business, and, the vehicle has been assigned to such place of business, or

c.   In the case of a commercial vehicle, including leased vehicles, the jurisdiction where, because of an agreement or arrangement between two or more jurisdictions, or pursuant to a declaration, the vehicle has been registered as required by said jurisdiction.

d.   In case of doubt or dispute as to the proper place of registration of a vehicle, the Division shall make the final determination, but in making such determination, may confer with departments of the other jurisdictions affected. (1961, c. 642, s. 1; 1975, c. 716, s. 5; 1979, c. 470, s. 2.)

§ 20-4.3. Commissioner may make reciprocity agreements, arrangements or declarations.

The Commissioner of Motor Vehicles shall have the authority to execute or make agreements, arrangements or declarations to carry out the provisions of this Article. (1961, c. 642, s. 1.)

§ 20-4.4. Authority for reciprocity agreements; provisions; reciprocity standards.

(a) The Commissioner may enter into an agreement or arrangement for interstate or intrastate operations with the duly authorized representatives of another jurisdiction, granting to vehicles or to owners of vehicles which are properly registered or licensed in such jurisdiction and for which evidence of compliance is supplied, benefits, privileges and exemptions from the payment, wholly or partially, of any taxes, fees, or other charges imposed upon such vehicles or owners with respect to the operation or ownership of such vehicles under the laws of this State. Such an agreement or arrangement shall provide that vehicles properly registered or licensed in this State when operated upon highways of such other jurisdiction shall receive exemptions, benefits and privileges of a similar kind or to a similar degree as are extended to vehicles properly registered or licensed in such jurisdiction when operated in this State. Each such agreement or arrangement shall, in the judgment of the Commissioner, be in the best interest of this State and the citizens thereof and shall be fair and equitable to this State and the citizens thereof, and all of the same shall be determined on the basis and recognition of the benefits which accrue to the economy of this State from the uninterrupted flow of commerce.

(b) When the Commissioner enters into a reciprocal registration agreement or arrangement with another jurisdiction which has a motor vehicle tax, license or fee which is not subject to waiver by a reciprocity agreement, the Commissioner is empowered and authorized to provide as a condition of the agreement or arrangement that owners of vehicles licensed in such other jurisdiction shall pay some equalizing tax or fee to the Division. The failure of any owner or operator of a vehicle to pay the taxes or fees provided in the agreement or arrangement shall prohibit them from receiving any benefits therefrom and they shall be required to register their vehicles and pay taxes as if there was no agreement or arrangement. (1961, c. 642, s. 1; 1971, c. 588; 1975, c. 716, s. 5.)

§ 20-4.5. Base-state registration reciprocity.

An agreement or arrangement entered into, or a declaration issued under the authority of this Article may contain provisions authorizing the registration or licensing in another jurisdiction of vehicles located in or operated from a base in such other jurisdiction which vehicles otherwise would be required to be registered or licensed in some other state; and in such event the exemptions, benefits and privileges extended by such agreement, arrangement or declaration shall apply to such vehicles, when properly licensed or registered in such base jurisdiction. (1961, c. 642, s. 1.)

§ 20-4.6. Repealed by Session Laws 1997-122, s. 1.

§ 20-4.7. Extension of reciprocal privileges to lessees authorized.

An agreement or arrangement entered into, or a declaration issued under the authority of this Article, may contain provisions under which a leased vehicle properly registered by the lessor thereof may be entitled, subject to terms and conditions stated therein, to the exemptions, benefits and privileges extended by such agreement, arrangement or declaration. (1961, c. 642, s. 1.)

§ 20-4.8. Automatic reciprocity, when.

On and after July 1, 1961, if no agreement, arrangement or declaration is in effect with respect to another jurisdiction as authorized by this Article, any vehicle properly registered or licensed in such other jurisdiction and for which evidence of compliance supplied shall receive, when operated in this State, the same exemptions, benefits and privileges granted by such other jurisdiction to vehicles properly registered in this State. Reciprocity extended under this section shall apply to commercial vehicles only when engaged exclusively in interstate operations. (1961, c. 642, s. 1.)

§ 20-4.9. Suspension of reciprocity benefits.

Agreements, arrangements or declarations made under the authority of this Article may include provisions authorizing the Division to suspend or cancel the exemptions, benefits or privileges granted thereunder to a vehicle which is in violation of any of the conditions or terms of such agreements, arrangements or declarations or is in violation of the laws of this State relating to motor vehicles or rules and regulations lawfully promulgated thereunder. (1961, c. 642, s. 1; 1975, c. 716, s. 5.)

§ 20-4.10. Agreements to be written, filed and available for distribution.

All agreements, arrangements or declarations or amendments thereto shall be in writing and shall be filed in the office of the Commissioner. Copies thereof shall be made available by the Commissioner upon request and upon payment of a fee therefor in an amount necessary to defray the costs of reproduction thereof. (1961, c. 642, s. 1.)

§ 20-4.11. Reciprocity agreements in effect at time of Article.

All reciprocity registration agreements, arrangements and declarations relating to vehicles in force and effect July 1, 1961, shall continue in force and effect until specifically amended or revoked as provided by law or by such agreements or arrangements. (1961, c. 642, s. 1.)

§ 20-4.12. Article part of and supplemental to motor vehicle registration law.

This Article shall be, and construed as, a part of and supplemental to the motor vehicle registration law of this State. (1961, c. 642, s. 1.)

§§ 20-4.13 through 20-4.17. Reserved for future codification purposes.

Article 1B.

Reciprocal Provisions as to Arrest of Nonresidents.

§ 20-4.18. Definitions.

Unless the context otherwise requires, the following words and phrases, for the purpose of this Article, shall have the following meanings:

(1) Citation. - Any citation, summons, ticket, or other document issued by a law-enforcement officer for the violation of a traffic law, ordinance, rule or regulation.

(2) Collateral or Bond. - Any cash or other security deposited to secure an appearance following a citation by a law-enforcement officer.

(3) Repealed by Session Laws 1979, c. 667, s. 2.

(4) Nonresident. - A person who holds a license issued by a reciprocating state.

(5) Personal Recognizance. - An agreement by a nonresident to comply with the terms of the citation issued to the nonresident.

(6) Reciprocating State. - Any state or other jurisdiction which extends by its laws to residents of North Carolina substantially the rights and privileges provided by this Article.

(7) State. - The State of North Carolina. (1973, c. 736; 1979, c. 667, s. 2; 1981, c. 508; 1999-452, s. 6.)

§ 20-4.19. Issuance of citation to nonresident; officer to report noncompliance.

(a) Notwithstanding other provisions of this Chapter, a law-enforcement officer observing a violation of this Chapter or other traffic regulation by a nonresident shall issue a citation as appropriate and shall not, subject to the provisions of subsection (b) of this section, require such nonresident to post collateral or bond to secure appearance for trial, but shall accept such nonresident's personal recognizance; provided, however, that the nonresident shall have the right upon request to post collateral or bond in a manner provided by law and in such case the provisions of this Article shall not apply.

(b) A nonresident may be required to post collateral or bond to secure appearance for trial if the offense is one which would result in the suspension or revocation of a person's license under the laws of this State.

(c) Upon the failure of the nonresident to comply with the citation, the clerk of court shall report the noncompliance to the Division. The report of noncompliance shall clearly identify the nonresident; describe the violation, specifying the section of the statute, code, or ordinance violated; indicate the location and date of offense; and identify the vehicle involved. (1973, c. 736; 1975, c. 716, s. 5; 1991, c. 682, s. 1; 1999-452, s. 7.)

§ 20-4.20. Division to transmit report to reciprocating state; suspension of license for noncompliance with citation issued by reciprocating state.

(a) Upon receipt of a report of noncompliance, the Division shall transmit a certified copy of such report to the official in charge of the issuance of licenses in the reciprocating state in which the nonresident resides or by which he is licensed.

(b) When the licensing authority of a reciprocating state reports that a person holding a North Carolina license has failed to comply with a citation issued in such state, the Commissioner shall forthwith suspend such person's license. The order of suspension shall indicate the reason for the order, and shall notify the person that his license shall remain suspended until he has furnished evidence satisfactory to the Commissioner that he has complied with the terms of the citation which was the basis for the suspension order by appearing before the tribunal to which he was cited and complying with any order entered by said tribunal.

(c) A copy of any suspension order issued hereunder may be furnished to the licensing authority of the reciprocating state.

(d) The Commissioner shall maintain a current listing of reciprocating states hereunder. Such lists shall from time to time be disseminated among the appropriate departments, divisions, bureaus, and agencies of this State; the principal law-enforcement officers of the several counties, cities, and towns of this State; and the licensing authorities in reciprocating states.

(e)   The Commissioner shall have the authority to execute or make agreements, arrangements, or declarations to carry out the provisions of this Article. (1973, c. 736; 1975, c. 716, s. 5; 1979, c. 104.)

Article 1C.

Drivers License Compact.

§ 20-4.21. Title of Article.

This Article is the Drivers License Compact and may be cited by that name. (1993, c. 533, s. 1.)

§ 20-4.22. Commissioner may make reciprocity agreements, arrangements, or declarations.

The Commissioner may execute or make agreements, arrangements, or declarations to implement this Article. (1993, c. 533, s. 1.)

§ 20-4.23. Legislative findings and policy.

(a)   Findings. - The General Assembly and the states that are members of the Drivers License Compact find that:

(1)   The safety of their streets and highways is materially affected by the degree of compliance with state laws and local ordinances relating to the operation of motor vehicles.

(2)   The violation of a law or an ordinance relating to the operation of a motor vehicle is evidence that the violator engages in conduct that is likely to endanger the safety of persons and property.

(3) The continuance in force of a license to drive is predicated upon compliance with laws and ordinances relating to the operation of motor vehicles in whichever jurisdiction the vehicle is operated.

(b) Policy. - It is the policy of the General Assembly and of each of the states that is a member of the Drivers License Compact to:

(1) Promote compliance with the laws, ordinances, and administrative rules and regulations of a member state relating to the operation of motor vehicles.

(2) Make the reciprocal recognition of licenses to drive and the eligibility for a license to drive more just and equitable by making consideration of overall compliance with motor vehicle laws, ordinances, and administrative rules and regulations a condition precedent to the continuance or issuance of any license that authorizes the holder of the license to operate a motor vehicle in a member state. (1993, c. 533, s. 1.)

§ 20-4.24. Reports of convictions; effect of reports.

(a) Reports. - A state that is a member of the Drivers License Compact shall report to another member state of the compact a conviction for any of the following:

(1) Manslaughter or negligent homicide resulting from the operation of a motor vehicle.

(2) Driving a motor vehicle while impaired.

(3) A felony in the commission of which a motor vehicle was used.

(4) Failure to stop and render aid in the event of a motor vehicle accident resulting in the death or personal injury of another.

If the laws of a member state do not describe the listed violations in precisely the words used in this subsection, the member state shall construe the descriptions to apply to offenses of the member state that are substantially similar to the ones described.

A state that is a member of the Drivers License Compact shall report to another member state of the compact a conviction for any other offense or any other information concerning convictions that the member states agree to report.

(b)   Effect. - A state that is a member of the Drivers License Compact shall treat a report of a conviction received from another member state of the compact as a report of the conduct that resulted in the conviction. For a conviction required to be reported under subsection (a), a member state shall give the same effect to the report as if the conviction had occurred in that state. For a conviction that is not required to be reported under subsection (a), a member state shall give the effect to the report that is required by the laws of that state. G.S. 20-23 governs the effect in this State of convictions that are not required to be reported under subsection (a). (1993, c. 533, s. 1.)

§ 20-4.25. Review of license status in other states upon application for license in member state.

Upon application for a license to drive, the licensing authority of a state that is a member of the Drivers License Compact must determine if the applicant has ever held, or currently holds, a license to drive issued by another member state. The licensing authority of the member state where the application is made may not issue the applicant a license to drive if:

(1)   The applicant has held a license, but it has been revoked for a violation and the revocation period has not ended. If the revocation period is for more than one year and it has been at least one year since the license was revoked, the licensing authority may allow the applicant to apply for a new license if the laws of the licensing authority's state permit the application.

(2)   The applicant currently holds a license to drive issued by another member state and does not surrender that license. (1993, c. 533, s. 1.)

§ 20-4.26. Effect on other laws or agreements.

Except as expressly required by the provisions of this Article, this Article does not affect the right of a member state to the Drivers License Compact to apply any of its other laws relating to licenses to drive to any person or circumstance, nor does it invalidate or prevent any driver license agreement or other cooperative arrangement between a member state and a state that is not a member. (1993, c. 533, s. 1.)

§ 20-4.27. Effect on other State driver license laws.

To the extent that this Article conflicts with general driver licensing provisions in this Chapter, this Article prevails. Where this Article is silent, the general driver licensing provisions apply. (1993, c. 533, s. 1.)

§ 20-4.28. Administration and exchange of information.

The head of the licensing authority of each member state is the administrator of the Drivers License Compact for that state. The administrators, acting jointly, have the power to formulate all necessary procedures for the exchange of information under this compact. The administrator of each member state shall furnish to the administrator of each other member state any information or documents reasonably necessary to facilitate the administration of this compact. (1993, c. 533, s. 1.)

§ 20-4.29. Withdrawal from Drivers License Compact.

A member state may withdraw from the Drivers License Compact. A withdrawal may not become effective until at least six months after the heads of all other member states have received notice of the withdrawal. Withdrawal does not affect the validity or applicability by the licensing authorities of states remaining members of the compact of a report of a conviction occurring prior to the withdrawal. (1993, c. 533, s. 1.)

§ 20-4.30. Construction and severability.

This Article shall be liberally construed to effectuate its purposes. The provisions of this Article are severable; if any part of this Article is declared to be invalid by a court, the invalidity does not affect other parts of this Article that can be given effect without the invalid provision. If the Drivers License Compact is declared invalid by a court in a member state, the compact remains in full force and effect in the remaining member states and in full force and effect for all severable matters in that member state. (1993, c. 533, s. 1.)

Article 2.

Uniform Driver's License Act.

§ 20-5. Title of Article.

This Article may be cited as the Uniform Driver's License Act. (1935, c. 52, s. 31.)

§ 20-6. Repealed by Session Laws 1973, c. 1330, s. 39.

§ 20-7. (See notes) Issuance and renewal of drivers licenses.

(a) License Required. - To drive a motor vehicle on a highway, a person must be licensed by the Division under this Article or Article 2C of this Chapter to drive the vehicle and must carry the license while driving the vehicle. The Division issues regular drivers licenses under this Article and issues commercial drivers licenses under Article 2C.

A license authorizes the holder of the license to drive any vehicle included in the class of the license and any vehicle included in a lesser class of license, except a vehicle for which an endorsement is required. To drive a vehicle for which an endorsement is required, a person must obtain both a license and an endorsement for the vehicle. A regular drivers license is considered a lesser class of license than its commercial counterpart.

The classes of regular drivers licenses and the motor vehicles that can be driven with each class of license are:

(1) Class A. - A Class A license authorizes the holder to drive any of the following:

a. A Class A motor vehicle that is exempt under G.S. 20-37.16 from the commercial drivers license requirements.

b. A Class A motor vehicle that has a combined GVWR of less than 26,001 pounds and includes as part of the combination a towed unit that has a GVWR of at least 10,001 pounds.

(2) Class B. - A Class B license authorizes the holder to drive any Class B motor vehicle that is exempt under G.S. 20-37.16 from the commercial drivers license requirements.

(3) Class C. - A Class C license authorizes the holder to drive any of the following:

a. A Class C motor vehicle that is not a commercial motor vehicle.

b. When operated by a volunteer member of a fire department, a rescue squad, or an emergency medical service (EMS) in the performance of duty, a Class A or Class B fire-fighting, rescue, or EMS motor vehicle or a combination of these vehicles.

c. A combination of noncommercial motor vehicles that have a GVWR of more than 10,000 pounds but less than 26,001 pounds. This sub-subdivision does not apply to a Class C license holder less than 18 years of age.

The Commissioner may assign a unique motor vehicle to a class that is different from the class in which it would otherwise belong.

A person holding a commercial drivers license issued by another jurisdiction must apply for a transfer and obtain a North Carolina issued commercial drivers license within 30 days of becoming a resident. Any other new resident of North Carolina who has a drivers license issued by another jurisdiction must obtain a license from the Division within 60 days after becoming a resident.

(a1) Motorcycles and Mopeds. - To drive a motorcycle, a person shall have one of the following:

(1) A full provisional license with a motorcycle learner's permit.

(2) A regular drivers license with a motorcycle learner's permit.

(3) A full provisional license with a motorcycle endorsement.

(4) A regular drivers license with a motorcycle endorsement.

Subsection (a2) of this section sets forth the requirements for a motorcycle learner's permit. To obtain a motorcycle endorsement, a person shall pay the fee set in subsection (i) of this section. In addition, to obtain an endorsement, a person age 18 or older shall demonstrate competence to drive a motorcycle by passing a knowledge test concerning motorcycles, and by passing a road test or providing proof of successful completion of one of the following:

(1) The North Carolina Motorcycle Safety Education Program Basic Rider Course or Experienced Rider Course.

(2) Any course approved by the Commissioner consistent with the instruction provided through the Motorcycle Safety Instruction Program established under G.S. 115D-72.

A person less than 18 years of age shall demonstrate competence to drive a motorcycle by passing a knowledge test concerning motorcycles and providing proof of successful completion of one of the following:

(1) Repealed by Session Laws 2012-85, s. 1, effective July 1, 2012.

(2) The North Carolina Motorcycle Safety Education Program Basic Rider Course or Experienced Rider Course.

(3) Any course approved by the Commissioner consistent with the instruction provided through the Motorcycle Safety Instruction Program established under G.S. 115D-72.

A person less than 18 years of age with a motorcycle endorsement may not drive a motorcycle with a passenger.

Neither a drivers license nor a motorcycle endorsement is required to drive a moped.

(a2) Motorcycle Learner's Permit. - The following persons are eligible for a motorcycle learner's permit:

(1) A person who is at least 16 years old but less than 18 years old and has a full provisional license issued by the Division.

(2) A person who is at least 18 years old and has a license issued by the Division.

To obtain a motorcycle learner's permit, an applicant shall pass a vision test, a road sign test, and a knowledge test specified by the Division. An applicant who is less than 18 years old shall successfully complete the North Carolina Motorcycle Safety Education Program Basic Rider Course or any course approved by the Commissioner consistent with the instruction provided through the Motorcycle Safety Instruction Program established under G.S. 115D-72. A motorcycle learner's permit expires twelve months after it is issued and may be renewed for one additional six-month period. The holder of a motorcycle learner's permit may not drive a motorcycle with a passenger. The fee for a motorcycle learner's permit is the amount set in G.S. 20-7(l) for a learner's permit.

(b) Repealed by Session Laws 1993, c. 368, s. 1, c. 533, s. 12.

(b1) Application. - To obtain an identification card, learners permit, or drivers license from the Division, a person shall complete an application form provided by the Division, present at least two forms of identification approved by the Commissioner, be a resident of this State, and, except for an identification card, demonstrate his or her physical and mental ability to drive safely a motor vehicle included in the class of license for which the person has applied. At least one of the forms of identification shall indicate the applicant's residence address. The Division may copy the identification presented or hold it for a brief period of time to verify its authenticity. To obtain an endorsement, a person shall demonstrate his or her physical and mental ability to drive safely the type of motor vehicle for which the endorsement is required.

The application form shall request all of the following information, and it shall contain the disclosures concerning the request for an applicant's social security number required by section 7 of the federal Privacy Act of 1974, Pub. L. No. 93-579:

(1) The applicant's full name.

(2)   The applicant's mailing address and residence address.

(3)   A physical description of the applicant, including the applicant's sex, height, eye color, and hair color.

(4)   The applicant's date of birth.

(5)   The applicant's valid social security number.

(6)   The applicant's signature.

The Division shall not issue an identification card, learners permit, or drivers license to an applicant who fails to provide the applicant's valid social security number.

(b2)   Disclosure of Social Security Number. - The social security number of an applicant is not a public record. The Division may not disclose an applicant's social security number except as allowed under federal law. A violation of the disclosure restrictions is punishable as provided in 42 U.S.C. § 408, and amendments to that law.

In accordance with 42 U.S.C. 405 and 42 U.S.C. 666, and amendments thereto, the Division may disclose a social security number obtained under subsection (b1) of this section only as follows:

(1)   For the purpose of administering the drivers license laws.

(2)   To the Department of Health and Human Services, Child Support Enforcement Program for the purpose of establishing paternity or child support or enforcing a child support order.

(3)   To the Department of Revenue for the purpose of verifying taxpayer identity.

(4)   To the Office of Indigent Defense Services of the Judicial Department for the purpose of verifying the identity of a represented client and enforcing a court order to pay for the legal services rendered.

(5)   To each county jury commission for the purpose of verifying the identity of deceased persons whose names should be removed from jury lists.

(6) To the Office of the State Controller for the purposes of G.S. 143B-426.38A.

(b3) The Division shall adopt rules implementing the provisions of subsection (b1) of this section with respect to proof of residency in this State. Those rules shall ensure that applicants submit verified or verifiable residency and address information that can be reasonably considered to be valid and that is provided on any of the following:

(1) A document issued by an agency of the United States or by the government of another nation.

(2) A document issued by another state.

(3) A document issued by the State of North Carolina, or a political subdivision of this State. This includes an agency or instrumentality of this State.

(4) A preprinted bank or other corporate statement.

(5) A preprinted business letterhead.

(6) Any other document deemed reliable by the Division.

(b4) Examples of documents that are reasonably reliable indicators of residency include, but are not limited to, any of the following:

(1) A pay stub with the payee's address.

(2) A utility bill showing the address of the applicant-payor.

(3) A contract for an apartment, house, modular unit, or manufactured home with a North Carolina address signed by the applicant.

(4) A receipt for personal property taxes paid.

(5) A receipt for real property taxes paid to a North Carolina locality.

(6) A current automobile insurance policy issued to the applicant and showing the applicant's address.

(7) A monthly or quarterly financial statement from a North Carolina regulated financial institution.

(8) A matricula consular or substantially similar document issued by the Mexican Consulate for North Carolina.

(9) A document similar to that described in subsection (8) of this section, issued by the consulate or embassy of another country. This subdivision only applies if the Division has consulted with the United State Department of State and is satisfied with the reliability of such document.

(b5) The Division rules adopted pursuant to subsection (b3) of this section shall also provide that if an applicant cannot produce any documentation specified in subsection (b3) or (b4) of this section, the applicant, or in the case of a minor applicant a parent or legal guardian of the applicant, may complete an affidavit, on a form provided by the Division and sworn to before an official of the Division, indicating the applicant's current residence address. The affidavit shall contain the provisions of G.S. 20-15(a) and G.S. 20-17(a)(5) and shall indicate the civil and criminal penalties for completing a false affidavit.

(c) Tests. - To demonstrate physical and mental ability, a person must pass an examination. The examination may include road tests, vision tests, oral tests, and, in the case of literate applicants, written tests, as the Division may require. The tests must ensure that an applicant recognizes the handicapped international symbol of access, as defined in G.S. 20-37.5. The Division may not require a person who applies to renew a license that has not expired to take a written test or a road test unless one or more of the following applies:

(1) The person has been convicted of a traffic violation since the person's license was last issued.

(2) The applicant suffers from a mental or physical condition that impairs the person's ability to drive a motor vehicle.

The Division may not require a person who is at least 60 years old to parallel park a motor vehicle as part of a road test.

(c1) Insurance. - The Division may not issue a drivers license to a person until the person has furnished proof of financial responsibility. Proof of financial responsibility shall be in one of the following forms:

(1) A written certificate or electronically-transmitted facsimile thereof from any insurance carrier duly authorized to do business in this State certifying that there is in effect a nonfleet private passenger motor vehicle liability policy for the benefit of the person required to furnish proof of financial responsibility. The certificate or facsimile shall state the effective date and expiration date of the nonfleet private passenger motor vehicle liability policy and shall state the date that the certificate or facsimile is issued. The certificate or facsimile shall remain effective proof of financial responsibility for a period of 30 consecutive days following the date the certificate or facsimile is issued but shall not in and of itself constitute a binder or policy of insurance.

(2) A binder for or policy of nonfleet private passenger motor vehicle liability insurance under which the applicant is insured, provided that the binder or policy states the effective date and expiration date of the nonfleet private passenger motor vehicle liability policy.

The preceding provisions of this subsection do not apply to applicants who do not own currently registered motor vehicles and who do not operate nonfleet private passenger motor vehicles that are owned by other persons and that are not insured under commercial motor vehicle liability insurance policies. In such cases, the applicant shall sign a written certificate to that effect. Such certificate shall be furnished by the Division and may be incorporated into the license application form. Any material misrepresentation made by such person on such certificate shall be grounds for suspension of that person's license for a period of 90 days.

For the purpose of this subsection, the term "nonfleet private passenger motor vehicle" has the definition ascribed to it in Article 40 of General Statute Chapter 58.

The Commissioner may require that certificates required by this subsection be on a form approved by the Commissioner.

The requirement of furnishing proof of financial responsibility does not apply to a person who applies for a renewal of his or her drivers license.

Nothing in this subsection precludes any person from showing proof of financial responsibility in any other manner authorized by Articles 9A and 13 of this Chapter.

(d) Repealed by Session Laws 1993, c. 368, s. 1.

(e) Restrictions. - The Division may impose any restriction it finds advisable on a drivers license. It is unlawful for the holder of a restricted license to operate a motor vehicle without complying with the restriction and is the equivalent of operating a motor vehicle without a license. If any applicant shall suffer from any physical defect or disease which affects his or her operation of a motor vehicle, the Division may require to be filed with it a certificate of such applicant's condition signed by some medical authority of the applicant's community designated by the Division. This certificate shall in all cases be treated as confidential. Nothing in this subsection shall be construed to prevent the Division from refusing to issue a license, either restricted or unrestricted, to any person deemed to be incapable of safely operating a motor vehicle. This subsection does not prohibit deaf persons from operating motor vehicles who in every other way meet the requirements of this section.

(f) Duration and Renewal of Licenses. - Drivers licenses shall be issued and renewed pursuant to the provisions of this subsection:

(1) Duration of license for persons under age 18. - A full provisional license issued to a person under the age of 18 expires on the person's twenty-first birthday.

(2) Duration of original license for persons at least 18 years of age or older. - A drivers license issued to a person at least 18 years old but less than 66 years old expires on the birthday of the licensee in the eighth year after issuance. A drivers license issued to a person at least 66 years old expires on the birthday of the licensee in the fifth year after issuance. A commercial drivers license expires on the birthday of the licensee in the fifth year after issuance. A commercial drivers license that has a vehicles carrying passengers (P) and school bus (S) endorsement issued pursuant to G.S. 20-37.16 expires on the birthday of the licensee in the third year after issuance, if the licensee is certified to drive a school bus in North Carolina.

(2a) Duration of renewed licenses. - A renewed drivers license that was issued by the Division to a person at least 18 years old but less than 66 years old expires eight years after the expiration date of the license that is renewed. A renewed drivers license that was issued by the Division to a person at least 66 years old expires five years after the expiration date of the license that is renewed. A renewed commercial drivers license expires five years after the expiration date of the license that is renewed.

(3)   Duration of license for certain other drivers. - The durations listed in subdivisions (1), (2) and (2a) of this subsection are valid unless the Division determines that a license of shorter duration should be issued when the applicant holds valid documentation issued by, or under the authority of, the United States government that demonstrates the applicant's legal presence of limited duration in the United States. In no event shall a license of limited duration expire later than the expiration of the authorization for the applicant's legal presence in the United States.

(3a)   When to renew. - A person may apply to the Division to renew a license during the 180-day period before the license expires. The Division may not accept an application for renewal made before the 180-day period begins.

(3b)   Renewal for certain members of the Armed Forces of the United States and reserve components of the Armed Forces of the United States.

a.   The Division may renew a drivers license, without limitation on the period of time before the license expires, if the person applying for renewal is a member of the Armed Forces of the United States or of a reserve component of the Armed Forces of the United States and provides orders that place the member on active duty and duty station outside this State.

b.   A person who is a member of a reserve component of the Armed Forces of the United States whose license bears an expiration date that occurred while the person was on active duty outside this State shall be considered to have a valid license until 60 days after the date of release from active duty upon showing proof of the release date, unless the license was rescinded, revoked, or otherwise invalidated under some other provision of law. Notwithstanding the provisions of this sub-subdivision, no license shall be considered valid more than 18 months after the date of expiration.

(4)   Renewal by mail. - The Division may renew by mail a drivers license issued by the Division to a person who meets any of the following descriptions:

a.   Is a member of the Armed Forces of the United States or a reserve component of the Armed Forces of the United States serving on active duty and is stationed outside this State.

b.   Is a resident of this State and has been residing outside the State for at least 30 continuous days.

When renewing a license by mail, the Division may waive the examination that would otherwise be required for the renewal and may impose any conditions it finds advisable. A license renewed by mail is a temporary license that expires 60 days after the person to whom it is issued returns to this State.

(5) License to be sent by mail. - The Division shall issue to the applicant a temporary driving certificate valid for 20 days, and 60 days for a commercial drivers license, unless the applicant is applying for renewal by mail under subdivision (4) of this subsection. The temporary driving certificate shall be valid for driving purposes only and shall not be valid for identification purposes. The Division shall produce the applicant's drivers license at a central location and send it to the applicant by first-class mail at the residence address provided by the applicant, unless the applicant is ineligible for mail delivery by the United States Postal Service at the applicant's residence. If the United States Postal Service documents that it does not deliver to the residential address provided by the applicant, and the Division has verified the applicant's residential address by other means, the Division may mail the drivers license to the post office box provided by the applicant. Applicants whose only mailing address prior to July 1, 2008, was a post office box in this State may continue to receive their license at that post office box, provided the applicant's residential address has been verified by the Division.

(g) Repealed by Session Laws 1979, c. 667, s. 6.

(h) Repealed by Session Laws 1979, c. 113, s. 1.

(i) Fees. - The fee for a regular drivers license is the amount set in the following table multiplied by the number of years in the period for which the license is issued:

Class of Regular License	Fee for Each Year
Class A	$4.00
Class B	$4.00
Class C	$4.00

The fee for a motorcycle endorsement is one dollar and seventy-five cents ($1.75) for each year of the period for which the endorsement is issued. The appropriate fee shall be paid before a person receives a regular drivers license or an endorsement.

(i1) Restoration Fee. - Any person whose drivers license has been revoked pursuant to the provisions of this Chapter, other than G.S. 20-17(a)(2) shall pay a restoration fee of fifty dollars ($50.00). A person whose drivers license has been revoked under G.S. 20-17(a)(2) shall pay a restoration fee of one hundred dollars ($100.00). The fee shall be paid to the Division prior to the issuance to such person of a new drivers license or the restoration of the drivers license. The restoration fee shall be paid to the Division in addition to any and all fees which may be provided by law. This restoration fee shall not be required from any licensee whose license was revoked or voluntarily surrendered for medical or health reasons whether or not a medical evaluation was conducted pursuant to this Chapter. The fifty-dollar ($50.00) fee, and the first fifty dollars ($50.00) of the one-hundred-dollar ($100.00) fee, shall be deposited in the Highway Fund. Twenty-five dollars ($25.00) of the one-hundred-dollar ($100.00) fee shall be used to fund a statewide chemical alcohol testing program administered by the Forensic Tests for Alcohol Branch of the Chronic Disease and Injury Section of the Department of Health and Human Services. The remainder of the one-hundred-dollar ($100.00) fee shall be deposited in the General Fund. The Office of State Budget and Management shall annually report to the General Assembly the amount of fees deposited in the General Fund and transferred to the Forensic Tests for Alcohol Branch of the Chronic Disease and Injury Section of the Department of Health and Human Services under this subsection.

Effective with the 2011-2012 fiscal year, from the funds deposited in the General Fund under this subsection the sum of five hundred thirty-seven thousand four hundred fifty-five dollars ($537,455) shall be transferred annually to the Board of Governors of The University of North Carolina to be used for the operating expenses of the Bowles Center for Alcohol Studies at The University of North Carolina at Chapel Hill.

(j) Highway Fund. - The fees collected under this section and G.S. 20-14 shall be placed in the Highway Fund.

(k) Repealed by Session Laws 1991, c. 726, s. 5.

(l) Learner's Permit. - A person who is at least 18 years old may obtain a learner's permit. A learner's permit authorizes the permit holder to drive a specified type or class of motor vehicle while in possession of the permit. A learner's permit is valid for a period of 18 months after it is issued. The fee for a learner's permit is fifteen dollars ($15.00). A learner's permit may be renewed, or a second learner's permit may be issued, for an additional period of 18 months. The permit holder must, while operating a motor vehicle over the highways, be accompanied by a person who is licensed to operate the motor vehicle being driven and is seated beside the permit holder.

(l-1) Repealed by Session Laws 1991, c. 726, s. 5.

(m) Instruction Permit. - The Division upon receiving proper application may in its discretion issue a restricted instruction permit effective for a school year or a lesser period to any of the following applicants:

(1) An applicant who is less than 18 years old and is enrolled in a drivers education program that is approved by the State Superintendent of Public Instruction and is offered at a public high school, a nonpublic secondary school, or a licensed drivers training school.

(2) An applicant for certification under G.S. 20-218 as a school bus driver.

A restricted instruction permit authorizes the holder of the permit to drive a specified type or class of motor vehicle when in possession of the permit, subject to any restrictions imposed by the Division. The restrictions the Division may impose on a permit include restrictions to designated areas and highways and restrictions prohibiting operation except when an approved instructor is occupying a seat beside the permittee. A restricted instruction permit is not required to have a distinguishing number or a picture of the person to whom the permit is issued.

(n) Format. - A drivers license issued by the Division must be tamperproof and must contain all of the following information:

(1) An identification of this State as the issuer of the license.

(2) The license holder's full name.

(3) The license holder's residence address.

(4) A color photograph, or a properly applied laser engraved picture on polycarbonate material, of the license holder, taken by the Division.

(5) A physical description of the license holder, including sex, height, eye color, and hair color.

(6) The license holder's date of birth.

(7) An identifying number for the license holder assigned by the Division. The identifying number may not be the license holder's social security number.

(8) Each class of motor vehicle the license holder is authorized to drive and any endorsements or restrictions that apply.

(9) The license holder's signature.

(10) The date the license was issued and the date the license expires.

The Commissioner shall ensure that applicants 21 years old or older are issued drivers licenses and special identification cards that are printed in a horizontal format. The Commissioner shall ensure that applicants under the age of 21 are issued drivers licenses and special identification cards that are printed in a vertical format, that distinguishes them from the horizontal format, for ease of identification of individuals under age 21 by members of industries that regulate controlled products that are sale restricted by age and law enforcement officers enforcing these laws.

At the request of an applicant for a drivers license, a license issued to the applicant must contain the applicant's race.

(o) Repealed by Session Laws 1991, c. 726, s. 5.

(p) The Division must give the clerk of superior court in each county at least 50 copies of the driver license handbook free of charge. The clerk must give a copy to a person who requests it.

(q) (See note) Military Designation. - The Division shall develop a military designation for drivers licenses that may, upon request, be granted to North Carolina residents on active duty and to their spouses and dependent children. A drivers license with a military designation on it may be renewed by mail no more than two times during the license holder's lifetime. A license renewed by mail under this subsection is a permanent license and does not expire when the license holder returns to the State. A drivers license with a military designation on it issued to a person on active duty may be renewed up to one year prior to its expiration upon presentation of military or Department of Defense credentials.

(q) (See note for delayed effective date and applicability) Active Duty Military Designation. - The Division shall develop a military designation for drivers licenses that may, upon request, be granted to North Carolina residents on active duty and to their spouses and dependent children. A drivers license with a military designation on it may be renewed by mail no more than two times during the license holder's lifetime. A license renewed by mail under this subsection is a permanent license and does not expire when the license holder returns to the State. A drivers license with a military designation on it issued to a person on active duty may be renewed up to one year prior to its expiration upon presentation of military or Department of Defense credentials.

(q1) (See note for delayed effective date and applicability) Veteran Military Designation. - The Division shall develop a military designation for drivers licenses and identification cards that may, upon request, be granted to North Carolina residents who are honorably discharged from military service in the Armed Forces of the United States. An applicant requesting this designation must produce a Form DD-214 showing the applicant has been honorably discharged from the Armed Forces of the United States.

(r) Waiver of Vision Test. - The following license holders shall be exempt from any required eye exam when renewing a drivers license by mail under either subsection (f) of this section or subsection (q) of this section if, at the time of renewal, the license holder is serving in a combat zone or a qualified hazardous duty zone:

(1) A member of the Armed Forces of the United States.

(2) A member of a reserve component of the Armed Forces of the United States.

(s) Notwithstanding the requirements of subsection (b1) of this section that an applicant present a valid social security number, the Division shall issue a drivers license of limited duration, under subsection (f) of this section, to an applicant present in the United States who holds valid documentation issued by, or under the authority of, the United States government that demonstrates the applicant's legal presence of limited duration in the United States if the applicant presents that valid documentation and meets all other requirements for a license of limited duration. Notwithstanding the requirements of subsection (n) of this section addressing background colors and borders, a drivers license of limited duration issued under this section shall bear a distinguishing mark or other designation on the face of the license clearly denoting the limited duration of the license.

(t)   Use of Bioptic Telescopic Lenses. -

(1)   An applicant using bioptic telescopic lenses shall be eligible for a regular Class C drivers license under this section if the applicant meets all of the following:

a.   Demonstrates a visual acuity of at least 20/200 in one or both eyes and a field of 70 degrees horizontal vision with or without corrective carrier lenses, or if the person has vision in one eye only, the person demonstrates a field of at least 40 degrees temporal and 30 degrees nasal horizontal vision.

b.   Demonstrates a visual acuity of at least 20/70 in one or both eyes with the bioptic telescopic lenses and without the use of field expanders.

c.   Provides a report of examination by an ophthalmologist or optometrist, on a form prescribed by the Division, for the Division to determine if all field of vision requirements are met or additional testing is needed.

d.   Successfully passes a road test administered by the Division. This requirement is waived if the applicant is a new resident of North Carolina who has a valid drivers license issued by another jurisdiction that requires a road test.

e.   Meets all other criteria for licensure.

(2)   In addition to the requirements listed in subdivision (1) of this subsection, the Division shall require an applicant using bioptic telescopic lenses to successfully complete a behind-the-wheel training and assessment program prescribed by the Division. This requirement is waived if the applicant has successfully completed a behind-the-wheel training and assessment program as a condition of licensure in another jurisdiction.

(3)   Applicants using bioptic telescopic lenses shall be eligible for a limited learner's permit or provisional drivers license issued pursuant to G.S. 20-11, provided the requirements of this subsection are met and any other required testing or documentation is completed and submitted with the application.

(4) Applicants issued a regular Class C drivers license, limited learner's permit, or provisional drivers license shall be subject to the following restrictions on the license issued:

a. The license or permit holder shall not be eligible for any endorsements.

b. The license or permit shall permit the operation of motor vehicles only during the period beginning one-half hour after sunrise and ending one-half hour before sunset.

(5) Applicants issued a regular Class C drivers license may drive motor vehicles between the period beginning one-half hour before sunset and ending one-half hour after sunrise if the applicant meets the following requirements:

a. Demonstrates a visual acuity of at least 20/40 in one or both eyes with the bioptic telescopic lenses and without the use of field expanders.

b. Provides a report of examination by an ophthalmologist or optometrist in accordance with sub-subdivision c. of subdivision (1) of this subsection that does not recommend restricting the applicant to driving a motor vehicle only during the period beginning one-half hour after sunrise and ending one-half hour before sunset. (1935, c. 52, s. 2; 1943, c. 649, s. 1; c. 787, s. 1; 1947, c. 1067, s. 10; 1949, c. 583, ss. 9, 10; c. 826, ss. 1, 2; 1951, c. 542, ss. 1, 2; c. 1196, ss. 1-3; 1953, cc. 839, 1284, 1311; 1955, c. 1187, ss. 2-6; 1957, c. 1225; 1963, cc. 754, 1007, 1022; 1965, c. 410, s. 5; 1967, c. 509; 1969, c. 183; c. 783, s. 1; c. 865; 1971, c. 158; 1973, cc. 73, 705; c. 1057, ss. 1, 3; 1975, c. 162, s. 1; c. 295; c. 296, ss. 1, 2; c. 684; c. 716, s. 5; c. 841; c. 875, s. 4; c. 879, s. 46; 1977, c. 6; c. 340, s. 3; c. 865, ss. 1, 3; 1979, c. 37, s. 1; c. 113; c. 178, s. 2; c. 667, ss. 3-11, 41; c. 678, ss. 1-3; c. 801, ss. 5, 6; 1981, c. 42; c. 690, ss. 8-10; c. 792, s. 3; 1981 (Reg. Sess., 1982), c. 1257, s. 1; 1983, c. 443, s. 1; 1985, c. 141, s. 4; c. 682, ss. 1, 2; 1987, c. 869, ss. 10, 11; 1989, c. 436, ss. 1, 2; c. 771, s. 5; c. 786, s. 4; 1991, c. 478, s. 1; c. 689, s. 325; c. 726, s. 5; 1991 (Reg. Sess., 1992), c. 1007, s. 27; c. 1030, s. 10; 1993, c. 368, s. 1; c. 533, ss. 2, 3, 12; 1993 (Reg. Sess., 1994), c. 595, ss. 1, 2; c. 750, s. 1; c. 761, s. 1.1; 1995 (Reg. Sess., 1996), c. 675, s. 1; 1997-16, ss. 5, 8, 9; 1997-122, ss. 2, 3; 1997-377, s. 1; 1997-433, s. 4; 1997-443, ss. 11A.122, 32.20; 1997-456, s. 32, 33; 1998-17, s. 1; 1998-149, s. 2; 2000-120, ss. 14, 15; 2000-140, s. 93.1(a); 2001-424, ss. 12.2(b), 27.10A(a)-(d); 2001-513, s. 32(a); 2003-152, ss. 1, 2; 2003-284, s. 36.1; 2004-189, s. 5(a); 2004-203, s. 2; 2005-276, s. 44.1(a); 2005-349, s. 4; 2006-257, ss. 1, 2; 2006-264, s. 35.2; 2007-56, ss. 1-3; 2007-249, s. 1; 2007-

350, s. 1; 2007-512, s. 5; 2008-202, ss. 2, 3; 2008-217, s. 1; 2008-221, s. 1; 2009-274, ss. 2, 3; 2009-451, s. 9.5(a); 2009-492, ss. 1, 2; 2010-130, s. 1; 2010-131, ss. 1, 2; 2010-132, s. 1; 2011-35, ss. 1, 2; 2011-183, ss. 21, 127(a); 2011-326, s. 28; 2011-381, s. 2; 2012-78, s. 1; 2012-85, ss. 1, 2; 2012-142, s. 9.16; 2012-145, s. 2.2; 2013-195, s. 2; 2013-231, s. 1; 2013-360, s. 7.10(a).)

§ 20-7.01: Repealed by Session Laws 1979, c. 667, s. 43.

§ 20-7.1. Notice of change of address or name.

(a)   Address. - A person whose address changes from the address stated on a drivers license must notify the Division of the change within 60 days after the change occurs. If the person's address changed because the person moved, the person must obtain a duplicate license within that time limit stating the new address. A person who does not move but whose address changes due to governmental action may not be charged with violating this subsection.

(b)   Name. - A person whose name changes from the name stated on a drivers license must notify the Division of the change within 60 days after the change occurs and obtain a duplicate drivers license stating the new name.

(c)   Fee. - G.S. 20-14 sets the fee for a duplicate license. (1975, c. 223, s. 1; 1979, c. 970; 1983, c. 521, s. 1; 1997-122, s. 4.)

§ 20-7.2. Repealed by Session Laws 1987, c. 581, s. 2.

§ 20-7.3. Availability of organ, eye, and tissue donor cards at motor vehicle offices.

The Division shall make organ, eye, and tissue donor cards available to interested individuals in each office authorized to issue drivers licenses or special identification cards. The Division shall obtain donor cards from qualified organ, eye, or tissue procurement organizations or tissue banks, as defined in

G.S. 130A-412.4(31). The Division shall offer organ donation information and a donor card to each applicant for a drivers license. The organ donation information shall include the following:

(1)   A statement informing the individual that federally designated organ procurement organizations and eye banks have read-only access to the Department-operated Organ Donor Registry Internet site (hereafter "Donor Registry") listing those individuals who have stated to the Division of Motor Vehicles the individual's intent to be an organ donor and have an organ donation symbol on the individual's drivers license or special identification card.

(2)   The type of information that will be made available on the Donor Registry. (2001-481, s. 3; 2004-189, s. 3; 2007-538, s. 7.)

§ 20-7.4. License to Give Trust Fund established.

(a)   There is established the License to Give Trust Fund. Revenue in the Fund includes amounts credited by the Division as required by law, and other funds. Any surplus in the Fund shall not revert but shall be used for the purposes stated in this section. The Fund shall be kept on deposit with the State Treasurer, as in the case of other State Funds, and may be invested by the State Treasurer in any lawful securities for investment of State funds. The License to Give Trust Fund is subject to oversight by the State Auditor pursuant to Article 5A of Chapter 147 of the General Statutes.

(b)   The purposes for which funds may be expended by the License to Give Trust Fund Commission from the License to Give Trust Fund are as follows:

(1)   As grants-in-aid for initiatives that educate about and promote organ and tissue donation and health care decision making at life's end.

(2)   Expenses of the License to Give Trust Fund Commission as authorized in G.S. 20-7.5. (2004-189, s. 4(a).)

§ 20-7.5. License to Give Trust Fund Commission established.

(a) There is established the License to Give Trust Fund Commission. The Commission shall be located in the Department of Administration for budgetary and administrative purposes only. The Commission may allocate funds from the License to Give Trust Fund for the purposes authorized in G.S. 20-7.4. The Commission shall have 15 members, appointed as follows:

(1) Four members by the General Assembly, upon the recommendation of the President Pro Tempore of the Senate:

a. One representative of Carolina Donor Services.

b. One representative of LifeShare of The Carolinas.

c. Two members who have demonstrated an interest in organ and tissue donation and education.

(2) Four members by the General Assembly, upon the recommendation of the Speaker of the House of Representatives:

a. One representative of The North Carolina Eye Bank, Inc.

b. One representative of The Carolinas Center for Hospice and End-of-Life Care.

c. Two members who have demonstrated an interest in promoting advance care planning education.

(3) Seven members by the Governor:

a. Three members representing organ, tissue, and eye recipients, families of recipients, or families of donors. Of these three, one each from the mountain, heartland, and coastal regions of the State.

b. One member who is a transplant physician licensed to practice medicine in this State.

c. One member who has demonstrated an interest in organ and tissue donation and education.

d. One member who has demonstrated an interest in promoting advance care planning education.

e. A representative of the North Carolina Department of Transportation.

(b) The Commission shall elect from its membership a chair and a vice-chair for two-year terms. The Secretary of Administration shall provide meeting facilities for the Commission as required by the Chair.

(c) The members of the Commission shall receive per diem and necessary travel and subsistence expenses in accordance with G.S. 138-5 and G.S. 138-6, as applicable. Per diem, subsistence, and travel expenses of the members shall be paid from the License to Give Trust Fund.

(d) The members of the Commission shall comply with G.S. 14-234 prohibiting conflicts of interest. In addition to the restrictions imposed under G.S. 14-234, a member shall not vote on, participate in the deliberations of, or otherwise attempt through his or her official capacity to influence the vote on allocations of moneys from the License to Give Trust Fund to a nonprofit entity of which the member is an officer, director, or employee, or to a governmental entity of which the member is an employee or a member of the governing board. A violation of this subsection is a Class 1 misdemeanor. (2004-189, s. 4(b).)

§ 20-7.6. Powers and duties of the License to Give Trust Fund Commission.

The License to Give Trust Fund Commission has the following powers and duties:

(1) Establish general policies and guidelines for awarding grants-in-aid to nonprofit entities to conduct education and awareness activities on organ and tissue donation and advance care planning.

(2) Accept gifts or grants from other sources to further the purposes of the License to Give Trust Fund. Such gifts or grants shall be transmitted to the State Treasurer for credit to the Fund.

(3) Hire staff or contract for other expertise for the administration of the Fund. Expenses related to staffing shall be paid from the License to Give Trust Fund. (2004-189, s. 4(b).)

§ 20-8. Persons exempt from license.

The following are exempt from license hereunder:

(1) Any person while operating a motor vehicle the property of and in the service of the Armed Forces of the United States. This shall not be construed to exempt any operators of the United States Civilian Conservation Corps motor vehicles;

(2) Any person while driving or operating any road machine, farm tractor, or implement of husbandry temporarily operated or moved on a highway;

(3) A nonresident who is at least 16 years of age who has in his immediate possession a valid driver's license issued to him in his home state or country if the nonresident is operating a motor vehicle in this State in accordance with the license restrictions and vehicle classifications that would be applicable to him under the laws and regulations of his home state or country if he were driving in his home state or country. This exemption specifically applies to nonresident military spouses, regardless of their employment status, who are temporarily residing in North Carolina due to the active duty military orders of a spouse.

(4) to (6) Repealed by Session Laws 1979, c. 667, s. 13.

(7) Any person who is at least 16 years of age and while operating a moped. (1935, c. 52, s. 3; 1963, c. 1175; 1973, c. 1017; 1975, c. 859, s. 2; 1979, c. 574, s. 7; c. 667, s. 13; 1983, c. 436; 2009-274, s. 4.)

§ 20-9. What persons shall not be licensed.

(a) To obtain a regular drivers license, a person must have reached the minimum age set in the following table for the class of license sought:

Class of Regular License	Minimum Age
Class A	18
Class B	18

Class C   16

G.S. 20-37.13 sets the age qualifications for a commercial drivers license.

(b)   The Division shall not issue a driver's license to any person whose license has been suspended or revoked during the period for which the license was suspended or revoked.

(b1)   The Division shall not issue a drivers license to any person whose permit or license has been suspended or revoked under G.S. 20-13.2(c1) during the suspension or revocation period, unless the Division has restored the person's permit or license under G.S. 20-13.2(c1).

(c)   The Division shall not issue a driver's license to any person who is an habitual drunkard or is an habitual user of narcotic drugs or barbiturates, whether or not such use be in accordance with the prescription of a physician.

(d)   Repealed by Session Laws 2012-194, s. 8, effective July 17, 2012.

(e)   The Division shall not issue a driver's license to any person when in the opinion of the Division such person is afflicted with or suffering from such physical or mental disability or disease as will serve to prevent such person from exercising reasonable and ordinary control over a motor vehicle while operating the same upon the highways, nor shall a license be issued to any person who is unable to understand highway warnings or direction signs.

(f)   The Division shall not issue a driver's license to any person whose license or driving privilege is in a state of cancellation, suspension or revocation in any jurisdiction, if the acts or things upon which the cancellation, suspension or revocation in such other jurisdiction was based would constitute lawful grounds for cancellation, suspension or revocation in this State had those acts or things been done or committed in this State; provided, however, any such cancellation shall not prohibit issuance for a period in excess of 18 months.

(g)   The Division may issue a driver's license to any applicant covered by subsection (e) of this section under the following conditions:

(1)   The Division may issue a license to any person who is afflicted with or suffering from a physical or mental disability set out in subsection (e) of this section who is otherwise qualified to obtain a license, provided such person submits to the Division a certificate in the form prescribed in subdivision (2).

Until a license issued under this subdivision expires or is revoked, the license continues in force as long as the licensee presents to the Division a certificate in the form prescribed in subdivision (2) of this subsection at the intervals determined by the Division to be in the best interests of public safety.

(2)   The Division shall not issue a license pursuant to this section unless the applicant has submitted to a physical examination by a physician or surgeon duly licensed to practice medicine in this State or in any other state of the United States and unless such examining physician or surgeon has completed and signed the certificate required by subdivision (1). Such certificate shall be devised by the Commissioner with the advice of qualified experts in the field of diagnosing and treating physical and mental disorders as he may select to assist him and shall be designed to elicit the maximum medical information necessary to aid in determining whether or not it would be a hazard to public safety to permit the applicant to operate a motor vehicle, including, if such is the fact, the examining physician's statement that the applicant is under medication and treatment and that such person's physical or mental disability is controlled. The certificate shall contain a waiver of privilege and the recommendation of the examining physician to the Commissioner as to whether a license should be issued to the applicant.

(3)   The Commissioner is not bound by the recommendation of the examining physician but shall give fair consideration to such recommendation in exercising his discretion in acting upon the application, the criterion being whether or not, upon all the evidence, it appears that it is safe to permit the applicant to operate a motor vehicle. The burden of proof of such fact is upon the applicant. In deciding whether to issue or deny a license, the Commissioner may be guided by opinion of experts in the field of diagnosing and treating the specific physical or mental disorder suffered by an applicant and such experts may be compensated for their services on an equitable basis. The Commissioner may also take into consideration any other factors which bear on the issue of public safety.

(4)   Whenever a license is denied by the Commissioner, such denial may be reviewed by a reviewing board upon written request of the applicant filed with the Division within 10 days after receipt of such denial. The reviewing board shall consist of the Commissioner or his authorized representative and four persons designated by the chairman of the Commission for Public Health. The persons designated by the chairman of the Commission for Public Health shall be either members of the Commission for Public Health or physicians duly licensed to practice medicine in this State. The members so designated by the

chairman of the Commission for Public Health shall receive the same per diem and expenses as provided by law for members of the Commission for Public Health, which per diem and expenses shall be charged to the same appropriation as per diems and expenses for members of the Commission for Public Health. The Commissioner or his authorized representative, plus any two of the members designated by the chairman of the Commission for Public Health, constitute a quorum. The procedure for hearings authorized by this section shall be as follows:

a. Applicants shall be afforded an opportunity for hearing, after reasonable notice of not less than 10 days, before the review board established by subdivision (4). The notice shall be in writing and shall be delivered to the applicant in person or sent by certified mail, with return receipt requested. The notice shall state the time, place, and subject of the hearing.

b. The review board may compel the attendance of witnesses and the production of such books, records and papers as it desires at a hearing authorized by the section. Upon request of an applicant, a subpoena to compel the attendance of any witness or a subpoena duces tecum to compel the production of any books, records, or papers shall be issued by the board. Subpoenas shall be directed to the sheriff of the county where the witness resides or is found and shall be served and returned in the same manner as a subpoena in a criminal case. Fees of the sheriff and witnesses shall be the same as that allowed in the district court in cases before that court and shall be paid in the same manner as other expenses of the Division of Motor Vehicles are paid. In any case of disobedience or neglect of any subpoena served on any person, or the refusal of any witness to testify to any matters regarding which he may be lawfully interrogated, the district court or superior court where such disobedience, neglect or refusal occurs, or any judge thereof, on application by the board, shall compel obedience or punish as for contempt.

c. A hearing may be continued upon motion of the applicant for good cause shown with approval of the board or upon order of the board.

d. The board shall pass upon the admissibility of evidence at a hearing but the applicant affected may at the time object to the board's ruling, and, if evidence offered by an applicant is rejected the party may proffer the evidence, and such proffer shall be made a part of the record. The board shall not be bound by common law or statutory rules of evidence which prevail in courts of law or equity and may admit and give probative value to evidence which possesses probative value commonly accepted by reasonably prudent men in the conduct of their affairs. They may exclude incompetent, immaterial, irrelevant and unduly repetitious evidence. Uncontested facts may be stipulated by agreement between an applicant and the board and evidence relating thereto may be excluded. All evidence, including records and documents in the possession of the Division of Motor Vehicles or the board, of which the board desires to avail itself shall be made a part of the record. Documentary evidence may be received in the form of copies or excerpts, or by incorporation by reference. The board shall prepare an official record, which shall include testimony and exhibits. A record of the testimony and other evidence submitted shall be taken, but it shall not be necessary to transcribe shorthand notes or electronic recordings unless requested for purposes of court review.

e.   Every decision and order adverse to an applicant shall be in writing or stated in the record and shall be accompanied by findings of fact and conclusions of law. The findings of fact shall consist of a concise statement of the board's conclusions on each contested issue of fact. Counsel for applicant, or applicant, if he has no counsel, shall be notified of the board's decision in person or by registered mail with return receipt requested. A copy of the board's decision with accompanying findings and conclusions shall be delivered or mailed upon request to applicant's attorney of record or to applicant, if he has no attorney.

f.   Actions of the reviewing board are subject to judicial review as provided under Chapter 150B of the General Statutes.

g.   Repealed by Session Laws 1977, c. 840.

h.   All records and evidence collected and compiled by the Division and the reviewing board shall not be considered public records within the meaning of Chapter [section] 132-1, and following, of the General Statutes of North Carolina and may be made available to the public only upon an order of a court of competent jurisdiction. All information furnished by or on behalf of an applicant under this section shall be without prejudice and shall be for the use of the Division, the reviewing board or the court in administering this section and shall not be used in any manner as evidence, or for any other purposes in any trial, civil or criminal.

(h)   The Division shall not issue a drivers license to an applicant who currently holds a license to drive issued by another state unless the applicant surrenders the license.

(i) The Division shall not issue a drivers license to an applicant who has resided in this State for less than 12 months until the Division has searched the National Sex Offender Public Registry to determine if the person is currently registered as a sex offender in another state.

(1) If the Division finds that the person is currently registered as a sex offender in another state, the Division shall not issue a drivers license to the person until the person submits proof of registration pursuant to Article 27A of Chapter 14 of the General Statutes issued by the sheriff of the county where the person resides.

(2) If the person does not appear on the National Sex Offender Public Registry, the Division shall issue a drivers license but shall require the person to sign an affidavit acknowledging that the person has been notified that if the person is a sex offender, then the person is required to register pursuant to Article 27A of Chapter 14 of the General Statutes.

(3) If the Division is unable to access all states' information contained in the National Sex Offender Public Registry, but the person is otherwise qualified to obtain a drivers license, then the Division shall issue the drivers license but shall first require the person to sign an affidavit stating that: (i) the person does not appear on the National Sex Offender Public Registry and (ii) acknowledging that the person has been notified that if the person is a sex offender, then the person is required to register pursuant to Article 27A of Chapter 14 of the General Statutes. The Division shall search the National Sex Offender Public Registry for the person within a reasonable time after access to the Registry is restored. If the person does appear in the National Sex Offender Public Registry, the person is in violation of G.S. 20-30, and the Division shall immediately revoke the drivers license and shall promptly notify the sheriff of the county where the person resides of the offense.

(4) Any person denied a license or whose license has been revoked by the Division pursuant to this subsection shall have a right to file a petition within 30 days thereafter for a hearing in the matter in the superior court of the county wherein such person shall reside, or to the resident judge of the district or judge holding the court of that district, or special or emergency judge holding a court in such district, and such court or judge is hereby vested with jurisdiction, and it shall be its or his duty to set the matter for hearing upon 30 days' written notice to the Division, and thereupon to take testimony and examine into the facts of the case and to determine whether the petitioner is entitled to a license under the provisions of this subsection and whether the petitioner is in violation of G.S.

20-30. (1935, c. 52, s. 4; 1951, c. 542, s. 3; 1953, c. 773; 1955, c. 118, s. 7; 1967, cc. 961, 966; 1971, c. 152; c. 528, s. 11; 1973, cc. 135, 441; c. 476, s. 128; c. 1331, s. 3; 1975, c. 716, s. 5; 1979, c. 667, ss. 14, 41; 1983, c. 545; 1987, c. 827, s. 1; 1989, c. 771, s. 7; 1991, c. 726, s. 6; 1993, c. 368, s. 2; c. 533, s. 4; 1999-243, s. 4; 1999-452, s. 8; 2003-14, s. 1; 2006-247, s. 19(c); 2007-182, s. 2; 2012-194, s. 8.)

§ 20-9.1. Physicians and psychologists providing medical information on drivers with physical and mental disabilities.

(a) Notwithstanding G.S. 8-53 for physicians and G.S. 8-53.3 for psychologists, or any other law relating to confidentiality of communications between physicians or psychologists and their patients, a physician or a psychologist duly licensed in the State of North Carolina may disclose after consultation with the patient to the Commissioner information about a patient who has a mental or physical disability that the physician or psychologist believes may affect the patient's ability to safely operate a motor vehicle. This information shall be limited to the patient's name, address, date of birth, and diagnosis.

(b) The information provided to the Commissioner pursuant to subsection (a) of this section shall be confidential and shall be used only for the purpose of determining the qualifications of the patient to operate a motor vehicle.

(c) A physician or psychologist disclosing or not disclosing information pursuant to this section is immune from any civil or criminal liability that might otherwise be incurred or imposed based on the disclosure or lack of disclosure provided that the physician or psychologist was acting in good faith and without malice. In any proceeding involving liability, good faith and lack of malice are presumed. (1997-464, s. 1.)

§ 20-9.2. Selective service system registration requirements.

(a) Any male United States citizen or immigrant who is at least 18 years of age but less than 26 years of age shall be registered in compliance with the requirements of the Military Selective Service Act, 50 U.S.C. § 453 (1948), when applying for the issuance, renewal, or duplication of a drivers license, commercial drivers license, or identification card.

(b) The Division shall forward in an electronic format the necessary personal information of the applicants identified in subsection (a) of this section required for registration to the Selective Service System. An application for the issuance, renewal, or duplication of a drivers license, commercial drivers license, or identification card constitutes an affirmation that the applicant has already registered with the Selective Service System or that he authorizes the Division to forward the necessary information to the Selective Service System for registration. The Division shall notify the applicant that his application for the issuance, renewal, or duplication of a drivers license, commercial drivers license, or identification card serves as his consent to be registered with the Selective Service System pursuant to this section. (2002-162, s. 1.)

§ 20-9.3. Notification of requirements for sex offender registration.

The Division shall provide notice to each person who applies for the issuance of a drivers license, learner's permit, or instruction permit to operate a motor vehicle, and to each person who applies for an identification card, that if the person is a sex offender, then the person is required to register pursuant to Article 27A of Chapter 14 of the General Statutes. (2006-247, s. 19(b).)

§ 20-10. Age limits for drivers of public passenger-carrying vehicles.

It shall be unlawful for any person, whether licensed under this Article or not, who is under the age of 18 years to drive a motor vehicle while in use as a public passenger-carrying vehicle. For purposes of this section, an ambulance when operated for the purpose of transporting persons who are sick, injured, or otherwise incapacitated shall not be treated as a public passenger-carrying vehicle.

No person 14 years of age or under, whether licensed under this Article or not, shall operate any road machine, farm tractor or motor driven implement of husbandry on any highway within this State. Provided any person may operate a road machine, farm tractor, or motor driven implement of husbandry upon a highway adjacent to or running in front of the land upon which such person lives when said person is actually engaged in farming operations. (1935, c. 52, s. 5; 1951, c. 764; 1967, c. 343, s. 4; 1971, c. 1231, s. 1.)

§ 20-10.1. Mopeds.

It shall be unlawful for any person who is under the age of 16 years to operate a moped as defined in G.S. 105-164.3 upon any highway or public vehicular area of this State. (1979, c. 574, s. 8; 2002-72, s. 6.)

§ 20-11. Issuance of limited learner's permit and provisional drivers license to person who is less than 18 years old.

(a) Process. - Safe driving requires instruction in driving and experience. To ensure that a person who is less than 18 years old has both instruction and experience before obtaining a drivers license, driving privileges are granted first on a limited basis and are then expanded in accordance with the following process:

(1) Level 1. - Driving with a limited learner's permit.

(2) Level 2. - Driving with a limited provisional license.

(3) Level 3. - Driving with a full provisional license.

A permit or license issued under this section must indicate the level of driving privileges granted by the permit or license.

(b) Level 1. - A person who is at least 15 years old but less than 18 years old may obtain a limited learner's permit if the person meets all of the following requirements:

(1) Passes a course of driver education prescribed in G.S. 115C-215 or a course of driver instruction at a licensed commercial driver training school.

(2) Passes a written test administered by the Division.

(3) Has a driving eligibility certificate or a high school diploma or its equivalent.

(c) Level 1 Restrictions. - A limited learner's permit authorizes the permit holder to drive a specified type or class of motor vehicle only under the following conditions:

(1) The permit holder must be in possession of the permit.

(2) A supervising driver must be seated beside the permit holder in the front seat of the vehicle when it is in motion. No person other than the supervising driver can be in the front seat.

(3) For the first six months after issuance, the permit holder may drive only between the hours of 5:00 a.m. and 9:00 p.m.

(4) After the first six months after issuance, the permit holder may drive at any time.

(5) Every person occupying the vehicle being driven by the permit holder must have a safety belt properly fastened about his or her body, or be restrained by a child passenger restraint system as provided in G.S. 20-137.1(a), when the vehicle is in motion.

(6) The permit holder shall not use a mobile telephone or other additional technology associated with a mobile telephone while operating the motor vehicle on a public street or highway or public vehicular area.

(d) Level 2. - A person who is at least 16 years old but less than 18 years old may obtain a limited provisional license if the person meets all of the following requirements:

(1) Has held a limited learner's permit issued by the Division for at least 12 months.

(2) Has not been convicted of a motor vehicle moving violation or seat belt infraction or a violation of G.S. 20-137.3 during the preceding six months.

(3) Passes a road test administered by the Division.

(4) Has a driving eligibility certificate or a high school diploma or its equivalent.

(5) Has completed a driving log, on a form approved by the Division, detailing a minimum of 60 hours as the operator of a motor vehicle of a class for which the driver has been issued a limited learner's permit. The log must show at least 10 hours of the required driving occurred during nighttime hours. No more than 10 hours of driving per week may be counted toward the 60-hour requirement. The driving log must be signed by the supervising driver and submitted to the Division at the time the applicant seeks to obtain a limited provisional license. If the Division has cause to believe that a driving log has been falsified, the limited learner's permit holder shall be required to complete a new driving log with the same requirements and shall not be eligible to obtain a limited provisional license for six months.

(e) Level 2 Restrictions. - A limited provisional license authorizes the license holder to drive a specified type or class of motor vehicle only under the following conditions:

(1) The license holder shall be in possession of the license.

(2) The license holder may drive without supervision in any of the following circumstances:

a. From 5:00 a.m. to 9:00 p.m.

b. When driving directly to or from work.

c. When driving directly to or from an activity of a volunteer fire department, volunteer rescue squad, or volunteer emergency medical service, if the driver is a member of the organization.

(3) The license holder may drive with supervision at any time. When the license holder is driving with supervision, the supervising driver shall be seated beside the license holder in the front seat of the vehicle when it is in motion. The supervising driver need not be the only other occupant of the front seat, but shall be the person seated next to the license holder.

(4) When the license holder is driving the vehicle and is not accompanied by the supervising driver, there may be no more than one passenger under 21 years of age in the vehicle. This limit does not apply to passengers who are

members of the license holder's immediate family or whose primary residence is the same household as the license holder. However, if a family member or member of the same household as the license holder who is younger than 21 years of age is a passenger in the vehicle, no other passengers under 21 years of age, who are not members of the license holder's immediate family or members of the license holder's household, may be in the vehicle.

(5) Every person occupying the vehicle being driven by the license holder shall have a safety belt properly fastened about his or her body, or be restrained by a child passenger restraint system as provided in G.S. 20-137.1(a), when the vehicle is in motion.

(6) The license holder shall not use a mobile telephone or other additional technology associated with a mobile telephone while operating the vehicle on a public street or highway or public vehicular area.

(f) Level 3. - A person who is at least 16 years old but less than 18 years old may obtain a full provisional license if the person meets all of the following requirements:

(1) Has held a limited provisional license issued by the Division for at least six months.

(2) Has not been convicted of a motor vehicle moving violation or seat belt infraction or a violation of G.S. 20-137.3 during the preceding six months.

(3) Has a driving eligibility certificate or a high school diploma or its equivalent.

(4) Has completed a driving log, on a form approved by the Division, detailing a minimum of 12 hours as the operator of a motor vehicle of a class for which the driver is licensed. The log must show at least six hours of the required driving occurred during nighttime hours. The driving log must be signed by the supervising driver for any hours driven outside the provisions of subdivision (e)(2) of this section and submitted to the Division at the time the applicant seeks to obtain a full provisional license. If the Division has cause to believe that a driving log has been falsified, the limited provisional licensee shall be required to complete a new driving log with the same requirements and shall not be eligible to obtain a full provisional license for six months.

A person who meets these requirements may obtain a full provisional license by mail.

(g)   Level 3 Restrictions. - The restrictions on Level 1 and Level 2 drivers concerning time of driving, supervision, and passenger limitations do not apply to a full provisional license. However, the prohibition against operating a motor vehicle while using a mobile telephone under G.S. 20-137.3(b) shall apply to a full provisional license.

(h)   Exception for Persons 16 to 18 Who Have an Unrestricted Out-of-State License. - A person who is at least 16 years old but less than 18 years old, who was a resident of another state and has an unrestricted drivers license issued by that state, and who becomes a resident of this State may obtain one of the following upon the submission of a driving eligibility certificate or a high school diploma or its equivalent:

(1)   A temporary permit, if the person has not completed a drivers education program that meets the requirements of the Superintendent of Public Instruction but is currently enrolled in a drivers education program that meets these requirements. A temporary permit is valid for the period specified in the permit and authorizes the holder of the permit to drive a specified type or class of motor vehicle when in possession of the permit, subject to any restrictions imposed by the Division concerning time of driving, supervision, and passenger limitations. The period must end within 10 days after the expected completion date of the drivers education program in which the applicant is enrolled.

(2)   A full provisional license, if the person has completed a drivers education program that meets the requirements of the Superintendent of Public Instruction, has held the license issued by the other state for at least 12 months, and has not been convicted during the preceding six months of a motor vehicle moving violation, a seat belt infraction, or an offense committed in another jurisdiction that would be a motor vehicle moving violation or seat belt infraction if committed in this State.

(2a)   A full provisional license, if the person has completed a drivers education program that meets the requirements of the Superintendent of Public Instruction, has held both a learner's permit and a restricted license from another state for at least six months each, the Commissioner finds that the requirements for the learner's permit and restricted license are comparable to the requirements for a learner's permit and restricted license in this State, and the person has not been convicted during the preceding six months of a motor vehicle moving violation, a seat belt infraction, or an offense committed in another jurisdiction that would be a moving violation or a seat belt infraction if committed in this State.

(3)   A limited provisional license, if the person has completed a drivers education program that meets the requirements of the Superintendent of Public Instruction but either did not hold the license issued by the other state for at least 12 months or was convicted during the preceding six months of a motor vehicle moving violation, a seat belt infraction, or an offense committed in another jurisdiction that would be a motor vehicle moving violation or seat belt infraction if committed in this State.

(h1)   Exception for Persons 16 to 18 Who Have an Out-of-State Restricted License. - A person who is at least 16 years old but less than 18 years old, who was a resident of another state and has a restricted drivers license issued by that state, and who becomes a resident of this State may obtain one of the following:

(1)   A limited provisional license, if the person has completed a drivers education program that meets the requirements of the Superintendent of Public Instruction, held the restricted license issued by the other state for at least 12 months, and whose parent or guardian certifies that the person has not been convicted during the preceding six months of a motor vehicle moving violation, a seat belt infraction, or an offense committed in another jurisdiction that would be a motor vehicle moving violation or seat belt infraction if committed in this State.

(2)   A limited learners permit, if the person has completed a drivers education program that meets the requirements of the Superintendent of Public Instruction but either did not hold the restricted license issued by the other state for at least 12 months or was convicted during the preceding six months of a motor vehicle moving violation, a seat belt infraction, or an offense committed in another jurisdiction that would be a motor vehicle moving violation or seat belt infraction if committed in this State. A person who qualifies for a limited learners permit under this subdivision and whose parent or guardian certifies that the person has not been convicted of a moving violation in the preceding six months shall be deemed to have held a limited learners permit in this State for each month the person held a restricted license in another state.

(h2)   Exception for Persons Age 15 Who Have an Out-of-State Unrestricted or Restricted License. - A person who is age 15, who was a resident of another state, has an unrestricted or restricted drivers license issued by that state, and who becomes a resident of this State may obtain a limited learners permit if the person has completed a drivers education program that meets the requirements of the Superintendent of Public Instruction. A person who qualifies for a limited learners permit under this subsection and whose parent or guardian certifies that the person has not been convicted of a moving violation in the preceding six months shall be deemed to have held a limited learners permit in this State for each month the person held an unrestricted or restricted license in another state.

(h3) Exception for Persons Less Than Age 18 Who Have a Federally Issued Unrestricted or Restricted License. - A person who is less than age 18, who has an unrestricted or restricted drivers license issued by the federal government, and who becomes a resident of this State may obtain a limited provisional license or a provisional license if the person has completed a drivers education program substantially equivalent to the drivers education program that meets the requirements of the Superintendent of Public Instruction. A person who qualifies for a limited provisional license or a provisional license under this subsection and whose parent or guardian certifies that the person has not been convicted of a moving violation in the preceding six months shall be deemed to have held a limited provisional license or a provisional license in this State for each month the person held an unrestricted or restricted license issued by the federal government.

(i) Application. - An application for a permit or license authorized by this section must be signed by both the applicant and another person. That person must be:

(1) The applicant's parent or guardian;

(2) A person approved by the applicant's parent or guardian; or

(3) A person approved by the Division.

(j) Duration and Fee. - A limited learner's permit expires on the eighteenth birthday of the permit holder. A limited provisional license expires on the eighteenth birthday of the license holder. A limited learner's permit or limited provisional license issued under this section that expires on a weekend or State holiday shall remain valid through the fifth regular State business day following the date of expiration. A full provisional license expires on the date set under G.S. 20-7(f). The fee for a limited learner's permit or a limited provisional license is fifteen dollars ($15.00). The fee for a full provisional license is the amount set under G.S. 20-7(i).

(k)   Supervising Driver. - A supervising driver shall be a parent, grandparent, or guardian of the permit holder or license holder or a responsible person approved by the parent or guardian or the Division. A supervising driver shall be a licensed driver who has been licensed for at least five years. At least one supervising driver shall sign the application for a permit or license.

(l)   Violations. - It is unlawful for the holder of a limited learner's permit, a temporary permit, or a limited provisional license to drive a motor vehicle in violation of the restrictions that apply to the permit or license. Failure to comply with a restriction concerning the time of driving or the presence of a supervising driver in the vehicle constitutes operating a motor vehicle without a license. Failure to comply with the restriction regarding the use of a mobile telephone while operating a motor vehicle is an infraction punishable by a fine of twenty-five dollars ($25.00). Failure to comply with any other restriction, including seating and passenger limitations, is an infraction punishable by a monetary penalty as provided in G.S. 20-176. Failure to comply with the provisions of subsections (e) and (g) of this section shall not constitute negligence per se or contributory negligence by the driver or passenger in any action for the recovery of damages arising out of the operation, ownership or maintenance of a motor vehicle. Any evidence of failure to comply with the provisions of subdivisions (1), (2), (3), (4), and (5) of subsection (e) of this section shall not be admissible in any criminal or civil trial, action, or proceeding except in an action based on a violation of this section. No drivers license points or insurance surcharge shall be assessed for failure to comply with seating and occupancy limitations in subsection (e) of this section. No drivers license points or insurance surcharge shall be assessed for failure to comply with subsection (e) or (g) of this section regarding the use of a mobile telephone while operating a motor vehicle.

(m)   Insurance Status. - The holder of a limited learner's permit is not considered a licensed driver for the purpose of determining the inexperienced operator premium surcharge under automobile insurance policies.

(n)   Driving Eligibility Certificate. - A person who desires to obtain a permit or license issued under this section must have a high school diploma or its equivalent or must have a driving eligibility certificate. A driving eligibility certificate must meet the following conditions:

(1) The person who is required to sign the certificate under subdivision (4) of this subsection must show that he or she has determined that one of the following requirements is met:

a. The person is currently enrolled in school and is making progress toward obtaining a high school diploma or its equivalent.

b. A substantial hardship would be placed on the person or the person's family if the person does not receive a certificate.

c. The person cannot make progress toward obtaining a high school diploma or its equivalent.

(1a) The person who is required to sign the certificate under subdivision (4) of this subsection also must show that one of the following requirements is met:

a. The person who seeks a permit or license issued under this section is not subject to subsection (n1) of this section.

b. The person who seeks a permit or license issued under this section is subject to subsection (n1) of this section and is eligible for the certificate under that subsection.

(2) It must be on a form approved by the Division.

(3) It must be dated within 30 days of the date the person applies for a permit or license issuable under this section.

(4) It must be signed by the applicable person named below:

a. The principal, or the principal's designee, of the public school in which the person is enrolled.

b. The administrator, or the administrator's designee, of the nonpublic school in which the person is enrolled.

c. The person who provides the academic instruction in the home school in which the person is enrolled.

c1. The person who provides the academic instruction in the home in accordance with an educational program found by a court, prior to July 1, 1998, to comply with the compulsory attendance law.

d. The designee of the board of directors of the charter school in which the person is enrolled.

e. The president, or the president's designee, of the community college in which the person is enrolled.

Notwithstanding any other law, the decision concerning whether a driving eligibility certificate was properly issued or improperly denied shall be appealed only as provided under the rules adopted in accordance with G.S. 115C-12(28), 115D-5(a3), or 115C-566, whichever is applicable, and may not be appealed under this Chapter.

(n1) Lose Control; Lose License.

(1) The following definitions apply in this subsection:

a. Applicable State entity. - The State Board of Education for public schools and charter schools, the State Board of Community Colleges for community colleges, or the Secretary of Administration for nonpublic schools and home schools.

b. Certificate. - A driving eligibility certificate that meets the conditions of subsection (n) of this section.

c. Disciplinary action. - An expulsion, a suspension for more than 10 consecutive days, or an assignment to an alternative educational setting for more than 10 consecutive days.

d. Enumerated student conduct. - One of the following behaviors that results in disciplinary action:

1. The possession or sale of an alcoholic beverage or an illegal controlled substance on school property.

2. The bringing, possession, or use on school property of a weapon or firearm that resulted in disciplinary action under G.S. 115C-390.10 or that could

have resulted in that disciplinary action if the conduct had occurred in a public school.

3. The physical assault on a teacher or other school personnel on school property.

e. School. - A public school, charter school, community college, nonpublic school, or home school.

f. School administrator. - The person who is required to sign certificates under subdivision (4) of subsection (n) of this section.

g. School property. - The physical premises of the school, school buses or other vehicles under the school's control or contract and that are used to transport students, and school-sponsored curricular or extracurricular activities that occur on or off the physical premises of the school.

h. Student. - A person who desires to obtain a permit or license issued under this section.

(2) Any student who was subject to disciplinary action for enumerated student conduct that occurred either after the first day of July before the school year in which the student enrolled in the eighth grade or after the student's fourteenth birthday, whichever event occurred first, is subject to this subsection.

(3) A student who is subject to this subsection is eligible for a certificate when the school administrator determines that the student has exhausted all administrative appeals connected to the disciplinary action and that one of the following conditions is met:

a. The enumerated student conduct occurred before the student reached the age of 15, and the student is now at least 16 years old.

b. The enumerated student conduct occurred after the student reached the age of 15, and it is at least one year after the date the student exhausted all administrative appeals connected to the disciplinary action.

c. The student needs the certificate in order to drive to and from school, a drug or alcohol treatment counseling program, as appropriate, or a mental health treatment program, and no other transportation is available.

(4) A student whose permit or license is denied or revoked due to ineligibility for a certificate under this subsection may otherwise be eligible for a certificate if, after six months from the date of the ineligibility, the school administrator determines that one of the following conditions is met:

a. The student has returned to school or has been placed in an alternative educational setting, and has displayed exemplary student behavior, as defined by the applicable State entity.

b. The disciplinary action was for the possession or sale of an alcoholic beverage or an illegal controlled substance on school property, and the student subsequently attended and successfully completed, as defined by the applicable State entity, a drug or alcohol treatment counseling program, as appropriate. (1935, c. 52, s. 6; 1953, c. 355; 1955, c. 1187, s. 8; 1963, c. 968, ss. 2, 2A; 1965, c. 410, s. 3; c. 1171; 1967, c. 694; 1969, c. 37; 1973, c. 191, ss. 1, 2; c. 664, ss. 1, 2; 1975, c. 79; c. 716, s. 5; 1979, c. 101; c. 667, ss. 15, 16, 41; 1981 (Reg. Sess., 1982), c. 1257, s. 2; 1989 (Reg. Sess., 1990), c. 1021, s. 11; 1991, c. 689, s. 326; 1993, c. 539, s. 319; 1994, Ex. Sess., c. 24, s. 14(c); 1997-16, s. 1; 1997-443, s. 32.20; 1997-507, s. 1; 1998-149, ss. 2.1, 2.2, 2.3, 2.4, 2.5; 1998-212, s. 9.21(c); 1999-243, ss. 1, 2; 1999-276, s. 1; 1999-387, s. 4; 1999-452, s. 9; 2001-194, s. 1; 2001-487, s. 51.5(a); 2002-73, ss. 1, 2; 2002-159, s. 30; 2005-276, s. 44.1(b); 2006-177, ss. 2-7; 2011-145, s. 28.37(d); 2011-282, s. 15; 2011-381, s. 3; 2011-385, ss. 1-3; 2011-412, s. 3.2.)

§ 20-11.1. Repealed by Session Laws 1965, c. 410, s. 4.

§ 20-12: Repealed by Session Laws 1997-16, s. 6.

§ 20-12.1. Impaired supervision or instruction.

(a) It is unlawful for a person to serve as a supervising driver under G.S. 20-7(l) or G.S. 20-11 or as an approved instructor under G.S. 20-7(m) in any of the following circumstances:

(1) While under the influence of an impairing substance.

(2) After having consumed sufficient alcohol to have, at any relevant time after the driving, an alcohol concentration of 0.08 or more.

(b) An offense under this section is an implied-consent offense under G.S. 20-16.2. (1977, c. 116, ss. 1, 2; 1981, c. 412, s. 4; c. 747, s. 66; 1983, c. 435, s. 9; 1993, c. 285, s. 2; 1997-16, s. 7; 1997-443, s. 32.20.)

§ 20-13. Suspension of license of provisional licensee.

(a) The Division may suspend, with or without a preliminary hearing, the operator's license of a provisional licensee upon receipt of notice of the licensee's conviction of a motor vehicle moving violation, in accordance with subsection (b), if the offense was committed while the person was still a provisional licensee. As used in this section, the phrase "motor vehicle moving violation" does not include the offenses listed in the third paragraph of G.S. 20-16(c) for which no points are assessed, nor does it include equipment violations specified in Part 9 of Article 3 of this Chapter. However, if the Division revokes without a preliminary hearing and the person whose license is being revoked requests a hearing before the effective date of the revocation, the licensee retains his license unless it is revoked under some other provision of the law, until the hearing is held, the person withdraws his request, or he fails to appear at a scheduled hearing.

(b) The Division may suspend the license of a provisional licensee as follows:

(1) For the first motor vehicle moving violation, the Division may not suspend the license of the provisional licensee.

(2) For conviction of a second motor vehicle moving violation committed within 12 months of the date the first offense was committed, the Division may suspend the licensee's license for up to 30 days.

(3) For conviction of a third motor vehicle moving violation committed within 12 months of the date the first offense was committed, the Division may suspend the licensee's license for up to 90 days.

(4) For conviction of a fourth motor vehicle moving violation committed within 12 months of the date the first offense was committed, the Division may suspend the licensee's license for up to six months.

The Division may, in lieu of suspension and with the written consent of the licensee, place the licensee on probation for a period of not more than 12 months on such terms and conditions as the Division sees fit to impose.

If the Division suspends the provisional licensee's license for at least 90 days without a preliminary hearing, the parent, guardian or other person standing in loco parentis of the provisional licensee may request a hearing to determine if the provisional licensee's license should be restored on a probationary status. The Division may wait until one-half the period of suspension has expired to hold the hearing. The Division may place the licensee on probation for up to 12 months on such terms and conditions as the Division sees fit to impose, if the licensee consents in writing to the terms and conditions of probation.

(c) In the event of conviction of two or more motor vehicle moving offenses committed on a single occasion, a licensee shall be charged, for purposes of this section, with only one moving offense, except as otherwise provided.

(d) The suspension provided for in this section is in addition to any other remedies which the Division may have against a licensee under other provisions of law; however, when the license of any person is suspended under this section and at the same time is also suspended under other provisions of law, the suspensions run concurrently.

(e) Repealed by Session Laws 1987, c. 869, s. 14. (1963, c. 968, s. 1; 1965, c. 897; 1967, c. 295, s. 1; 1971, c. 120, ss. 1, 2; 1973, c. 439; 1975, c. 716, s. 5; 1979, c. 555, s. 1; 1983, c. 538, ss. 1, 2; 1983 (Reg. Sess., 1984), c. 1101, s. 3; 1987, c. 744, ss. 3, 4; c. 869, s. 14.)

§ 20-13.1. Repealed by Session Laws 1979, c. 555, s. 2.

§ 20-13.2. Grounds for revoking provisional license.

(a) The Division must revoke the license of a person convicted of violating the provisions of G.S. 20-138.3 upon receipt of a record of the licensee's conviction.

(b) If a person is convicted of an offense involving impaired driving and the offense occurs while he is less than 21 years old, his license must be revoked under this section in addition to any other revocation required or authorized by law.

(c) If a person willfully refuses to submit to a chemical analysis pursuant to G.S. 20-16.2 while he is less than 21 years old, his license must be revoked under this section, in addition to any other revocation required or authorized by law. A revocation order entered under authority of this subsection becomes effective at the same time as a revocation order issued under G.S. 20-16.2 for the same willful refusal.

(c1) Upon receipt of notification from the proper school authority that a person no longer meets the requirements for a driving eligibility certificate under G.S. 20-11(n), the Division must expeditiously notify the person that his or her permit or license is revoked effective on the tenth calendar day after the mailing of the revocation notice. The Division must revoke the permit or license of that person on the tenth calendar day after the mailing of the revocation notice. Notwithstanding subsection (d) of this section, the length of revocation must last for the following periods:

(1) If the revocation is because of ineligibility for a driving eligibility certificate under G.S. 20-11(n)(1), then the revocation shall last until the person's eighteenth birthday.

(2) If the revocation is because of ineligibility for a driving eligibility certificate under G.S. 20-11(n1), then the revocation shall be for a period of one year.

For a person whose permit or license was revoked due to ineligibility for a driving eligibility certificate under G.S. 20-11(n)(1), the Division must restore a person's permit or license before the person's eighteenth birthday, if the person submits to the Division one of the following:

(1) A high school diploma or its equivalent.

(2) A driving eligibility certificate as required under G.S. 20-11(n).

If the Division restores a permit or license that was revoked due to ineligibility for a driving eligibility certificate under G.S. 20-11(n)(1), any record of revocation or suspension shall be expunged by the Division from the person's driving record. The Division shall not expunge a suspension or revocation record if a person has had a prior expunction from the person's driving record for any reason.

For a person whose permit or license was revoked due to ineligibility for a driving eligibility certificate under G.S. 20-11(n1), the Division shall restore a person's permit or license before the end of the revocation period, if the person submits to the Division a driving eligibility certificate as required under G.S. 20-11(n).

Notwithstanding any other law, the decision concerning whether a driving eligibility certificate was properly issued or improperly denied shall be appealed only as provided under the rules adopted in accordance with G.S. 115C-12(28), 115D-5(a3), or 115C-566, whichever is applicable, and may not be appealed under this Chapter.

(c2) The Division must revoke the permit or license of a person under the age of 18 upon receiving a record of the person's conviction for malicious use of an explosive or incendiary device to damage property (G.S. 14-49(b) and (b1)); conspiracy to injure or damage by use of an explosive or incendiary device (G.S. 14-50); making a false report concerning a destructive device in a public building (G.S. 14-69.1(c)); perpetrating a hoax concerning a destructive device in a public building (G.S. 14-69.2(c)); possessing or carrying a dynamite cartridge, bomb, grenade, mine, or powerful explosive on educational property (G.S. 14-269.2(b1)); or causing, encouraging, or aiding a minor to possess or carry a dynamite cartridge, bomb, grenade, mine, or powerful explosive on educational property (G.S. 14-269.2(c1)).

(d) The length of revocation under this section shall be one year. Revocations under this section run concurrently with any other revocations.

(e) Before the Division restores a driver's license that has been suspended or revoked under any provision of this Article, other than G.S. 20-24.1, the person seeking to have his driver's license restored shall submit to the Division proof that he has notified his insurance agent or company of his seeking the restoration and that he is financially responsible. Proof of financial responsibility shall be in one of the following forms:

(1)   A written certificate or electronically-transmitted facsimile thereof from any insurance carrier duly authorized to do business in this State certifying that there is in effect a nonfleet private passenger motor vehicle liability policy for the benefit of the person required to furnish proof of financial responsibility. The certificate or facsimile shall state the effective date and expiration date of the nonfleet private passenger motor vehicle liability policy and shall state the date that the certificate or facsimile is issued. The certificate or facsimile shall remain effective proof of financial responsibility for a period of 30 consecutive days following the date the certificate or facsimile is issued but shall not in and of itself constitute a binder or policy of insurance or

(2)   A binder for or policy of nonfleet private passenger motor vehicle liability insurance under which the applicant is insured, provided that the binder or policy states the effective date and expiration date of the nonfleet private passenger motor vehicle liability policy.

The preceding provisions of this subsection do not apply to applicants who do not own currently registered motor vehicles and who do not operate nonfleet private passenger motor vehicles that are owned by other persons and that are not insured under commercial motor vehicle liability insurance policies. In such cases, the applicant shall sign a written certificate to that effect. Such certificate shall be furnished by the Division and may be incorporated into the restoration application form. Any material misrepresentation made by such person on such certificate shall be grounds for suspension of that person's license for a period of 90 days.

For the purposes of this subsection, the term "nonfleet private passenger motor vehicle" has the definition ascribed to it in Article 40 of General Statute Chapter 58.

The Commissioner may require that certificates required by this subsection be on a form approved by the Commissioner. The financial responsibility required by this subsection shall be kept in effect for not less than three years after the date that the license is restored. Failure to maintain financial responsibility as required by this subsection shall be grounds for suspending the restored driver's license for a period of thirty (30) days. Nothing in this subsection precludes any person from showing proof of financial responsibility in any other manner authorized by Articles 9A and 13 of this Chapter. (1983, c. 435, s. 33; 1987, c. 869, s. 12; 1989, c. 436, s. 3; 1993, c. 285, s. 8; 1995, c. 506, ss. 3, 4, 5; 1997-507, s. 2; 1999-243, s. 3; 1999-257, s. 4; 2013-133, s. 1.)

§ 20-13.3. Immediate civil license revocation for provisional licensees charged with certain offenses.

(a) Definitions. - As used in this section, the following words and phrases have the following meanings:

(1) Clerk. - As defined in G.S. 15A-101(2).

(2) Criminal moving violation. - A violation of Part 9 or 10 of Article 3 of this Chapter which is punishable as a misdemeanor or a felony offense. This term does not include the offenses listed in the third paragraph of G.S. 20-16(c) for which no points are assessed, nor does it include equipment violations specified in Part 9 of Article 3 of this Chapter.

(3) Judicial official. - As defined in G.S. 15A-101(5).

(4) Provisional licensee. - A person under the age of 18 who has a limited learner's permit, a limited provisional license, or a full provisional license issued pursuant to G.S. 20-11.

(5) Revocation report. - A sworn statement by a law enforcement officer containing facts indicating that the conditions of subsection (b) of this section have been met.

(b) Revocations for Provisional Licensees Charged With Criminal Moving Violation. - A provisional licensee's permit or license is subject to revocation under this section if a law enforcement officer has reasonable grounds to believe that the provisional licensee has committed a criminal moving violation, the provisional licensee is charged with that offense, and the provisional licensee is not subject to a civil revocation pursuant to G.S. 20-16.5.

(c) Duty of Law Enforcement Officers to Notify Provisional Licensee and Report to Judicial Officials. - If a provisional licensee's permit or license is subject to revocation under this section, the law enforcement officer must execute a revocation report. It is the specific duty of the law enforcement officer to make sure that the report is expeditiously filed with a judicial official as required by this section. If no initial appearance is required on the underlying criminal moving violation at the time of the issuance of the charge, the law enforcement officer must verbally notify the provisional licensee that the provisional licensee's permit or license is subject to revocation pursuant to this section and must provide the provisional licensee with a written form containing notice of the process for revocation and hearing under this section.

(c1)   Which Judicial Official Must Receive Report. - The judicial official with whom the revocation report must be filed is:

(1)   The judicial official conducting the initial appearance on the underlying criminal moving violation.

(2)   The clerk of superior court in the county in which the underlying criminal charge has been brought if no initial appearance is required.

(d)   Procedure If Report Filed With Judicial Official When Provisional Licensee Is Present. - If an initial appearance is required, the law enforcement officer must file the revocation report with the judicial official conducting the initial appearance on the underlying criminal moving violation. If a properly executed revocation report concerning a provisional licensee is filed with a judicial official when the person is present before that official, the judicial official shall, after completing any other proceedings involving the provisional licensee, determine whether there is probable cause to believe that the conditions of subsection (b) of this section have been met. If the judicial official determines there is such probable cause, the judicial official shall enter an order revoking the provisional licensee's permit or license. In addition to setting it out in the order, the judicial official shall personally inform the provisional licensee of the right to a hearing as specified in subsection (d2) of this section and that the provisional licensee's permit or license remains revoked pending the hearing. The period of revocation is for 30 days and begins at the time the revocation order is issued and continues for 30 additional calendar days. The judicial official shall give the provisional licensee a copy of the revocation order, which shall include the beginning date of the revocation and shall clearly state the final day of the revocation period and the date on which the provisional licensee's permit or license will again become valid. The provisional licensee shall not be required to surrender the provisional licensee's permit or license; however, the provisional licensee shall not be authorized to drive at any time or for any purpose during the period of revocation.

(d1)   Procedure If Report Filed With Clerk of Court When Provisional Licensee Not Present. - When a clerk receives a properly executed report under subdivision (2) of subsection (c1) of this section and the provisional licensee named in the revocation report is not present before the clerk, the clerk shall determine whether there is probable cause to believe that the conditions of subsection (b) of this section have been met. If the clerk determines there is such probable cause, the clerk shall mail to the provisional licensee a revocation order by first-class mail. The order shall inform the provisional licensee that the period of revocation is for 30 days, that the revocation becomes effective on the fourth day after the order is deposited in the United States mail and continues for 30 additional calendar days, of the right to a hearing as specified in subsection (d2) of this section, and that the revocation remains in effect pending the hearing. The provisional licensee shall not be required to surrender the provisional licensee's permit or license; however, the provisional licensee shall not be authorized to drive at any time or for any purpose during the period of revocation.

(d2) Hearing Before Magistrate or Judge If Provisional Licensee Contests Validity of Revocation. - A provisional licensee whose permit or license is revoked under this section may request in writing a hearing to contest the validity of the revocation. The request may be made at the time of the person's initial appearance, or within 10 days of the effective date of the revocation to the clerk or a magistrate designated by the clerk, and may specifically request that the hearing be conducted by a district court judge. The Administrative Office of the Courts must develop a hearing request form for any provisional licensee requesting a hearing. Unless a district court judge is requested, the hearing must be conducted within the county by a magistrate assigned by the chief district court judge to conduct such hearings. If the provisional licensee requests that a district court judge hold the hearing, the hearing must be conducted within the district court district as defined in G.S. 7A-133 by a district court judge assigned to conduct such hearings. The revocation remains in effect pending the hearing, but the hearing must be held within three working days following the request if the hearing is before a magistrate or within ten working days if the hearing is before a district court judge. The request for the hearing must specify the grounds upon which the validity of the revocation is challenged, and the hearing must be limited to the grounds specified in the request. A witness may submit his evidence by affidavit unless he is subpoenaed to appear. Any person who appears and testifies is subject to questioning by the judicial official conducting the hearing, and the judicial official may adjourn the hearing to seek additional evidence if the judicial official is not satisfied with the accuracy or completeness of evidence. The provisional licensee contesting the validity of the revocation may, but is not required to, testify in his own behalf. Unless contested by the person requesting the hearing, the judicial official may accept as true any matter stated in the revocation report. If any relevant condition under subsection (b) of this section is contested, the judicial official must find by the greater weight of the evidence that the condition was met in order to sustain the revocation. At the conclusion of the hearing, the judicial official must enter an order sustaining or rescinding the revocation. The judicial official's findings are without prejudice to the provisional licensee contesting the revocation and to any other potential party as to any other proceedings, civil or criminal, that may involve facts bearing upon the conditions in subsection (b) of this section considered by the judicial official. The decision of the judicial official is final and may not be appealed in the General Court of Justice. If the hearing is not held and completed within three working days of the written request for a hearing before a magistrate or within ten working days of the written request for a hearing before a district court judge, the judicial official must enter an order rescinding the revocation, unless the provisional licensee contesting the revocation contributed to the delay in completing the hearing. If the provisional licensee requesting the hearing fails to appear at the hearing or any rescheduling thereof after having been properly notified, the provisional licensee forfeits the right to a hearing.

(e)   Report to Division. - The clerk shall notify the Division of the issuance of a revocation order pursuant to this section within two business days of the issuance of the revocation order. The notification shall identify the person whose provisional license has been revoked and specify the beginning and end date of the revocation period.

(f)   Effect of Revocations. - A revocation under this section revokes a provisional licensee's privilege to drive in North Carolina. Revocations under this section are independent of and run concurrently with any other revocations, except for a revocation pursuant to G.S. 20-16.5. Any civil revocation issued pursuant to G.S. 20-16.5 for the same underlying conduct as a revocation under this section shall have the effect of terminating a revocation pursuant to this section. No court imposing a period of revocation following conviction for an offense involving impaired driving may give credit for any period of revocation imposed under this section. A person whose license is revoked pursuant to this section is not eligible to receive a limited driving privilege.

(g)   Designation of Proceedings. - Proceedings under this section are civil actions and must be identified by the caption "In the Matter of _____" and filed as directed by the Administrative Office of the Courts.

(h)   No drivers license points or insurance surcharge shall be assessed for a revocation pursuant to this section. Possession of a drivers license revoked pursuant to this section shall not be a violation of G.S. 20-30.

(i) The Administrative Office of the Courts shall adopt forms to implement this section. (2011-385, s. 4; 2011-412, s. 3.2; 2012-168, s. 3.)

§ 20-14. Duplicate licenses.

A person may obtain a duplicate of a license issued by the Division by paying a fee of ten dollars ($10.00) and giving the Division satisfactory proof that any of the following has occurred:

(1) The person's license has been lost or destroyed.

(2) It is necessary to change the name or address on the license.

(3) Because of age, the person is entitled to a license with a different color photographic background or a different color border.

(4) The Division revoked the person's license, the revocation period has expired, and the period for which the license was issued has not expired. (1935, c. 52, s. 9; 1943, c. 649, s. 2; 1969, c. 783, s. 2; 1975, c. 716, s. 5; 1979, c. 667, s. 41; 1981, c. 690, s. 11; 1983, c. 443, s. 3; 1991, c. 682, s. 2; c. 689, s. 327; 1991 (Reg. Sess., 1992), c. 1007, s. 28; 1995 (Reg. Sess., 1996), c. 675, s. 2; 2004-189, s. 5(b); 2005-276, s. 44.1(c).)

§ 20-15. Authority of Division to cancel license or endorsement.

(a) The Division shall have authority to cancel any driver's license upon determining any of the following:

(1) The licensee was not entitled to the issuance of the license under this Chapter.

(2) The licensee failed to give the required or correct information on the license application or committed fraud in making the application.

(3) The licensee is no longer authorized under federal law to be legally present in the United States.

(b) Upon such cancellation, the licensee must surrender the license so cancelled to the Division.

(c) Any person whose license is canceled under this section for failure to give the required or correct information, or for committing fraud, in an application for a commercial drivers license shall be prohibited from reapplying for a commercial drivers license for a period of 60 days from the date of cancellation.

(d) The Division shall have authority to revoke an H endorsement of a commercial drivers license holder if the person with the endorsement is determined by the federal Transportation Security Administration to constitute a security threat, as specified in 49 C.F.R. § 1572.5(d)(4). (1935, c. 52, s. 10; 1943, c. 649, s. 3; 1975, c. 716, s. 5; 1979, c. 667, s. 41; 2005-349, s. 5; 2007-56, s. 5.)

§ 20-15.1. Revocations when licensing privileges forfeited.

The Division shall revoke the license of a person whose licensing privileges have been forfeited under G.S. 15A-1331.1, 50-13.12, and 110-142.2. If a revocation period set by this Chapter is longer than the revocation period resulting from the forfeiture of licensing privileges, the revocation period in this Chapter applies. (1994, Ex. Sess., c. 20, s. 2; 1995, c. 538, s. 2(a); 2012-194, s. 45(b).)

§ 20-16. Authority of Division to suspend license.

(a) The Division shall have authority to suspend the license of any operator with or without a preliminary hearing upon a showing by its records or other satisfactory evidence that the licensee:

(1) through (4) Repealed by Session Laws 1979, c. 36;

(5) Has, under the provisions of subsection (c) of this section, within a three-year period, accumulated 12 or more points, or eight or more points in the three-year period immediately following the reinstatement of a license which has

been suspended or revoked because of a conviction for one or more traffic offenses;

(6) Has made or permitted an unlawful or fraudulent use of such license or a learner's permit, or has displayed or represented as his own, a license or learner's permit not issued to him;

(7) Has committed an offense in another state, which if committed in this State would be grounds for suspension or revocation;

(8) Has been convicted of illegal transportation of alcoholic beverages;

(8a) Has been convicted of impaired instruction under G.S. 20-12.1;

(8b) Has violated on a military installation a regulation of that installation prohibiting conduct substantially similar to conduct that constitutes impaired driving under G.S. 20-138.1 and, as a result of that violation, has had his privilege to drive on that installation revoked or suspended after an administrative hearing authorized by the commanding officer of the installation and that commanding officer has general court martial jurisdiction;

(9) Has, within a period of 12 months, been convicted of (i) two or more charges of speeding in excess of 55 and not more than 80 miles per hour, (ii) one or more charges of reckless driving and one or more charges of speeding in excess of 55 and not more than 80 miles per hour, or (iii) one or more charges of aggressive driving and one or more charges of speeding in excess of 55 and not more than 80 miles per hour;

(10) Has been convicted of operating a motor vehicle at a speed in excess of 75 miles per hour on a public road or highway where the maximum speed is less than 70 miles per hour;

(10a) Has been convicted of operating a motor vehicle at a speed in excess of 80 miles per hour on a public highway where the maximum speed is 70 miles per hour; or

(11) Has been sentenced by a court of record and all or a part of the sentence has been suspended and a condition of suspension of the sentence is that the operator not operate a motor vehicle for a period of time.

However, if the Division revokes without a preliminary hearing and the person whose license is being revoked requests a hearing before the effective date of the revocation, the licensee retains his license unless it is revoked under some other provision of the law, until the hearing is held, the person withdraws his request, or he fails to appear at a scheduled hearing.

(b) Pending an appeal from a conviction of any violation of the motor vehicle laws of this State, no driver's license shall be suspended by the Division of Motor Vehicles because of such conviction or because of evidence of the commission of the offense for which the conviction has been had.

(c) The Division shall maintain a record of convictions of every person licensed or required to be licensed under the provisions of this Article as an operator and shall enter therein records of all convictions of such persons for any violation of the motor vehicle laws of this State and shall assign to the record of such person, as of the date of commission of the offense, a number of points for every such conviction in accordance with the following schedule of convictions and points, except that points shall not be assessed for convictions resulting in suspensions or revocations under other provisions of laws: Further, any points heretofore charged for violation of the motor vehicle inspection laws shall not be considered by the Division of Motor Vehicles as a basis for suspension or revocation of driver's license:

Schedule of Point Values

Passing stopped school bus.. 5

Aggressive driving.. 5

Reckless driving... 4

Hit and run, property damage only... 4

Following too close.. 4

Driving on wrong side of road... 4

Illegal passing.. 4

Failure to yield right-of-way to pedestrian pursuant to G.S. 20-158(b)(2)b. 4

Failure to yield right-of-way to bicycle, motor scooter, or motorcycle.. 4

Running through stop sign.. 3

Speeding in excess of 55 miles per hour... 3

Failing to yield right-of-way... 3

Running through red light.. 3

No driver's license or license expired more than one year............................ 3

Failure to stop for siren.. 3

Driving through safety zone... 3

No liability insurance... 3

Failure to report accident where such report is required.. 3

Speeding in a school zone in excess of the posted school zone speed limit.. 3

Failure to properly restrain a child in a restraint or seat belt.. 2

All other moving violations.. 2

Littering pursuant to G.S. 14-399 when the littering involves the use of a motor vehicle.. 1

Schedule of Point Values for Violations While Operating a Commercial Motor Vehicle

Passing stopped school bus.. 8

Rail-highway crossing violation... 6

Careless and reckless driving in violation of G.S. 20-140(f)... 6

Speeding in violation of G.S. 20-141(j3)... 6

Aggressive driving.. 6

Reckless driving... 5

Hit and run, property damage only.. 5

Following too close.. 5

Driving on wrong side of road.. 5

Illegal passing.. 5

Failure to yield right-of-way to pedestrian pursuant to G.S. 20-158(b)(2)b........ 5

Failure to yield right-of-way to bicycle, motor scooter, or motorcycle............ 5

Running through stop sign... 4

Speeding in excess of 55 miles per hour... 4

Failing to yield right-of-way... 4

Running through red light... 4

No driver's license or license expired more than one year... 4

Failure to stop for siren.. 4

Driving through safety zone.. 4

No liability insurance... 4

Failure to report accident where such report is required... 4

Speeding in a school zone in excess of the posted school zone speed limit.. 4

Possessing alcoholic beverages in the passenger area of a commercial motor vehicle.. 4

All other moving violations.. 3

Littering pursuant to G.S. 14-399 when the littering involves the use of a motor vehicle... 1

The above provisions of this subsection shall only apply to violations and convictions which take place within the State of North Carolina. The Schedule of Point Values for Violations While Operating a Commercial Motor Vehicle shall not apply to any commercial motor vehicle known as an "aerial lift truck" having a hydraulic arm and bucket station, and to any commercial motor vehicle known as a "line truck" having a hydraulic lift for cable, if the vehicle is owned, operated by or under contract to a public utility, electric or telephone membership corporation or municipality and used in connection with installation, restoration or maintenance of utility services.

No points shall be assessed for conviction of the following offenses:

Overloads

Over length

Over width

Over height

Illegal parking

Carrying concealed weapon

Improper plates

Improper registration

Improper muffler

Improper display of license plates or dealers' tags

Unlawful display of emblems and insignia

Failure to display current inspection certificate.

In case of the conviction of a licensee of two or more traffic offenses committed on a single occasion, such licensee shall be assessed points for one offense only and if the offenses involved have a different point value, such licensee shall be assessed for the offense having the greater point value.

Upon the restoration of the license or driving privilege of such person whose license or driving privilege has been suspended or revoked because of conviction for a traffic offense, any points that might previously have been accumulated in the driver's record shall be cancelled.

Whenever any licensee accumulates as many as seven points or accumulates as many as four points during a three-year period immediately following reinstatement of his license after a period of suspension or revocation, the Division may request the licensee to attend a conference regarding such licensee's driving record. The Division may also afford any licensee who has accumulated as many as seven points or any licensee who has accumulated as many as four points within a three-year period immediately following reinstatement of his license after a period of suspension or revocation an opportunity to attend a driver improvement clinic operated by the Division and, upon the successful completion of the course taken at the clinic, three points shall be deducted from the licensee's conviction record; provided, that only one deduction of points shall be made on behalf of any licensee within any five-year period.

When a license is suspended under the point system provided for herein, the first such suspension shall be for not more than 60 days; the second such suspension shall not exceed six months and any subsequent suspension shall not exceed one year.

Whenever the driver's license of any person is subject to suspension under this subsection and at the same time also subject to suspension or revocation under other provisions of laws, such suspensions or revocations shall run concurrently.

In the discretion of the Division, a period of probation not to exceed one year may be substituted for suspension or for any unexpired period of suspension under subsections (a)(1) through (a)(10a) of this section. Any violation of probation during the probation period shall result in a suspension for the unexpired remainder of the suspension period. Any accumulation of three or more points under this subsection during a period of probation shall constitute a violation of the condition of probation.

(d) Upon suspending the license of any person as authorized in this section, the Division shall immediately notify the licensee in writing and upon his request shall afford him an opportunity for a hearing, not to exceed 60 days after receipt of the request, unless a preliminary hearing was held before his license was suspended. Upon such hearing the duly authorized agents of the Division may administer oaths and may issue subpoenas for the attendance of witnesses and the production of relevant books and papers and may require a reexamination of the licensee. Upon such hearing the Division shall either rescind its order of suspension, or good cause appearing therefor, may extend the suspension of such license. Provided further upon such hearing, preliminary or otherwise, involving subsections (a)(1) through (a)(10a) of this section, the Division may for good cause appearing in its discretion substitute a period of probation not to exceed one year for the suspension or for any unexpired period of suspension. Probation shall mean any written agreement between the suspended driver and a duly authorized representative of the Division and such period of probation shall not exceed one year, and any violation of the probation agreement during the probation period shall result in a suspension for the unexpired remainder of the suspension period. The authorized agents of the Division shall have the same powers in connection with a preliminary hearing prior to suspension as this subsection provided in connection with hearings held after suspension. These agents shall also have the authority to take possession of a surrendered license on behalf of the Division if the suspension is upheld and the licensee requests that the suspension begin immediately.

(e) The Division may conduct driver improvement clinics for the benefit of those who have been convicted of one or more violations of this Chapter. Each driver attending a driver improvement clinic shall pay a fee of fifty dollars ($50.00).

(e1) Notwithstanding any other provision of this Chapter, if the Division suspends the license of an operator pursuant to subdivisions (a)(9), (a)(10), or (a)(10a) of this section, upon the first suspension only, a district court judge may allow the licensee a limited driving privilege or license for a period not to exceed 12 months, provided he has not been convicted of any other motor vehicle moving violation within the previous 12 months. The limited driving privilege shall be issued in the same manner and under the terms and conditions prescribed in G.S. 20-16.1(b)(1), (2), (3), (4), and (5).

(e2) If the Division revokes a person's drivers license pursuant to G.S. 20-17(a)(16), a judge may allow the licensee a limited driving privilege for a period not to exceed the period of revocation. The limited driving privilege shall be issued in the same manner and under the terms and conditions prescribed in G.S. 20-16.1(b)(1), (2), (3), (4), (5), and (g). (1935, c. 52, s. 11; 1947, c. 893, ss. 1, 2; c. 1067, s. 13; 1949, c. 373, ss. 1, 2; c. 1032, s. 2; 1953, c. 450; 1955, c. 1152, s. 15; c. 1187, ss. 9-12; 1957, c. 499, s. 1; 1959, c. 1242, ss. 1-2; 1961, c. 460, ss. 1, 2(a); 1963, c. 1115; 1965, c. 130; 1967, c. 16; 1971, c. 234, ss. 1, 2; c. 793, ss. 1, 2; c. 1198, ss. 1, 2; 1973, c. 17, ss. 1, 2; 1975, c. 716, s. 5; 1977,

c. 902, s. 1; 1979, c. 36; c. 667, ss. 18, 41; 1981, c. 412, s. 4; c. 747, ss. 33, 66; 1981 (Reg. Sess., 1982), c. 1256; 1983, c. 435, s. 10; c. 538, ss. 3-5; c. 798; 1983 (Reg. Sess., 1984), c. 1101, s. 4; 1987, c. 744, ss. 1, 2; 1987 (Reg. Sess., 1988), c. 1037, s. 75; 1989, c. 784, s. 9; 1991, c. 682, s. 3; 1999-330, s. 7; 1999-452, s. 10; 2000-109, s. 7(d); 2000-117, s. 2; 2000-155, s. 10; 2001-352, s. 2; 2004-172, s. 3; 2004-193, ss. 2, 3; 2005-276, s. 44.1(d).)

§ 20-16.01. Double penalties for offenses committed while operating a commercial motor vehicle.

Any person who commits an offense for which points may be assessed pursuant to the Schedule of Point Values for Violations While Operating a Commercial Motor Vehicle as provided in G.S. 20-16(c) may be assessed double the amount of any fine or penalty authorized by statute. (1999-330, s. 8.)

§ 20-16.4: Repealed by Session Laws 1989, c. 691, s. 4.

§ 20-16.5. Immediate civil license revocation for certain persons charged with implied-consent offenses.

(a)   Definitions. - As used in this section the following words and phrases have the following meanings:

(1)   Law Enforcement Officer. - As described in G.S. 20-16.2(a1).

(2)   Clerk. - As defined in G.S. 15A-101(2).

(3)   Judicial Official. - As defined in G.S. 15A-101(5).

(4)   Revocation Report. - A sworn statement by a law enforcement officer and a chemical analyst containing facts indicating that the conditions of subsection (b) have been met, and whether the person has a pending offense for which the person's license had been or is revoked under this section. When one chemical analyst analyzes a person's blood and another chemical analyst informs a person of his rights and responsibilities under G.S. 20-16.2, the report must include the statements of both analysts.

(5)   Surrender of a Driver's License. - The act of turning over to a court or a law-enforcement officer the person's most recent, valid driver's license or

learner's permit issued by the Division or by a similar agency in another jurisdiction, or a limited driving privilege issued by a North Carolina court. A person who is validly licensed but who is unable to locate his license card may file an affidavit with the clerk setting out facts that indicate that he is unable to locate his license card and that he is validly licensed; the filing of the affidavit constitutes a surrender of the person's license.

(b) Revocations for Persons Who Refuse Chemical Analyses or Who Are Charged With Certain Implied-Consent Offenses. - A person's driver's license is subject to revocation under this section if:

(1) A law enforcement officer has reasonable grounds to believe that the person has committed an offense subject to the implied-consent provisions of G.S. 20-16.2;

(2) The person is charged with that offense as provided in G.S. 20-16.2(a);

(3) The law enforcement officer and the chemical analyst comply with the procedures of G.S. 20-16.2 and G.S. 20-139.1 in requiring the person's submission to or procuring a chemical analysis; and

(4) The person:

a. Willfully refuses to submit to the chemical analysis;

b. Has an alcohol concentration of 0.08 or more within a relevant time after the driving;

c. Has an alcohol concentration of 0.04 or more at any relevant time after the driving of a commercial motor vehicle; or

d. Has any alcohol concentration at any relevant time after the driving and the person is under 21 years of age.

(b1) Precharge Test Results as Basis for Revocation. - Notwithstanding the provisions of subsection (b), a person's driver's license is subject to revocation under this section if:

(1) The person requests a precharge chemical analysis pursuant to G.S. 20-16.2(i); and

(2) The person has:

a. An alcohol concentration of 0.08 or more at any relevant time after driving;

b. An alcohol concentration of 0.04 or more at any relevant time after driving a commercial motor vehicle; or

c. Any alcohol concentration at any relevant time after driving and the person is under 21 years of age; and

(3) The person is charged with an implied-consent offense.

(c) Duty of Law Enforcement Officers and Chemical Analysts to Report to Judicial Officials. - If a person's driver's license is subject to revocation under this section, the law enforcement officer and the chemical analyst must execute a revocation report. If the person has refused to submit to a chemical analysis, a copy of the affidavit to be submitted to the Division under G.S. 20-16.2(c) may be substituted for the revocation report if it contains the information required by this section. It is the specific duty of the law enforcement officer to make sure that the report is expeditiously filed with a judicial official as required by this section.

(d) Which Judicial Official Must Receive Report. - The judicial official with whom the revocation report must be filed is:

(1) The judicial official conducting the initial appearance on the underlying criminal charge if:

a. No revocation report has previously been filed; and

b. At the time of the initial appearance the results of the chemical analysis, if administered, or the reports indicating a refusal, are available.

(2) A judicial official conducting any other proceeding relating to the underlying criminal charge at which the person is present, if no report has previously been filed.

(3) The clerk of superior court in the county in which the underlying criminal charge has been brought if subdivisions (1) and (2) are not applicable at the time the law enforcement officer must file the report.

(e) Procedure if Report Filed with Judicial Official When Person Is Present. - If a properly executed revocation report concerning a person is filed with a judicial official when the person is present before that official, the judicial official shall, after completing any other proceedings involving the person, determine whether there is probable cause to believe that each of the conditions of subsection (b) has been met. If he determines that there is such probable cause, he shall enter an order revoking the person's driver's license for the period required in this subsection. The judicial official shall order the person to surrender his license and if necessary may order a law-enforcement officer to seize the license. The judicial official shall give the person a copy of the revocation order. In addition to setting it out in the order the judicial official shall personally inform the person of his right to a hearing as specified in subsection (g), and that his license remains revoked pending the hearing. The revocation under this subsection begins at the time the revocation order is issued and continues until the person's license has been surrendered for the period specified in this subsection, and the person has paid the applicable costs. The period of revocation is 30 days, if there are no pending offenses for which the person's license had been or is revoked under this section. If at the time of the current offense, the person has one or more pending offenses for which his license had been or is revoked under this section, the revocation shall remain in effect until a final judgment, including all appeals, has been entered for the current offense and for all pending offenses. In no event, may the period of revocation under this subsection be less than 30 days. If within five working days of the effective date of the order, the person does not surrender his license or demonstrate that he is not currently licensed, the clerk shall immediately issue a pick-up order. The pick-up order shall be issued to a member of a local law-enforcement agency if the law enforcement officer was employed by the agency at the time of the charge and the person resides in or is present in the agency's territorial jurisdiction. In all other cases, the pick-up order shall be issued to an officer or inspector of the Division. A pick-up order issued pursuant to this section is to be served in accordance with G.S. 20-29 as if the order had been issued by the Division.

(f) Procedure if Report Filed with Clerk of Court When Person Not Present. - When a clerk receives a properly executed report under subdivision (d)(3) and the person named in the revocation report is not present before the clerk, the clerk shall determine whether there is probable cause to believe that each of the conditions of subsection (b) has been met. For purposes of this subsection, a properly executed report under subdivision (d)(3) may include a sworn statement by the law enforcement officer along with an affidavit received directly by the Clerk from the chemical analyst. If he determines that there is such probable cause, he shall mail to the person a revocation order by first-class mail. The order shall direct that the person on or before the effective date of the order either surrender his license to the clerk or appear before the clerk and demonstrate that he is not currently licensed, and the order shall inform the person of the time and effective date of the revocation and of its duration, of his right to a hearing as specified in subsection (g), and that the revocation remains in effect pending the hearing. Revocation orders mailed under this subsection become effective on the fourth day after the order is deposited in the United States mail. If within five working days of the effective date of the order, the person does not surrender his license to the clerk or appear before the clerk to demonstrate that he is not currently licensed, the clerk shall immediately issue a pick-up order. The pick-up order shall be issued and served in the same manner as specified in subsection (e) for pick-up orders issued pursuant to that subsection. A revocation under this subsection begins at the date specified in the order and continues until the person's license has been revoked for the period specified in this subsection and the person has paid the applicable costs. If the person has no pending offenses for which his license had been or is revoked under this section, the period of revocation under this subsection is:

(1) Thirty days from the time the person surrenders his license to the court, if the surrender occurs within five working days of the effective date of the order; or

(2) Thirty days after the person appears before the clerk and demonstrates that he is not currently licensed to drive, if the appearance occurs within five working days of the effective date of the revocation order; or

(3) Forty-five days from the time:

a. The person's drivers license is picked up by a law-enforcement officer following service of a pick-up order; or

b. The person demonstrates to a law-enforcement officer who has a pick-up order for his license that he is not currently licensed; or

c. The person's drivers license is surrendered to the court if the surrender occurs more than five working days after the effective date of the revocation order; or

d. The person appears before the clerk to demonstrate that he is not currently licensed, if he appears more than five working days after the effective date of the revocation order.

If at the time of the current offense, the person has one or more pending offenses for which his license had been or is revoked under this section, the revocation shall remain in effect until a final judgment, including all appeals, has been entered for the current offense and for all pending offenses. In no event may the period of revocation for the current offense be less than the applicable period of revocation in subdivision (1), (2), or (3) of this subsection. When a pick-up order is issued, it shall inform the person of his right to a hearing as specified in subsection (g), and that the revocation remains in effect pending the hearing. An officer serving a pick-up order under this subsection shall return the order to the court indicating the date it was served or that he was unable to serve the order. If the license was surrendered, the officer serving the order shall deposit it with the clerk within three days of the surrender.

(g) Hearing before Magistrate or Judge if Person Contests Validity of Revocation. - A person whose license is revoked under this section may request in writing a hearing to contest the validity of the revocation. The request may be made at the time of the person's initial appearance, or within 10 days of the effective date of the revocation to the clerk or a magistrate designated by the clerk, and may specifically request that the hearing be conducted by a district court judge. The Administrative Office of the Courts must develop a hearing request form for any person requesting a hearing. Unless a district court judge is requested, the hearing must be conducted within the county by a magistrate assigned by the chief district court judge to conduct such hearings. If the person requests that a district court judge hold the hearing, the hearing must be conducted within the district court district as defined in G.S. 7A-133 by a district court judge assigned to conduct such hearings. The revocation remains in effect pending the hearing, but the hearing must be held within three working days following the request if the hearing is before a magistrate or within five working days if the hearing is before a district court judge. The request for the hearing must specify the grounds upon which the validity of the revocation is challenged and the hearing must be limited to the grounds specified in the request. A witness may submit his evidence by affidavit unless he is subpoenaed to appear. Any person who appears and testifies is subject to questioning by the judicial official conducting the hearing, and the judicial official may adjourn the hearing to seek additional evidence if he is not satisfied with the accuracy or completeness of evidence. The person contesting the validity of the revocation may, but is not required to, testify in his own behalf. Unless contested by the person requesting the hearing, the judicial official may accept as true any matter stated in the revocation report. If any relevant condition under subsection (b) is contested, the judicial official must find by the greater weight of the evidence that the condition was met in order to sustain the revocation. At the conclusion of the hearing the judicial official must enter an order sustaining or rescinding the revocation. The judicial official's findings are without prejudice to the person contesting the revocation and to any other potential party as to any other proceedings, civil or criminal, that may involve facts bearing upon the conditions in subsection (b) considered by the judicial official. The decision of the judicial official is final and may not be appealed in the General Court of Justice. If the hearing is not held and completed within three working days of the written request for a hearing before a magistrate or within five working days of the written request for a hearing before a district court judge, the judicial official must enter an order rescinding the revocation, unless the person contesting the revocation contributed to the delay in completing the hearing. If the person requesting the hearing fails to appear at the hearing or any rescheduling thereof after having been properly notified, he forfeits his right to a hearing.

(h)   Return of License. - After the applicable period of revocation under this section, or if the magistrate or judge orders the revocation rescinded, the person whose license was revoked may apply to the clerk for return of his surrendered license. Unless the clerk finds that the person is not eligible to use the surrendered license, he must return it if:

(1)   The applicable period of revocation has passed and the person has tendered payment for the costs under subsection (j); or

(2)   The magistrate or judge has ordered the revocation rescinded.

If the license has expired, he may return it to the person with a caution that it is no longer valid. Otherwise, if the person is not eligible to use the license and the license was issued by the Division or in another state, the clerk must mail it to the Division. If the person has surrendered his copy of a limited driving privilege and he is no longer eligible to use it, the clerk must make a record that he has withheld the limited driving privilege and forward that record to the clerk in the county in which the limited driving privilege was issued for filing in the case file. If the person's license is revoked under this section and under another section of this Chapter, the clerk must surrender the license to the Division if the revocation under this section can terminate before the other revocation; in such cases, the costs required by subsection (j) must still be paid before the revocation under this section is terminated.

(i) Effect of Revocations. - A revocation under this section revokes a person's privilege to drive in North Carolina whatever the source of his authorization to drive. Revocations under this section are independent of and run concurrently with any other revocations. No court imposing a period of revocation following conviction of an offense involving impaired driving may give credit for any period of revocation imposed under this section. A person whose license is revoked pursuant to this section is not eligible to receive a limited driving privilege except as specifically authorized by G.S. 20-16.5(p).

(j) Costs. - Unless the magistrate or judge orders the revocation rescinded, a person whose license is revoked under this section must pay a fee of one hundred dollars ($100.00) as costs for the action before the person's license may be returned under subsection (h) of this section. Fifty percent (50%) of the costs collected under this section shall be credited to the General Fund. Twenty-five percent (25%) of the costs collected under this section shall be used to fund a statewide chemical alcohol testing program administered by the Injury Control Section of the Department of Health and Human Services. The remaining twenty-five percent (25%) of the costs collected under this section shall be remitted to the county for the sole purpose of reimbursing the county for jail expenses incurred due to enforcement of the impaired driving laws.

(k) Report to Division. - Except as provided below, the clerk shall mail a report to the Division:

(1) If the license is revoked indefinitely, within 10 working days of the revocation of the license; and

(2) In all cases, within 10 working days of the return of a license under this section or of the termination of a revocation of the driving privilege of a person not currently licensed.

The report shall identify the person whose license has been revoked, specify the date on which his license was revoked, and indicate whether the license has been returned. The report must also provide, if applicable, whether the license is revoked indefinitely. No report need be made to the Division, however, if there was a surrender of the driver's license issued by the Division, a 30-day minimum revocation was imposed, and the license was properly returned to the person under subsection (h) within five working days after the 30-day period had elapsed.

(l) Restoration Fee for Unlicensed Persons. - If a person whose license is revoked under this section has no valid license, he must pay the restoration fee required by G.S. 20-7 before he may apply for a license from the Division.

(m) Modification of Revocation Order. - Any judicial official presiding over a proceeding under this section may issue a modified order if he determines that an inappropriate order has been issued.

(n) Exception for Revoked Licenses. - Notwithstanding any other provision of this section, if the judicial official required to issue a revocation order under this section determines that the person whose license is subject to revocation under subsection (b):

(1) Has a currently revoked driver's license;

(2) Has no limited driving privilege; and

(3) Will not become eligible for restoration of his license or for a limited driving privilege during the period of revocation required by this section,

the judicial official need not issue a revocation order under this section. In this event the judicial official must file in the records of the civil proceeding a copy of any documentary evidence and set out in writing all other evidence on which he relies in making his determination.

(o) Designation of Proceedings. - Proceedings under this section are civil actions, and must be identified by the caption "In the Matter of _____" and filed as directed by the Administrative Office of the Courts.

(p) Limited Driving Privilege. - A person whose drivers license has been revoked for a specified period of 30 or 45 days under this section may apply for a limited driving privilege if:

(1) At the time of the alleged offense the person held either a valid drivers license or a license that had been expired for less than one year;

(2) Does not have an unresolved pending charge involving impaired driving except the charge for which the license is currently revoked under this section or additional convictions of an offense involving impaired driving since being charged for the violation for which the license is currently revoked under this section;

(3) The person's license has been revoked for at least 10 days if the revocation is for 30 days or 30 days if the revocation is for 45 days; and

(4) The person has obtained a substance abuse assessment from a mental health facility and registers for and agrees to participate in any recommended training or treatment program.

A person whose license has been indefinitely revoked under this section may, after completion of 30 days under subsection (e) or the applicable period of time under subdivision (1), (2), or (3) of subsection (f), apply for a limited driving privilege. In the case of an indefinite revocation, a judge of the division in which the current offense is pending may issue the limited driving privilege only if the privilege is necessary to overcome undue hardship and the person meets the eligibility requirements of G.S. 20-179.3, except that the requirements in G.S. 20-179.3(b)(1)c. and G.S. 20-179.3(e) shall not apply. Except as modified in this subsection, the provisions of G.S. 20-179.3 relating to the procedure for application and conduct of the hearing and the restrictions required or authorized to be included in the limited driving privilege apply to applications under this subsection. Any district court judge authorized to hold court in the judicial district is authorized to issue such a limited driving privilege. A limited driving privilege issued under this section authorizes a person to drive if the person's license is revoked solely under this section. If the person's license is revoked for any other reason, the limited driving privilege is invalid. (1983, c. 435, s. 14; 1983 (Reg. Sess., 1984), c. 1101, ss. 11-17; 1985, c. 690, ss. 1, 2; 1987 (Reg. Sess., 1988), c. 1037, s. 80, c. 1112; 1989, c. 771, ss. 15, 16, 18; 1991, c. 689, s. 233.1(a); 1993, c. 285, ss. 5, 6; 1997-379, ss. 3.4-3.8; 1997-443, s. 11A.9; 1997-486, ss. 2-6; 1998-182, ss. 29, 30; 1999-406, s. 13; 2000-140, s. 103A; 2000-155, s. 15; 2001-487, ss. 6, 7; 2003-104, s. 1; 2007-323, s. 30.10(e); 2007-493, s. 17.)

§ 20-17. Mandatory revocation of license by Division.

(a) The Division shall forthwith revoke the license of any driver upon receiving a record of the driver's conviction for any of the following offenses:

(1) Manslaughter (or negligent homicide) resulting from the operation of a motor vehicle.

(2) Either of the following impaired driving offenses:

a. Impaired driving under G.S. 20-138.1.

b. Impaired driving under G.S. 20-138.2, if the driver's alcohol concentration level was .06 or higher. For the purposes of this sub-subdivision, the driver's alcohol concentration level result, obtained by chemical analysis, shall be conclusive and is not subject to modification by any party, with or without approval by the court.

(3) Any felony in the commission of which a motor vehicle is used.

(4) Failure to stop and render aid in violation of G.S. 20-166(a) or (b).

(5) Perjury or the making of a false affidavit or statement under oath to the Division under this Article or under any other law relating to the ownership of motor vehicles.

(6) Conviction, within a period of 12 months, of (i) two charges of reckless driving, (ii) two charges of aggressive driving, or (iii) one or more charges of reckless driving and one or more charges of aggressive driving.

(7) Conviction upon one charge of aggressive driving or reckless driving while engaged in the illegal transportation of intoxicants for the purpose of sale.

(8) Conviction of using a false or fictitious name or giving a false or fictitious address in any application for a drivers license, or learner's permit, or any renewal or duplicate thereof, or knowingly making a false statement or knowingly concealing a material fact or otherwise committing a fraud in any such application or procuring or knowingly permitting or allowing another to commit any of the foregoing acts.

(9) Any offense set forth under G.S. 20-141.4.

(10) Repealed by Session Laws 1997-443, s. 19.26(b).

(11) Conviction of assault with a motor vehicle.

(12) A second or subsequent conviction of transporting an open container of alcoholic beverage under G.S. 20-138.7.

(13)   A second or subsequent conviction, as defined in G.S. 20-138.2A(d), of driving a commercial motor vehicle after consuming alcohol under G.S. 20-138.2A.

(14)   A conviction of driving a school bus, school activity bus, or child care vehicle after consuming alcohol under G.S. 20-138.2B.

(15)   A conviction of malicious use of an explosive or incendiary device to damage property (G.S. 14-49(b) and (b1)); making a false report concerning a destructive device in a public building (G.S. 14-69.1(c)); perpetrating a hoax concerning a destructive device in a public building (G.S. 14-69.2(c)); possessing or carrying a dynamite cartridge, bomb, grenade, mine, or powerful explosive on educational property (G.S. 14-269.2(b1)); or causing, encouraging, or aiding a minor to possess or carry a dynamite cartridge, bomb, grenade, mine, or powerful explosive on educational property (G.S. 14-269.2(c1)).

(16)   A second or subsequent conviction of larceny of motor fuel under G.S. 14-72.5. A conviction for violating G.S. 14-72.5 is a second or subsequent conviction if at the time of the current offense the person has a previous conviction under G.S. 14-72.5 that occurred in the seven years immediately preceding the date of the current offense.

(b)   On the basis of information provided by the child support enforcement agency or the clerk of court, the Division shall:

(1)   Ensure that no license or right to operate a motor vehicle under this Chapter is renewed or issued to an obligor who is delinquent in making child support payments when a court of record has issued a revocation order pursuant to G.S. 110-142.2 or G.S. 50-13.12. The obligor shall not be entitled to any other hearing before the Division as a result of the revocation of his license pursuant to G.S. 110-142.2 or G.S. 50-13.12; or

(2)   Revoke the drivers license of any person who has willfully failed to complete court-ordered community service and a court has issued a revocation order. This revocation shall continue until the Division receives certification from the clerk of court that the person has completed the court-ordered community service. No person whose drivers license is revoked pursuant to this subdivision shall be entitled to any other hearing before the Division as a result of this revocation. (1935, c. 52, s. 12; 1947, c. 1067, s. 14; 1967, c. 1098, s. 2; 1971, c. 619, s. 7; 1973, c. 18, s. 1; c. 1081, s. 3; c. 1330, s. 2; 1975, c. 716, s. 5; c. 831; 1979, c. 667, ss. 20, 41; 1981, c. 412, s. 4; c. 747, s. 66; 1983, c. 435, s. 15;

1989, c. 771, s. 11; 1991, c. 726, s. 7; 1993 (Reg. Sess., 1994), c. 761, s. 1; 1995, c. 506, s. 7; c. 538, s. 2(b); 1997-234, s. 3; 1997-443, s. 19.26(b); 1998-182, s. 18; 1999-257, s. 4.1; 2001-352, s. 3; 2001-487, s. 52; 2004-193, ss. 4, 5; 2006-253, s. 22.2; 2007-493, s. 2.)

§ 20-17.1. Revocation of license of mental incompetents, alcoholics and habitual users of narcotic drugs.

(a)   The Commissioner, upon receipt of notice that any person has been legally adjudicated incompetent or has been involuntarily committed to an institution for the treatment of alcoholism or drug addiction, shall forthwith make inquiry into the facts for the purpose of determining whether such person is competent to operate a motor vehicle. If a person has been adjudicated incompetent under Chapter 35A of the General Statutes, in making an inquiry into the facts, the Commissioner shall consider the clerk of court's recommendation regarding whether the incompetent person should be allowed to retain his or her driving privilege. Unless the Commissioner is satisfied that such person is competent to operate a motor vehicle with safety to persons and property, he shall revoke such person's driving privilege. Provided that if such person requests, in writing, a hearing, he shall retain his license until after the hearing, and if the revocation is sustained after such hearing, the person whose driving privilege has been revoked under the provisions of this section, shall have the right to a review by the review board as provided in G.S. 20-9(g)(4) upon written request filed with the Division.

(b)   If any person shall be adjudicated as incompetent or is involuntarily committed for the treatment of alcoholism or drug addiction, the clerk of the court in which any such adjudication is made shall forthwith send a certified copy of abstract thereof to the Commissioner.

(c)   Repealed by Session Laws 1973, c. 475, s. 31/2.

(d)   It is the intent of this section that the provisions herein shall be carried out by the Commissioner of Motor Vehicles for the safety of the motoring public. The Commissioner shall have authority to make such agreements as are necessary with the persons in charge of every institution of any nature for the care and treatment of alcoholics or habitual users of narcotic drugs, to effectively carry out the duty hereby imposed and the person in charge of the institutions described above shall cooperate with and assist the Commissioner of Motor Vehicles.

(e)   Notwithstanding the provisions of G.S. 8-53, 8-53.2, and Article 3 of Chapter 122C of the General Statutes, the person or persons in charge of any institution as set out in subsection (a) hereinabove shall furnish such information as may be required for the effective enforcement of this section. Information furnished to the Division of Motor Vehicles as provided herein shall be confidential and the Commissioner of Motor Vehicles shall be subject to the same penalties and is granted the same protection as is the department, institution or individual furnishing such information. No criminal or civil action may be brought against any person or agency who shall provide or submit to the Commissioner of Motor Vehicles or his authorized agents the information as required herein.

(f)   Revocations under this section may be reviewed as provided in G.S. 20-9(g)(4). (1947, c. 1006, s. 9; 1953, c. 1300, s. 36; 1955, c. 1187, s. 16; 1969, c. 186, s. 1; c. 1125; 1971, c. 208, ss. 1, 11/2; c. 401, s. 1; c. 767; 1973, c. 475, s. 31/2; c. 1362; 1975, c. 716, s. 5; 1983, c. 768, s. 3; 1987, c. 720, s. 1; 2008-182, s. 1.)

§ 20-17.2: Repealed by Session Laws 2006-253, s. 25, effective December 1, 2006, and applicable to offenses committed on or after that date.

§ 20-17.3. Revocation for underage purchasers of alcohol.

The Division shall revoke for one year the driver's license of any person who has been convicted of violating any of the following:

(1)   G.S. 18B-302(c), (e), or (f).

(2)   G.S. 18B-302(b), if the violation occurred while the person was purchasing or attempting to purchase an alcoholic beverage.

(3)   G.S. 18B-302(a1).

If the person's license is currently suspended or revoked, then the revocation under this section shall begin at the termination of that revocation. A person whose license is revoked under this section for a violation of G.S. 18B-302(a1) or G.S. 18B-302(c) shall be eligible for a limited driving privilege under G.S. 20-179.3. (1983, c. 435, s. 36; 2007-537, s. 3.)

§ 20-17.4. Disqualification to drive a commercial motor vehicle.

(a) One Year. - Any of the following disqualifies a person from driving a commercial motor vehicle for one year if committed by a person holding a commercial drivers license, or, when applicable, committed while operating a commercial motor vehicle by a person who does not hold a commercial drivers license:

(1) A first conviction of G.S. 20-138.1, driving while impaired, for a holder of a commercial drivers license that occurred while the person was driving a motor vehicle that is not a commercial motor vehicle.

(2) A first conviction of G.S. 20-138.2, driving a commercial motor vehicle while impaired.

(3) A first conviction of G.S. 20-166, hit and run.

(4) A first conviction of a felony in the commission of which a commercial motor vehicle was used or the first conviction of a felony in which any motor vehicle is used by a holder of a commercial drivers license.

(5) Refusal to submit to a chemical test when charged with an implied-consent offense, as defined in G.S. 20-16.2.

(6) A second or subsequent conviction, as defined in G.S. 20-138.2A(d), of driving a commercial motor vehicle after consuming alcohol under G.S. 20-138.2A.

(7) A civil license revocation under G.S. 20-16.5, or a substantially similar revocation obtained in another jurisdiction, arising out of a charge that occurred while the person was either operating a commercial motor vehicle or while the person was holding a commercial drivers license.

(8) A first conviction of vehicular homicide under G.S. 20-141.4 or vehicular manslaughter under G.S. 14-18 occurring while the person was operating a commercial motor vehicle.

(9) Driving a commercial motor vehicle during a period when the person's commercial drivers license is revoked, suspended, cancelled, or the driver is otherwise disqualified from operating a commercial motor vehicle.

(a1) Ten-Day Disqualification. - A person who is convicted for a first offense of driving a commercial motor vehicle after consuming alcohol under G.S. 20-138.2A is disqualified from driving a commercial motor vehicle for 10 days.

(b) Modified Life. - A person who has been disqualified from driving a commercial motor vehicle for a conviction or refusal described in subsection (a) who, as the result of a separate incident, is subsequently convicted of an offense or commits an act requiring disqualification under subsection (a) is disqualified for life. The Division may adopt guidelines, including conditions, under which a disqualification for life under this subsection may be reduced to 10 years.

(b1) Life Without Reduction. - A person is disqualified from driving a commercial motor vehicle for life, without the possibility of reinstatement after 10 years, if that person is convicted of a third or subsequent violation of G.S. 20-138.2, a fourth or subsequent violation of G.S. 20-138.2A, or if the person refuses to submit to a chemical test a third time when charged with an implied-consent offense, as defined in G.S. 20-16.2, that occurred while the person was driving a commercial motor vehicle.

(c) Life. - A person is disqualified from driving a commercial motor vehicle for life if that person either uses a commercial motor vehicle in the commission of any felony involving the manufacture, distribution, or dispensing of a controlled substance, or possession with intent to manufacture, distribute, or dispense a controlled substance or is the holder of a commercial drivers license at the time of the commission of any such felony.

(c1) Life. - A person shall be disqualified from driving a commercial motor vehicle for life, without the possibility of reinstatement, if that person has had a commercial drivers license reinstated in the past and is convicted of another major disqualifying offense as defined in 49 C.F.R. § 383.51(b).

(d) Less Than a Year. - A person is disqualified from driving a commercial motor vehicle for 60 days if that person is convicted of two serious traffic violations, or 120 days if convicted of three or more serious traffic violations, arising from separate incidents occurring within a three-year period, committed in a commercial motor vehicle or while holding a commercial drivers license. This disqualification shall be in addition to, and shall be served at the end of, any other prior disqualification. For purposes of this subsection, a "serious violation" includes violations of G.S. 20-140(f) and G.S. 20-141(j3).

(e) Three Years. - A person is disqualified from driving a commercial motor vehicle for three years if that person is convicted of an offense or commits an act requiring disqualification under subsection (a) and the offense or act occurred while the person was transporting a hazardous material that required the motor vehicle driven to be placarded.

(f) Revocation Period. - A person is disqualified from driving a commercial motor vehicle for the period during which the person's regular or commercial drivers license is revoked, suspended, or cancelled.

(g) Violation of Out-of-Service Order. - Any person convicted for violating an out-of-service order, except as described in subsection (h) of this section, shall be disqualified as follows:

(1) A person is disqualified from driving a commercial vehicle for a period of 90 days if convicted of a first violation of an out-of-service order.

(2) A person is disqualified for a period of one year if convicted of a second violation of an out-of-service order during any 10-year period, arising from separate incidents.

(3) A person is disqualified for a period of three years if convicted of a third or subsequent violation of an out-of-service order during any 10-year period, arising from separate incidents.

(h) Violation of Out-of-Service Order; Special Rule for Hazardous Materials and Passenger Offenses. - Any person convicted for violating an out-of-service order while transporting hazardous materials or while operating a commercial vehicle designed or used to transport more than 15 passengers, including the driver, shall be disqualified as follows:

(1) A person is disqualified for a period of 180 days if convicted of a first violation of an out-of-service order.

(2) A person is disqualified for a period of three years if convicted of a second or subsequent violation of an out-of-service order during any 10-year period, arising from separate incidents.

(i) Disqualification for Out-of-State Violations. - The Division shall withdraw the privilege to operate a commercial vehicle of any resident of this State or person transferring to this State upon receiving notice of the person's conviction or Administrative Per Se Notice in another state for an offense that, if committed in this State, would be grounds for disqualification, even if the offense occurred in another jurisdiction prior to being licensed in this State where no action had been taken at that time in the other jurisdiction. The period of disqualification shall be the same as if the offense occurred in this State.

(j) Disqualification of Persons Without Commercial Drivers Licenses. - Any person convicted of an offense that requires disqualification under this section, but who does not hold a commercial drivers license, shall be disqualified from operating a commercial vehicle in the same manner as if the person held a valid commercial drivers license.

(k) Disqualification for Railroad Grade Crossing Offenses. - Any person convicted of a violation of G.S. 20-142.1 through G.S. 20-142.5, when the driver is operating a commercial motor vehicle, shall be disqualified from driving a commercial motor vehicle as follows:

(1) A person is disqualified for a period of 60 days if convicted of a first violation of a railroad grade crossing offense listed in this subsection.

(2) A person is disqualified for a period of 120 days if convicted during any three-year period of a second violation of any combination of railroad grade crossing offenses listed in this subsection.

(3) A person is disqualified for a period of one year if convicted during any three-year period of a third or subsequent violation of any combination of railroad grade crossing offenses listed in this subsection.

(l) Disqualification for Testing Positive in a Drug or Alcohol Test. - Upon receipt of notice of a positive drug or alcohol test, or of refusal to participate in a drug or alcohol test, pursuant to G.S. 20-37.19(c), the Division must disqualify a

CDL holder from operating a commercial motor vehicle for a minimum of 30 days and until receipt of proof of successful completion of assessment and treatment by a substance abuse professional in accordance with 49 C.F.R. § 382.503.

(m)   Disqualifications of Drivers Who Are Determined to Constitute an Imminent Hazard. - The Division shall withdraw the privilege to operate a commercial motor vehicle for any resident of this State for a period of 30 days in accordance with 49 C.F.R. § 383.52.

(n)   Disqualification for Conviction of Criminal Offense That Requires Registration Under the Sex Offender and Public Protection Registration Programs. - Effective December 1, 2009, except as otherwise provided by this subsection, a person convicted of a violation that requires registration under Article 27A of Chapter 14 of the General Statutes is disqualified from driving a commercial motor vehicle that requires a commercial drivers license with a P or S endorsement for the period of time during which the person is required to maintain registration under Article 27A of Chapter 14 of the General Statutes. If a person who is registered pursuant to Article 27A of Chapter 14 of the General Statutes on December 1, 2009, also has a valid commercial drivers license with a P or S endorsement that was issued on or before December 1, 2009, then the person is not disqualified under this subsection until that license expires, provided the person does not commit a subsequent offense that requires registration under Article 27A of Chapter 14 of the General Statutes.

(o)   Disqualification for Passing Stopped School Bus. - Any person whose drivers license is revoked under G.S. 20-217 is disqualified from driving a commercial motor vehicle for the period of time in which the person's drivers license remains revoked under G.S. 20-217. (1989, c. 771, s. 3; 1991, c. 726, s. 8; 1993, c. 533, s. 5; 1998-149, s. 3; 1998-182, s. 19; 2000-109, s. 7(e); 2002-72, s. 7; 2003-397, s. 2; 2005-156, s. 2; 2005-349, s. 6; 2007-492, s. 1; 2008-175, s. 1; 2009-416, s. 3; 2009-491, s. 2; 2013-293, s. 3.)

§ 20-17.5. Effect of disqualification.

(a)   When No Accompanying Revocation. - A person who is disqualified as the result of a conviction that requires disqualification but not revocation may keep any regular Class C drivers license the person had at the time of the offense resulting in disqualification. If the person had a Class A or Class B regular drivers license or a commercial drivers license when the offense occurred, all of the following apply:

(1) The person must give the license to the court that convicts the person or, if the person is not present when convicted, to the Division.

(2) The person may apply for a regular Class C drivers license.

(b) When Revocation and Disqualification. - When a person is disqualified as the result of a conviction that requires both disqualification and revocation, all of the following apply:

(1) The person must give any drivers license the person has to the court that convicts the person or, if the person is not present when convicted, to the Division.

(2) The person may obtain limited driving privileges to drive a noncommercial motor vehicle during the revocation period to the extent the law would allow limited driving privileges if the person had been driving a noncommercial motor vehicle when the offense occurred. The same procedure, eligibility requirements, and mandatory conditions apply to limited driving privileges authorized by this subdivision that would apply if the person had been driving a noncommercial motor vehicle when the offense occurred.

(3) If the disqualification period is longer than the revocation period, the person may apply for a regular Class C drivers license at the end of the revocation period.

(c) Refusal to Take Chemical Test. - When a person is disqualified for refusing to take a chemical test, all of the following apply:

(1) The person must give any license the person has to a court, a law enforcement officer, or the Division, in accordance with G.S. 20-16.2 and G.S. 20-16.5.

(2) The person may obtain limited driving privileges to drive a noncommercial motor vehicle during the period the person's license is revoked for the refusal that disqualified the person to the extent the law would allow limited driving privileges if the person had been driving a noncommercial motor vehicle at the time of the refusal. The same procedure, eligibility requirements, and mandatory conditions apply to limited driving privileges authorized by this

subdivision that would apply if the person had been driving a noncommercial motor vehicle at the time of the refusal.

(3)   If the disqualification period is longer than the revocation period, the person may apply for a regular Class C drivers license at the end of the revocation period.

(d)   Obtaining Class C Regular License. - A person who is authorized by this section to apply for a regular Class C drivers license and who meets all of the following criteria may obtain a regular Class C drivers license without taking a test:

(1)   The person must have had a Class A or Class B regular drivers license or a commercial drivers license when the person was disqualified.

(2)   The person's license must have been issued by the Division.

(3)   The person's license must not have expired by the date the person applies for a regular Class C drivers license.

Upon application and payment of the fee set in G.S. 20-14 for a duplicate license, the Division shall issue a person who meets these criteria a regular Class C drivers license. The license shall include the same endorsements and restrictions as the former Class A regular, Class B regular, or commercial drivers license, to the extent they apply to a regular Class C drivers license. A regular Class C drivers license issued to a person who meets these criteria expires the same day as the license it replaces.

G.S. 20-7 governs the issuance of a regular Class C drivers license to a person who is authorized by this section to apply for a regular Class C drivers license but who does not meet the listed criteria. In accordance with that statute, the Division may require the person to take a test and the person must pay the license fee.

(e)   Restoration Fee. - A person who is disqualified must pay the restoration fee set in G.S. 20-7(i1) the first time any of the following events occurs as a result of the same disqualification:

(1)   The Division reinstates a Class A regular drivers license, a Class B regular drivers license, or a commercial drivers license the person had at the time of the disqualification by issuing the person a duplicate license.

(2) The Division issues a Class A regular drivers license, a Class B regular drivers license, or a commercial drivers license to the person.

(3) If the person's license was revoked because of the conviction or act requiring disqualification, the Division issues a regular Class C drivers license to the person.

The restoration fee does not apply the second time any of these events occurs as a result of the same disqualification. (1991, c. 726, s. 9.)

§ 20-17.6. Restoration of a license after a conviction of driving while impaired or driving while less than 21 years old after consuming alcohol or drugs.

(a) Scope. - This section applies to a person whose license was revoked as a result of a conviction of any of the following offenses:

(1) G.S. 20-138.1, driving while impaired (DWI).

(2) G.S. 20-138.2, commercial DWI.

(3) G.S. 20-138.3, driving while less than 21 years old after consuming alcohol or drugs.

(4) G.S. 20-138.2A, driving a commercial motor vehicle with an alcohol concentration of greater than 0.00 and less than 0.04, if the person's drivers license was revoked under G.S. 20-17(a)(13).

(5) G.S. 20-138.2B, driving a school bus, a school activity bus, or a child care vehicle with an alcohol concentration of greater than 0.00, if the person's drivers license was revoked under G.S. 20-17(a)(14).

(b) Requirement for Restoring License. - The Division must receive a certificate of completion for a person who is subject to this section before the Division can restore that person's license. The revocation period for a person who is subject to this section is extended until the Division receives the certificate of completion.

(c)   Certificate of Completion. - To obtain a certificate of completion, a person must have a substance abuse assessment and, depending on the results of the assessment, must complete either an alcohol and drug education traffic (ADET) school or a substance abuse treatment program. The substance abuse assessment must be conducted by one of the entities authorized by the Department of Health and Human Services to conduct assessments. G.S. 122C-142.1 describes the procedure for obtaining a certificate of completion.

(d)   Notice of Requirement. - When a court reports to the Division a conviction of a person who is subject to this section, the Division must send the person written notice of the requirements of this section and of the consequences of failing to comply with these requirements. The notification must include a statement that the person may contact the local area mental health, developmental disabilities, and substance abuse program for a list of agencies and entities in the person's area that are authorized to make a substance abuse assessment and provide the education or treatment needed to obtain a certificate of completion.

(e)   Effect on Limited Driving Privileges. - A person who is subject to this section is not eligible for limited driving privileges if the revocation period for the offense that caused the person to become subject to this section has ended and the person's license remains revoked only because the Division has not obtained a certificate of completion for that person. The issuance of limited driving privileges during the revocation period for the offense that caused the person to become subject to this section is governed by the statutes that apply to that offense. (1995, c. 496, ss. 1, 11, 12; 1997-443, s. 11A.118(a); 1998-182, s. 20.)

§ 20-17.7. Commercial motor vehicle out-of-service fines authorized.

The Secretary of Public Safety may adopt rules implementing fines for violation of out-of-service criteria as defined in 49 C.F.R. § 390.5. These fines may not exceed the schedule of fines adopted by the Commercial Motor Vehicle Safety Alliance that is in effect on the date of the violations. (1999-330, s. 1; 2002-159, s. 31.5(b); 2002-190, s. 3; 2011-145, s. 19.1(g).)

§ 20-17.8. Restoration of a license after certain driving while impaired convictions; ignition interlock.

(a) Scope. - This section applies to a person whose license was revoked as a result of a conviction of driving while impaired, G.S. 20-138.1, and:

(1) The person had an alcohol concentration of 0.15 or more;

(2) The person has been convicted of another offense involving impaired driving, which offense occurred within seven years immediately preceding the date of the offense for which the person's license has been revoked; or

(3) The person was sentenced pursuant to G.S. 20-179(f3).

For purposes of subdivision (1) of this subsection, the results of a chemical analysis, as shown by an affidavit or affidavits executed pursuant to G.S. 20-16.2(c1), shall be used by the Division to determine that person's alcohol concentration.

(a1) (Expires December 1, 2014) Additional Scope. - This section applies to a person whose license was revoked as a result of a conviction of habitual impaired driving, G.S. 20-138.5.

(b) (Effective until December 1, 2014) Ignition Interlock Required. - Except as provided in subsection (l) of this section, when the Division restores the license of a person who is subject to this section, in addition to any other restriction or condition, it shall require the person to agree to and shall indicate on the person's drivers license the following restrictions for the period designated in subsection (c):

(1) A restriction that the person may operate only a vehicle that is equipped with a functioning ignition interlock system of a type approved by the Commissioner. The Commissioner shall not unreasonably withhold approval of an ignition interlock system and shall consult with the Division of Purchase and Contract in the Department of Administration to ensure that potential vendors are not discriminated against.

(2) A requirement that the person personally activate the ignition interlock system before driving the motor vehicle.

(3) An alcohol concentration restriction as follows:

a. If the ignition interlock system is required pursuant only to subdivision (a)(1) of this section, a requirement that the person not drive with an alcohol concentration of 0.04 or greater;

b. If the ignition interlock system is required pursuant to subdivision (a)(2) or (a)(3) of this section, or subsection (a1) of this section, a requirement that the person not drive with an alcohol concentration of greater than 0.00; or

c. If the ignition interlock system is required pursuant to subdivision (a)(1) of this section, and the person has also been convicted, based on the same set of circumstances, of: (i) driving while impaired in a commercial vehicle, G.S. 20-138.2, (ii) driving while less than 21 years old after consuming alcohol or drugs, G.S. 20-138.3, (iii) a violation of G.S. 20-141.4, or (iv) manslaughter or negligent homicide resulting from the operation of a motor vehicle when the offense involved impaired driving, a requirement that the person not drive with an alcohol concentration of greater than 0.00.

(b) (Effective December 1, 2014) Ignition Interlock Required. - Except as provided in subsection (l) of this section, when the Division restores the license of a person who is subject to this section, in addition to any other restriction or condition, it shall require the person to agree to and shall indicate on the person's drivers license the following restrictions for the period designated in subsection (c):

(1) A restriction that the person may operate only a vehicle that is equipped with a functioning ignition interlock system of a type approved by the Commissioner. The Commissioner shall not unreasonably withhold approval of an ignition interlock system and shall consult with the Division of Purchase and Contract in the Department of Administration to ensure that potential vendors are not discriminated against.

(2) A requirement that the person personally activate the ignition interlock system before driving the motor vehicle.

(3) An alcohol concentration restriction as follows:

a. If the ignition interlock system is required pursuant only to subdivision (a)(1) of this section, a requirement that the person not drive with an alcohol concentration of 0.04 or greater;

b. If the ignition interlock system is required pursuant to subdivision (a)(2) or (a)(3) of this section, a requirement that the person not drive with an alcohol concentration of greater than 0.00; or

c. If the ignition interlock system is required pursuant to subdivision (a)(1) of this section, and the person has also been convicted, based on the same set of circumstances, of: (i) driving while impaired in a commercial vehicle, G.S. 20-138.2, (ii) driving while less than 21 years old after consuming alcohol or drugs, G.S. 20-138.3, (iii) a violation of G.S. 20-141.4, or (iv) manslaughter or negligent homicide resulting from the operation of a motor vehicle when the offense involved impaired driving, a requirement that the person not drive with an alcohol concentration of greater than 0.00.

(c) Length of Requirement. - The requirements of subsection (b) shall remain in effect for:

(1) One year from the date of restoration if the original revocation period was one year;

(2) Three years from the date of restoration if the original revocation period was four years; or

(3) Seven years from the date of restoration if the original revocation was a permanent revocation.

(c1) Vehicles Subject to Requirement. - A person subject to this section shall have all registered vehicles owned by that person equipped with a functioning ignition interlock system of a type approved by the Commissioner. The Commissioner shall not issue a license to a person subject to this section until presented with proof of the installation of an ignition interlock system in all registered vehicles owned by the person. In order to avoid an undue financial hardship, a person subject to this section may seek a waiver from the Division for any vehicle registered to that person that is relied upon by another member of that person's family for transportation and that the vehicle is not in the possession of the person subject to this section. The Division shall determine such waiver on a case-by-case basis following an assessment of financial hardship to the person subject to this restriction. The Commissioner shall cancel the drivers license of any person subject to this section for registration of a motor vehicle owned by the person without an installed ignition interlock system or removal of the ignition interlock system from a motor vehicle owned by the person, other than when changing ignition interlock providers or upon sale of the vehicle.

(d) Effect of Limited Driving Privileges. - If the person was eligible for and received a limited driving privilege under G.S. 20-179.3, with the ignition interlock requirement contained in G.S. 20-179.3(g5), the period of time for which that limited driving privilege was held shall be applied towards the requirements of subsection (c).

(e) Notice of Requirement. - When a court reports to the Division a conviction of a person who is subject to this section, the Division must send the person written notice of the requirements of this section and of the consequences of failing to comply with these requirements. The notification must include a statement that the person may contact the Division for information on obtaining and having installed an ignition interlock system of a type approved by the Commissioner.

(f) Effect of Violation of Restriction. - A person subject to this section who violates any of the restrictions of this section commits the offense of driving while license revoked under G.S. 20-28(a) and is subject to punishment and license revocation as provided in that section. If a law enforcement officer has reasonable grounds to believe that a person subject to this section has consumed alcohol while driving or has driven while he has remaining in his body any alcohol previously consumed, the suspected offense of driving while license is revoked is an alcohol-related offense subject to the implied-consent provisions of G.S. 20-16.2. If a person subject to this section is charged with driving while license revoked by violating a condition of subsection (b) of this section, and a judicial official determines that there is probable cause for the charge, the person's license is suspended pending the resolution of the case, and the judicial official must require the person to surrender the license. The judicial official must also notify the person that he is not entitled to drive until his case is resolved. An alcohol concentration report from the ignition interlock system shall not be admissible as evidence of driving while license revoked, nor shall it be admissible in an administrative revocation proceeding as provided in subsection (g) of this section, unless the person operated a vehicle when the ignition interlock system indicated an alcohol concentration in violation of the restriction placed upon the person by subdivision (b)(3) of this section.

(g) Effect of Violation of Restriction When Driving While License Revoked Not Charged. - A person subject to this section who violates any of the restrictions of this section, but is not charged or convicted of driving while license revoked pursuant to G.S. 20-28(a), shall have the person's license revoked by the Division for a period of one year.

(h) Beginning of Revocation Period. - If the original period of revocation was imposed pursuant to G.S. 20-19(d) or (e), any remaining period of the original revocation, prior to its reduction, shall be reinstated and the revocation required by subsection (f) or (g) of this section begins after all other periods of revocation have terminated.

(i) Notification of Revocation. - If the person's license has not already been surrendered to the court, the Division must expeditiously notify the person that the person's license to drive is revoked pursuant to subsection (f) or (g) of this section effective on the tenth calendar day after the mailing of the revocation order.

(j) Right to Hearing Before Division; Issues. - If the person's license is revoked pursuant to subsection (g) of this section, before the effective date of the order issued under subsection (i) of this section, the person may request in writing a hearing before the Division. Except for the time referred to in G.S. 20-16.5, if the person shows to the satisfaction of the Division that the person's license was surrendered to the court and remained in the court's possession, then the Division shall credit the amount of time for which the license was in the possession of the court against the revocation period required by subsection (g) of this section. If the person properly requests a hearing, the person retains the person's license, unless it is revoked under some other provision of law, until the hearing is held, the person withdraws the request, or the person fails to appear at a scheduled hearing. The hearing officer may subpoena any witnesses or documents that the hearing officer deems necessary. The person may request the hearing officer to subpoena the charging officer, the chemical analyst, or both to appear at the hearing if the person makes the request in writing at least three days before the hearing. The person may subpoena any other witness whom the person deems necessary, and the provisions of G.S. 1A-1, Rule 45, apply to the issuance and service of all subpoenas issued under the authority of this section. The hearing officer is authorized to administer oaths to witnesses appearing at the hearing. The hearing must be conducted in the county where the charge was brought, and must be limited to consideration of whether:

(1) The drivers license of the person had an ignition interlock requirement; and

(2) The person:

a. Was driving a vehicle that was not equipped with a functioning ignition interlock system; or

b. Did not personally activate the ignition interlock system before driving the vehicle; or

c. Drove the vehicle in violation of an applicable alcohol concentration restriction prescribed by subdivision (b)(3) of this section.

If the Division finds that the conditions specified in this subsection are met, it must order the revocation sustained. If the Division finds that the condition of subdivision (1) is not met, or that none of the conditions of subdivision (2) are met, it must rescind the revocation. If the revocation is sustained, the person must surrender the person's license immediately upon notification by the Division. If the revocation is sustained, the person may appeal the decision of the Division pursuant to G.S. 20-25.

(k) Restoration After Violation. - When the Division restores the license of a person whose license was revoked pursuant to subsection (f) or (g) of this section and the revocation occurred prior to completion of time period required by subsection (c) of this section, in addition to any other restriction or condition, it shall require the person to comply with the conditions of subsection (b) of this section until the person has complied with those conditions for the cumulative period of time as set forth in subsection (c) of this section. The period of time for which the person successfully complied with subsection (b) of this section prior to revocation pursuant to subsection (f) or (g) of this section shall be applied towards the requirements of subsection (c) of this section.

(l) Medical Exception to Requirement. - A person subject to this section solely for the reason set forth in subdivision (a)(1) of this section and who has a medically diagnosed physical condition that makes the person incapable of personally activating an ignition interlock system may request an exception to the requirements of this section from the Division. The Division shall not issue an exception to this section unless the person has submitted to a physical examination by two or more physicians or surgeons duly licensed to practice medicine in this State or in any other state of the United States and unless such examining physicians or surgeons have completed and signed a certificate in the form prescribed by the Division. Such certificate shall be devised by the Commissioner with the advice of those qualified experts in the field of diagnosing and treating physical disorders that the Commissioner may select and shall be designed to elicit the maximum medical information necessary to aid in determining whether or not the person is capable of personally activating an ignition interlock system. The certificate shall contain a waiver of privilege and the recommendation of the examining physician to the Commissioner as to whether the person is capable of personally activating an ignition interlock system.

The Commissioner is not bound by the recommendations of the examining physicians but shall give fair consideration to such recommendations in acting upon the request for medical exception, the criterion being whether or not, upon all the evidence, it appears that the person is in fact incapable of personally activating an ignition interlock system. The burden of proof of such fact is upon the person seeking the exception.

Whenever an exception is denied by the Commissioner, such denial may be reviewed by a reviewing board upon written request of the person seeking the exception filed with the Division within 10 days after receipt of such denial. The composition, procedures, and review of the reviewing board shall be as provided in G.S. 20-9(g)(4). This subsection shall not apply to persons subject to an ignition interlock requirement under this section for the reasons set forth in subdivision (a)(2) or (a)(3) of this section. (1999-406, s. 3; 2000-155, ss. 1-3; 2001-487, s. 8; 2006-253, ss. 22.3, 22.4; 2007-493, ss. 5, 10, 28; 2009-369, ss. 5, 6; 2011-191, s. 3; 2013-348, s. 1.)

§ 20-17.8A. Tampering with ignition interlock systems.

Any person who tampers with, circumvents, or attempts to circumvent an ignition interlock device required to be installed on a motor vehicle pursuant to judicial order, statute, or as may be otherwise required as a condition for an individual to operate a motor vehicle, for the purpose of avoiding or altering testing on the ignition interlock device in the operation or attempted operation of a vehicle, or altering the testing results received or results in the process of being received on the ignition interlock device, is guilty of a Class 1 misdemeanor. Each act of tampering, circumvention, or attempted circumvention under this statute shall constitute a separate violation. (2011-381, s. 1.)

§ 20-17.9. Revocation of commercial drivers license with a P or S endorsement upon conviction of certain offenses.

The Division shall revoke the commercial drivers license with a P or S endorsement of any person convicted of any offense on or after December 1, 2009, that requires registration under Article 27A of Chapter 14 of the General Statutes. The person may apply for the issuance of a new commercial drivers license pursuant to this Chapter, but, pursuant to G.S. 20-17.4, shall remain disqualified from obtaining a commercial drivers license with a P or S endorsement for the period of time during which the person is required to maintain registration. (2009-491, s. 3.)

§ 20-18. Conviction of offenses described in § 20-181 not ground for suspension or revocation.

Conviction of offenses described in G.S. 20-181 shall not be cause for the suspension or revocation of driver's license under the terms of this Article. (1939, c. 351, s. 2; 1955, c. 913, s. 1; 1979, c. 667, s. 41.)

§ 20-19. Period of suspension or revocation; conditions of restoration.

(a)   When a license is suspended under subdivision (8) or (9) of G.S. 20-16(a), the period of suspension shall be in the discretion of the Division and for such time as it deems best for public safety but shall not exceed six months.

(b)   When a license is suspended under subdivision (10) of G.S. 20-16(a), the period of suspension shall be in the discretion of the Division and for such time as it deems best for public safety but shall not exceed a period of 12 months.

(c)   When a license is suspended under any other provision of this Article which does not specifically provide a period of suspension, the period of suspension shall be not more than one year.

(c1)   When a license is revoked under subdivision (2) of G.S. 20-17, and the period of revocation is not determined by subsection (d) or (e) of this section, the period of revocation is one year.

(c2) When a license is suspended under G.S. 20-17(a)(14), the period of revocation for a first conviction shall be for 10 days. For a second or subsequent conviction as defined in G.S. 20-138.2B(d), the period of revocation shall be one year.

(c3) (Effective until December 1, 2014) Restriction; Revocations. - When the Division restores a person's drivers license which was revoked pursuant to G.S. 20-13.2 (a), G.S. 20-23 when the offense involved impaired driving, G.S. 20-23.2, subdivision (2) of G.S. 20-17(a), subdivision (1) or (9) of G.S. 20-17(a) when the offense involved impaired driving, G.S. 20-138.5(d), or this subsection, in addition to any other restriction or condition, it shall place the applicable restriction on the person's drivers license as follows:

(1) For the first restoration of a drivers license for a person convicted of driving while impaired, G.S. 20-138.1, or a drivers license revoked pursuant to G.S. 20-23 or G.S. 20-23.2 when the offense for which the person's license was revoked prohibits substantially similar conduct which if committed in this State would result in a conviction of driving while impaired under G.S. 20-138.1, that the person not operate a vehicle with an alcohol concentration of 0.04 or more at any relevant time after the driving;

(2) For the second or subsequent restoration of a drivers license for a person convicted of driving while impaired, G.S. 20-138.1, or a drivers license revoked pursuant to G.S. 20-23 or G.S. 20-23.2 when the offense for which the person's license was revoked prohibits substantially similar conduct which if committed in this State would result in a conviction of driving while impaired under G.S. 20-138.1, that the person not operate a vehicle with an alcohol concentration greater than 0.00 at any relevant time after the driving;

(3) For any restoration of a drivers license for a person convicted of driving while impaired in a commercial motor vehicle, G.S. 20-138.2, habitual impaired driving, G.S. 20-138.5, driving while less than 21 years old after consuming alcohol or drugs, G.S. 20-138.3, felony death by vehicle, G.S. 20-141.4(a1), manslaughter or negligent homicide resulting from the operation of a motor vehicle when the offense involved impaired driving, or a revocation under this subsection, that the person not operate a vehicle with an alcohol concentration of greater than 0.00 at any relevant time after the driving;

(4) For any restoration of a drivers license revoked pursuant to G.S. 20-23 or G.S. 20-23.2 when the offense for which the person's license was revoked

prohibits substantially similar conduct which if committed in this State would result in a conviction of driving while impaired in a commercial motor vehicle, G.S. 20-138.2, driving while less than 21 years old after consuming alcohol or drugs, G.S. 20-138.3, a violation of G.S. 20-141.4, or manslaughter or negligent homicide resulting from the operation of a motor vehicle when the offense involved impaired driving, that the person not operate vehicle with an alcohol concentration of greater than 0.00 at any relevant time after the driving.

In addition, the person seeking restoration of a license must agree to submit to a chemical analysis in accordance with G.S. 20-16.2 at the request of a law enforcement officer who has reasonable grounds to believe the person is operating a motor vehicle on a highway or public vehicular area in violation of the restriction specified in this subsection. The person must also agree that, when requested by a law enforcement officer, the person will agree to be transported by the law enforcement officer to the place where chemical analysis is to be administered.

The restrictions placed on a license under this subsection shall be in effect (i) seven years from the date of restoration if the person's license was permanently revoked, (ii) until the person's twenty-first birthday if the revocation was for a conviction under G.S. 20-138.3, and (iii) three years in all other cases.

A law enforcement officer who has reasonable grounds to believe that a person has violated a restriction placed on the person's drivers license shall complete an affidavit pursuant to G.S. 20-16.2(c1). On the basis of information reported pursuant to G.S. 20-16.2, the Division shall revoke the drivers license of any person who violates a condition of reinstatement imposed under this subsection. An alcohol concentration report from an ignition interlock system shall not be used as the basis for revocation under this subsection. A violation of a restriction imposed under this subsection or the willful refusal to submit to a chemical analysis shall result in a one-year revocation. If the period of revocation was imposed pursuant to subsection (d) or (e), or G.S. 20-138.5(d), any remaining period of the original revocation, prior to its reduction, shall be reinstated and the one-year revocation begins after all other periods of revocation have terminated.

(c3)   (Effective December 1, 2014) Restriction; Revocations. - When the Division restores a person's drivers license which was revoked pursuant to G.S. 20-13.2 (a), G.S. 20-23 when the offense involved impaired driving, G.S. 20-23.2, subdivision (2) of G.S. 20-17(a), subdivision (1) or (9) of G.S. 20-17(a) when the offense involved impaired driving, or this subsection, in addition to any other restriction or condition, it shall place the applicable restriction on the person's drivers license as follows:

(1) For the first restoration of a drivers license for a person convicted of driving while impaired, G.S. 20-138.1, or a drivers license revoked pursuant to G.S. 20-23 or G.S. 20-23.2 when the offense for which the person's license was revoked prohibits substantially similar conduct which if committed in this State would result in a conviction of driving while impaired under G.S. 20-138.1, that the person not operate a vehicle with an alcohol concentration of 0.04 or more at any relevant time after the driving;

(2) For the second or subsequent restoration of a drivers license for a person convicted of driving while impaired, G.S. 20-138.1, or a drivers license revoked pursuant to G.S. 20-23 or G.S. 20-23.2 when the offense for which the person's license was revoked prohibits substantially similar conduct which if committed in this State would result in a conviction of driving while impaired under G.S. 20-138.1, that the person not operate a vehicle with an alcohol concentration greater than 0.00 at any relevant time after the driving;

(3) For any restoration of a drivers license for a person convicted of driving while impaired in a commercial motor vehicle, G.S. 20-138.2, driving while less than 21 years old after consuming alcohol or drugs, G.S. 20-138.3, felony death by vehicle, G.S. 20-141.4(a1), manslaughter or negligent homicide resulting from the operation of a motor vehicle when the offense involved impaired driving, or a revocation under this subsection, that the person not operate a vehicle with an alcohol concentration of greater than 0.00 at any relevant time after the driving;

(4) For any restoration of a drivers license revoked pursuant to G.S. 20-23 or G.S. 20-23.2 when the offense for which the person's license was revoked prohibits substantially similar conduct which if committed in this State would result in a conviction of driving while impaired in a commercial motor vehicle, G.S. 20-138.2, driving while less than 21 years old after consuming alcohol or drugs, G.S. 20-138.3, a violation of G.S. 20-141.4, or manslaughter or negligent homicide resulting from the operation of a motor vehicle when the offense involved impaired driving, that the person not operate vehicle with an alcohol concentration of greater than 0.00 at any relevant time after the driving.

In addition, the person seeking restoration of a license must agree to submit to a chemical analysis in accordance with G.S. 20-16.2 at the request of a law enforcement officer who has reasonable grounds to believe the person is operating a motor vehicle on a highway or public vehicular area in violation of the restriction specified in this subsection. The person must also agree that, when requested by a law enforcement officer, the person will agree to be transported by the law enforcement officer to the place where chemical analysis is to be administered.

The restrictions placed on a license under this subsection shall be in effect (i) seven years from the date of restoration if the person's license was permanently revoked, (ii) until the person's twenty-first birthday if the revocation was for a conviction under G.S. 20-138.3, and (iii) three years in all other cases.

A law enforcement officer who has reasonable grounds to believe that a person has violated a restriction placed on the person's drivers license shall complete an affidavit pursuant to G.S. 20-16.2(c1). On the basis of information reported pursuant to G.S. 20-16.2, the Division shall revoke the drivers license of any person who violates a condition of reinstatement imposed under this subsection. An alcohol concentration report from an ignition interlock system shall not be used as the basis for revocation under this subsection. A violation of a restriction imposed under this subsection or the willful refusal to submit to a chemical analysis shall result in a one-year revocation. If the period of revocation was imposed pursuant to subsection (d) or (e), any remaining period of the original revocation, prior to its reduction, shall be reinstated and the one-year revocation begins after all other periods of revocation have terminated.

(c4) Applicable Procedures. - When a person has violated a condition of restoration by refusing a chemical analysis, the notice and hearing procedures of G.S. 20-16.2 apply. When a person has submitted to a chemical analysis and the results show a violation of the alcohol concentration restriction, the notification and hearing procedures of this section apply.

(c5) Right to Hearing Before Division; Issues. - Upon receipt of a properly executed affidavit required by G.S. 20-16.2(c1), the Division must expeditiously notify the person charged that the person's license to drive is revoked for the period of time specified in this section, effective on the tenth calendar day after the mailing of the revocation order unless, before the effective date of the order, the person requests in writing a hearing before the Division. Except for the time referred to in G.S. 20-16.5, if the person shows to the satisfaction of the Division that the person's license was surrendered to the court and remained in the court's possession, then the Division shall credit the amount of time for which the license was in the possession of the court against the revocation period required by this section. If the person properly requests a hearing, the person retains the person's license, unless it is revoked under some other provision of law, until the hearing is held, the person withdraws the request, or the person fails to appear at a scheduled hearing. The hearing officer may subpoena any witnesses or documents that the hearing officer deems necessary. The person may request the hearing officer to subpoena the charging officer, the chemical analyst, or both to appear at the hearing if the person makes the request in writing at least three days before the hearing. The person may subpoena any other witness whom the person deems necessary, and the provisions of G.S. 1A-1, Rule 45, apply to the issuance and service of all subpoenas issued under the authority of this section. The hearing officer is authorized to administer oaths to witnesses appearing at the hearing. The hearing must be conducted in the county where the charge was brought, and must be limited to consideration of whether:

(1) The charging officer had reasonable grounds to believe that the person had violated the alcohol concentration restriction;

(2) The person was notified of the person's rights as required by G.S. 20-16.2(a);

(3) The drivers license of the person had an alcohol concentration restriction; and

(4) The person submitted to a chemical analysis upon the request of the charging officer, and the analysis revealed an alcohol concentration in excess of the restriction on the person's drivers license.

If the Division finds that the conditions specified in this subsection are met, it must order the revocation sustained. If the Division finds that any of the conditions (1), (2), (3), or (4) is not met, it must rescind the revocation. If the revocation is sustained, the person must surrender the person's license immediately upon notification by the Division.

(c6) Appeal to Court. - There is no right to appeal the decision of the Division. However, if the person properly requested a hearing before the Division under subsection (c5) and the Division held such a hearing, the person may within 30 days of the date the Division's decision is mailed to the person, petition the superior court of the county in which the hearing took place for discretionary review on the record of the revocation. The superior court may stay the imposition of the revocation only if the court finds that the person is likely to succeed on the merits of the case and will suffer irreparable harm if such a stay is not granted. The stay shall not exceed 30 days. The reviewing court shall review the record only and shall be limited to determining if the Division hearing officer followed proper procedures and if the hearing officer made sufficient findings of fact to support the revocation. There shall be no further appeal.

(d)   When a person's license is revoked under (i) G.S. 20-17(a)(2) and the person has another offense involving impaired driving for which he has been convicted, which offense occurred within three years immediately preceding the date of the offense for which his license is being revoked, or (ii) G.S. 20-17(a)(9) due to a violation of G.S. 20-141.4(a3), the period of revocation is four years, and this period may be reduced only as provided in this section. The Division may conditionally restore the person's license after it has been revoked for at least two years under this subsection if he provides the Division with satisfactory proof that:

(1)   He has not in the period of revocation been convicted in North Carolina or any other state or federal jurisdiction of a motor vehicle offense, an alcoholic beverage control law offense, a drug law offense, or any other criminal offense involving the possession or consumption of alcohol or drugs; and

(2)   He is not currently an excessive user of alcohol, drugs, or prescription drugs, or unlawfully using any controlled substance. The person may voluntarily submit themselves to continuous alcohol monitoring for the purpose of proving abstinence from alcohol consumption during a period of revocation immediately prior to the restoration consideration.

a.   Monitoring periods of 120 days or longer shall be accepted by the Division as evidence of abstinence if the Division receives sufficient documentation that reflects that the person abstained from alcohol use during the monitoring period.

b.   The continuous alcohol monitoring system shall be a system approved under G.S. 15A-1343.3.

c.   The Division may establish guidelines for the acceptance of evidence of abstinence under this subdivision.

If the Division restores the person's license, it may place reasonable conditions or restrictions on the person for the duration of the original revocation period.

(e) When a person's license is revoked under (i) G.S. 20-17(a)(2) and the person has two or more previous offenses involving impaired driving for which the person has been convicted, and the most recent offense occurred within the five years immediately preceding the date of the offense for which the person's license is being revoked, (ii) G.S. 20-17(a)(2) and the person was sentenced pursuant to G.S. 20-179(f3) for the offense resulting in the revocation, or (iii) G.S. 20-17(a)(9) due to a violation of G.S. 20-141.4(a4), the revocation is permanent.

(e1) Notwithstanding subsection (e) of this section, the Division may conditionally restore the license of a person to whom subsection (e) applies after it has been revoked for at least three years under subsection (e) if the person provides the Division with satisfactory proof of all of the following:

(1) In the three years immediately preceding the person's application for a restored license, the person has not been convicted in North Carolina or in any other state or federal court of a motor vehicle offense, an alcohol beverage control law offense, a drug law offense, or any criminal offense involving the consumption of alcohol or drugs.

(2) The person is not currently an excessive user of alcohol, drugs, or prescription drugs, or unlawfully using any controlled substance. The person may voluntarily submit themselves to continuous alcohol monitoring for the purpose of proving abstinence from alcohol consumption during a period of revocation immediately prior to the restoration consideration.

a. Monitoring periods of 120 days or longer shall be accepted by the Division as evidence of abstinence if the Division receives sufficient documentation that reflects that the person abstained from alcohol use during the monitoring period.

b. The continuous alcohol monitoring system shall be a system approved under G.S. 15A-1343.3.

c. The Division may establish guidelines for the acceptance of evidence of abstinence under this subdivision.

(e2) Notwithstanding subsection (e) of this section, the Division may conditionally restore the license of a person to whom subsection (e) applies after it has been revoked for at least 24 months under G.S. 20-17(a)(2) if the person provides the Division with satisfactory proof of all of the following:

(1) The person has not consumed any alcohol for the 12 months preceding the restoration while being monitored by a continuous alcohol monitoring device of a type approved by the Division of Adult Correction of the Department of Public Safety.

(2) The person has not in the period of revocation been convicted in North Carolina or any other state or federal jurisdiction of a motor vehicle offense, an alcoholic beverage control law offense, a drug law offense, or any other criminal offense involving the possession or consumption of alcohol or drugs.

(3) The person is not currently an excessive user of drugs or prescription drugs.

(4) The person is not unlawfully using any controlled substance.

(e3) (Effective until December 1, 2014) If the Division restores a person's license under subsection (e1), (e2), or (e4) of this section, it may place reasonable conditions or restrictions on the person for any period up to five years from the date of restoration.

(e3) (Effective December 1, 2014) If the Division restores a person's license under subsection (e1) or (e2) of this section, it may place reasonable conditions or restrictions on the person for any period up to five years from the date of restoration.

(e4) (Expires December 1, 2014) When a person's license is revoked under G.S. 20-138.5(d), the Division may conditionally restore the license of that person after it has been revoked for at least 10 years after the completion of any sentence imposed by the court, if the person provides the Division with satisfactory proof of all of the following:

(1) In the 10 years immediately preceding the person's application for a restored license, the person has not been convicted in North Carolina or in any other state or federal court of a motor vehicle offense, an alcohol beverage control law offense, a drug law offense, or any other criminal offense.

(2) The person is not currently a user of alcohol, unlawfully using any controlled substance, or an excessive user of prescription drugs.

(f)   When a license is revoked under any other provision of this Article which does not specifically provide a period of revocation, the period of revocation shall be one year.

(g)   When a license is suspended under subdivision (11) of G.S. 20-16(a), the period of suspension shall be for a period of time not in excess of the period of nonoperation imposed by the court as a condition of the suspended sentence; further, in such case, it shall not be necessary to comply with the Motor Vehicle Safety and Financial Responsibility Act in order to have such license returned at the expiration of the suspension period.

(g1)   When a license is revoked under subdivision (12) of G.S. 20-17, the period of revocation is six months for conviction of a second offense and one year for conviction of a third or subsequent offense.

(g2)   When a license is revoked under G.S. 20-17(a)(16), the period of revocation is 90 days for a second conviction and six months for a third or subsequent conviction. The term "second or subsequent conviction" shall have the same meaning as found in G.S. 20-17(a)(16).

(h)   Repealed by Session Laws 1983, c. 435, s. 17.

(i)   (For applicability, see Editor's note) When a person's license is revoked under G.S. 20-17(a)(1) or G.S. 20-17(a)(9), and the offense is one involving impaired driving and a fatality, the revocation is permanent. The Division may, however, conditionally restore the person's license after it has been revoked for at least five years under this subsection if he provides the Division with satisfactory proof that:

(1)   In the five years immediately preceding the person's application for a restored license, he has not been convicted in North Carolina or in any other state or federal court of a motor vehicle offense, an alcohol beverage control law offense, a drug law offense, or any criminal offense involving the consumption of alcohol or drugs; and

(2)   He is not currently an excessive user of alcohol or drugs.

If the Division restores the person's license, it may place reasonable conditions or restrictions on the person for any period up to seven years from the date of restoration.

(j)   The Division is authorized to issue amended revocation orders issued under subsections (d) and (e), if necessary because convictions do not respectively occur in the same order as offenses for which the license may be revoked under those subsections.

(k)   (Effective until December 1, 2014) Before the Division restores a driver's license that has been suspended or revoked under G.S. 20-138.5(d), or under any provision of this Article, other than G.S. 20-24.1, the person seeking to have his driver's license restored shall submit to the Division proof that he has notified his insurance agent or company of his seeking the restoration and that he is financially responsible. Proof of financial responsibility shall be in one of the following forms:

(1)   A written certificate or electronically-transmitted facsimile thereof from any insurance carrier duly authorized to do business in this State certifying that there is in effect a nonfleet private passenger motor vehicle liability policy for the benefit of the person required to furnish proof of financial responsibility. The certificate or facsimile shall state the effective date and expiration date of the nonfleet private passenger motor vehicle liability policy and shall state the date that the certificate or facsimile is issued. The certificate or facsimile shall remain effective proof of financial responsibility for a period of 30 consecutive days following the date the certificate or facsimile is issued but shall not in and of itself constitute a binder or policy of insurance or

(2)   A binder for or policy of nonfleet private passenger motor vehicle liability insurance under which the applicant is insured, provided that the binder or policy states the effective date and expiration date of the nonfleet private passenger motor vehicle liability policy.

The preceding provisions of this subsection do not apply to applicants who do not own currently registered motor vehicles and who do not operate nonfleet private passenger motor vehicles that are owned by other persons and that are not insured under commercial motor vehicle liability insurance policies. In such cases, the applicant shall sign a written certificate to that effect. Such certificate shall be furnished by the Division and may be incorporated into the restoration application form. Any material misrepresentation made by such person on such certificate shall be grounds for suspension of that person's license for a period of 90 days.

For the purposes of this subsection, the term "nonfleet private passenger motor vehicle" has the definition ascribed to it in Article 40 of General Statute Chapter 58.

The Commissioner may require that certificates required by this subsection be on a form approved by the Commissioner. The financial responsibility required by this subsection shall be kept in effect for not less than three years after the date that the license is restored. Failure to maintain financial responsibility as required by this subsection shall be grounds for suspending the restored driver's license for a period of thirty (30) days. Nothing in this subsection precludes any person from showing proof of financial responsibility in any other manner authorized by Articles 9A and 13 of this Chapter.

(k) (Effective December 1, 2014) Before the Division restores a driver's license that has been suspended or revoked under any provision of this Article, other than G.S. 20-24.1, the person seeking to have his driver's license restored shall submit to the Division proof that he has notified his insurance agent or company of his seeking the restoration and that he is financially responsible. Proof of financial responsibility shall be in one of the following forms:

(1) A written certificate or electronically-transmitted facsimile thereof from any insurance carrier duly authorized to do business in this State certifying that there is in effect a nonfleet private passenger motor vehicle liability policy for the benefit of the person required to furnish proof of financial responsibility. The certificate or facsimile shall state the effective date and expiration date of the nonfleet private passenger motor vehicle liability policy and shall state the date that the certificate or facsimile is issued. The certificate or facsimile shall remain effective proof of financial responsibility for a period of 30 consecutive days following the date the certificate or facsimile is issued but shall not in and of itself constitute a binder or policy of insurance or

(2) A binder for or policy of nonfleet private passenger motor vehicle liability insurance under which the applicant is insured, provided that the binder or policy states the effective date and expiration date of the nonfleet private passenger motor vehicle liability policy.

The preceding provisions of this subsection do not apply to applicants who do not own currently registered motor vehicles and who do not operate nonfleet private passenger motor vehicles that are owned by other persons and that are not insured under commercial motor vehicle liability insurance policies. In such cases, the applicant shall sign a written certificate to that effect. Such certificate shall be furnished by the Division and may be incorporated into the restoration application form. Any material misrepresentation made by such person on such certificate shall be grounds for suspension of that person's license for a period of 90 days.

For the purposes of this subsection, the term "nonfleet private passenger motor vehicle" has the definition ascribed to it in Article 40 of General Statute Chapter 58.

The Commissioner may require that certificates required by this subsection be on a form approved by the Commissioner. The financial responsibility required by this subsection shall be kept in effect for not less than three years after the date that the license is restored. Failure to maintain financial responsibility as required by this subsection shall be grounds for suspending the restored driver's license for a period of thirty (30) days. Nothing in this subsection precludes any person from showing proof of financial responsibility in any other manner authorized by Articles 9A and 13 of this Chapter. (1935, c. 52, s. 13; 1947, c. 1067, s. 15; 1951, c. 1202, ss. 2-4; 1953, c. 1138; 1955, c. 1187, ss. 13, 17, 18; 1957, c. 499, s. 2; c. 515, s. 1; 1959, c. 1264, s. 11A; 1969, c. 242; 1971, c. 619, ss. 8-10; 1973, c. 1445, ss. 1-4; 1975, c. 716, s. 5; 1979, c. 903, ss. 4-6; 1981, c. 412, s. 4; c. 747, ss. 34, 66; 1983, c. 435, s. 17; 1983 (Reg. Sess., 1984), c. 1101, s. 18; 1987, c. 869, s. 12; 1987 (Reg. Sess., 1988), c. 1112; 1989, c. 436, s. 5; c. 771, s. 18; 1995, c. 506, s. 8; 1998-182, s. 21; 1999-406, s. 2; 1999-452, ss. 11, 12; 2000-140, ss. 3, 4; 2000-155, s. 6; 2001-352, s. 4; 2007-165, ss. 1(a), (b); 2007-493, ss. 11-14; 2008-187, s. 9; 2009-99, s. 1; 2009-369, ss. 1-4; 2009-500, ss. 1, 2; 2011-145, s. 19.1(h); 2011-191, s. 2.)

§ 20-20: Repealed by Session Laws 1981, c. 938, s. 5.

§ 20-20.1. Limited driving privilege for certain revocations.

(a)   Definitions. - The following definitions apply in this section:

(1)   Limited driving privilege. - A judgment issued by a court authorizing a person with a revoked drivers license to drive under specified terms and conditions.

(2) Nonstandard working hours. - Anytime other than 6:00 A.M. until 8:00 P.M. on Monday through Friday.

(3) Standard working hours. - Anytime from 6:00 A.M. until 8:00 P.M. on Monday through Friday.

(4) Underlying offense. - The offense for which a person's drivers license was revoked when the person was charged under G.S. 20-28(a), driving with a revoked license, or under G.S. 20-28.1, committing a motor vehicle moving offense while driving with a revoked license.

(b) Eligibility. - A person is eligible to apply for a limited driving privilege under this section if all of the following conditions apply:

(1) The person's license is currently revoked under G.S. 20-28(a) or G.S. 20-28.1.

(2) The person has complied with the revocation for the period required in subsection (c) of this section immediately preceding the date the person files a petition for a limited driving privilege under this section.

(3) The person's underlying offense is not an offense involving impaired driving and, if the person's license is revoked under G.S. 20-28.1 for committing a motor vehicle moving offense while driving with a revoked license, the moving offense is not an offense involving impaired driving.

(4) The revocation period for the underlying offense has expired.

(5) The revocation under G.S. 20-28(a) or G.S. 20-28.1 is the only revocation in effect.

(6) The person is not eligible to receive a limited driving privilege under any other law.

(7) The person has not held a limited driving privilege issued under this section at anytime during the three years prior to the date the person files the current petition.

(8) The person has no pending charges for any motor vehicle offense in this or in any other state and has no unpaid motor vehicle fines or penalties in this or in any other state.

(9)   The person's drivers license issued by another state has not been revoked by that state.

(10)   G.S. 20-9(e) or G.S. 20-9(f) does not prohibit the Division from issuing the person a license.

(c)   Compliance Period. - The following table sets out the period during which a person must comply with a revocation under G.S. 20-28(a) or G.S. 20-28.1 to be eligible for a limited driving privilege under this section:

Revocation Period	Compliance Period
1 Year	90 Days
2 Years	1 Year
Permanent	2 Years

(d)   Petition. - A person may apply for a limited driving privilege under this section by filing a petition. A petition filed under this section is separate from the action that resulted in the initial revocation and is a civil action. A petition must be filed in district court in the county of the person's residence as reflected by the Division's records or, if the Division's records are inaccurate, in the county of the person's actual residence. A person must attach to a petition a copy of the person's motor vehicle record. A petition must include a sworn statement that the person filing the petition is eligible for a limited driving privilege under this section.

A court, for good cause shown, may issue a limited driving privilege to an eligible person in accordance with this section. The costs required under G.S. 7A-305(a) and G.S. 20-20.2 apply to a petition filed under this section. The clerk of court for the court that issues a limited driving privilege under this section must send a copy of the limited driving privilege to the Division.

(e)   Scope of Privilege. - A limited driving privilege restricts the person to essential driving related to one or more of the purposes listed in this subsection. Any driving that is not related to the purposes authorized in this subsection is unlawful even though done at times and upon routes that may be authorized by the privilege. Except as otherwise provided, all driving must be for a purpose and done within the restrictions specified in the privilege.

The permissible purposes for a limited driving privilege are:

(1) Travel to and from the person's place of employment and in the course of employment.

(2) Travel necessary for maintenance of the person's household.

(3) Travel to provide emergency medical care for the person or for an immediate family member of the person who resides in the same household with the person. Driving related to emergency medical care is authorized at anytime and without restriction as to routes.

(f) Employment Driving in Standard Working Hours. - The court may authorize driving for employment-related purposes during standard working hours without specifying times and routes for the driving. If the person is required to drive for essential employment-related purposes only during standard working hours, the limited driving privilege must prohibit driving during nonstandard working hours unless the driving is for emergency medical care or for authorized household maintenance. The limited driving privilege must state the name and address of the person's employer and may, in the discretion of the court, include other information and restrictions applicable to employment-related driving.

(g) Employment Driving in Nonstandard Working Hours. - If a person is required to drive during nonstandard working hours for an essential employment-related purpose and the person provides documentation of that fact to the court, the court may authorize the person to drive for that purpose during those hours. If the person is self-employed, the documentation must be attached to or made a part of the limited driving privilege. If the person is employed by another, the limited driving privilege must state the name and address of the person's employer and may, in the discretion of the court, include other information and restrictions applicable to employment-related driving. If the court determines that it is necessary for the person to drive during nonstandard working hours for an employment-related purpose, the court may authorize the person to drive subject to these limitations:

(1) If the person is required to drive to and from a specific place of employment at regular times, the limited driving privilege must specify the general times and routes by which the person may drive to and from work and must restrict driving to those times and routes.

(2) If the person is required to drive to and from work at a specific place but is unable to specify the times during which the driving will occur, the limited driving privilege must specify the general routes by which the person may drive to and from work and must restrict driving to those general routes.

(3) If the person is required to drive to and from work at regular times but is unable to specify the places at which work is to be performed, the limited driving privilege must specify the general times and geographic boundaries within which the person may drive and must restrict driving to those times and boundaries.

(4) If the person can specify neither the times nor places in which the person will be driving to and from work, the limited driving privilege must specify the geographic boundaries within which the person may drive and must restrict driving to those boundaries.

(h) Household Maintenance. - A limited driving privilege may allow driving for maintenance of the household only during standard working hours. The court, at its discretion, may impose additional restrictions on driving for the maintenance of the household.

(i) Restrictions. - A limited driving privilege that is not authorized by this section or that does not contain the restrictions required by law is invalid. A limited driving privilege issued under this section is subject to the following conditions:

(1) Financial responsibility. - A person applying for a limited driving privilege under this section must provide the court proof of financial responsibility acceptable under G.S. 20-16.1(g) and must maintain the financial responsibility during the period of the limited driving privilege.

(2) Alcohol restrictions. - A person who received a limited driving privilege under this section may not consume alcohol while driving or drive at anytime while the person has remaining in the person's body any alcohol or controlled substance previously consumed, unless the controlled substance was lawfully obtained and taken in therapeutically appropriate amounts.

(3) Others. - The court may impose any other reasonable restrictions or conditions necessary to achieve the purposes of this section.

(j) Term and Reinstatement. - The term of a limited driving privilege issued under this section is the shorter of one year or the length of time remaining in the revocation period imposed under G.S. 20-28(a) or G.S. 20-28.1. When the term of the limited driving privilege expires, the Division must reinstate the person's license if the person meets all of the conditions listed in this subsection. The Division may impose restrictions or conditions on the new license in accordance with G.S. 20-7(e). The conditions are:

(1) Payment of the restoration fee as required under G.S. 20-7(i1).

(2) Providing proof of financial responsibility as required under G.S. 20-7(c1).

(3) Providing the proof required for reinstatement of a license under G.S. 20-28(c1).

(k) Modification. - A court may modify or revoke a person's limited driving privilege issued under this section upon a showing that the circumstances have changed sufficiently to justify modification or revocation. If the judge who issued the privilege is not presiding in the court in which the privilege was issued, a presiding judge in that court may modify or revoke the privilege. The judge must indicate in the order of modification or revocation the reasons for the order or make specific findings indicating the reason for the order and enter those findings in the record of the case. When a court issues an order of modification or revocation, the clerk of court must send a copy of the order to the Division.

(l) Effect of Violation. - A violation of a limited driving privilege issued under this section constitutes the offense of driving while license revoked under G.S. 20-28. When a person is charged with operating a motor vehicle in violation of the limited driving privilege, the limited driving privilege is suspended pending the final disposition of the charge. (2007-293, s. 1; 2007-323, s. 30.11(d); 2007-345, s. 9.1(c); 2008-118, s. 2.9(b).)

§ 20-20.2. Processing fee for limited driving privilege.

Upon the issuance of a limited driving privilege by a court under this Chapter, the applicant or petitioner must pay, in addition to any other costs associated with obtaining the privilege, a processing fee of one hundred dollars ($100.00). The applicant or petitioner shall pay this fee to the clerk of superior court in the county in which the limited driving privilege is issued. The fee must be remitted to the State Treasurer and used for support of the General Court of Justice. The failure to pay this fee shall render the privilege invalid. (2007-323, s. 30.11(b); 2007-345, s. 9.1(b).)

§ 20-21. No operation under foreign license during suspension or revocation in this State.

Any resident or nonresident whose driver's license or right or privilege to operate a motor vehicle in this State has been suspended or revoked as provided in this Article shall not operate a motor vehicle in this State under a license, permit or registration issued by another jurisdiction or otherwise during such suspension, or after such revocation until a new license is obtained when and as permitted under this Article. (1935, c. 52, s. 15; 1979, c. 667, s. 41.)

§ 20-22. Suspending privileges of nonresidents and reporting convictions.

(a) The privilege of driving a motor vehicle on the highways of this State given to a nonresident hereunder shall be subject to suspension or revocation by the Division in like manner and for like cause as a driver's license issued hereunder may be suspended or revoked.

(b) The Division is further authorized, upon receiving a record of the conviction in this State of a nonresident driver of a motor vehicle of any offense under the motor vehicle laws of this State, to forward a certified copy of such record to the motor vehicle administrator in the state wherein the person so convicted is a resident. (1935, c. 52, s. 16; 1975, c. 716, s. 5; 1979, c. 667, s. 41.)

§ 20-23. Revoking resident's license upon conviction in another state.

The Division may revoke the license of any resident of this State upon receiving notice of the person's conviction in another state of an offense set forth in G.S. 20-26(a). (1935, c. 52, s. 17; 1971, c. 486, s. 2; 1975, c. 716, s. 5; 1979, c. 667, s. 22; 1993, c. 533, s. 6.)

§ 20-23.1. Suspending or revoking operating privilege of person not holding license.

In any case where the Division would be authorized to suspend or revoke the license of a person but such person does not hold a license, the Division is authorized to suspend or revoke the operating privilege of such a person in like manner as it could suspend or revoke his license if such person held a driver's license, and the provisions of this Chapter governing suspensions, revocations, issuance of a license, and driving after license suspended or revoked, shall apply in the discretion of the Division in the same manner as if the license has been suspended or revoked. (1955, c. 1187, s. 19; 1969, c. 186, s. 2; 1975, c. 716, s. 5; 1979, c. 667, s. 41.)

§ 20-23.2. Suspension of license for conviction of offense involving impaired driving in federal court.

Upon receipt of notice of conviction in any court of the federal government of an offense involving impaired driving, the Division is authorized to revoke the driving privilege of the person convicted in the same manner as if the conviction had occurred in a court of this State. (1969, c. 988; 1971, c. 619, s. 11; 1975, c. 716, s. 5; 1979, c. 903, s. 12; 1981, c. 412, s. 4; c. 747, s. 66; 1983, c. 435, s. 18.)

§ 20-24. When court or child support enforcement agency to forward license to Division and report convictions, child support delinquencies, and prayers for judgment continued.

(a) License. - A court that convicts a person of an offense that requires revocation of the person's drivers license or revokes a person's drivers license pursuant to G.S. 50-13.12 shall require the person to give the court any regular or commercial drivers license issued to that person. A court that convicts a person of an offense that requires disqualification of the person but would not require revocation of a regular drivers license issued to that person shall require the person to give the court any Class A or Class B regular drivers license and any commercial drivers license issued to that person.

The clerk of court in a non-IV-D case, and the child support enforcement agency in a IV-D case, shall accept a drivers license required to be given to the court under this subsection. A clerk of court or the child support enforcement agency who receives a drivers license shall give the person whose license is received a copy of a dated receipt for the license. The receipt must be on a form approved by the Commissioner. A revocation or disqualification for which a license is received under this subsection is effective as of the date on the receipt for the license.

The clerk of court or the child support enforcement agency shall notify the Division of a license received under this subsection either by forwarding to the Division the license, a record of the conviction for which the license was received, a copy of the court order revoking the license for failure to pay child support for which the license was received, and the original dated receipt for the license or by electronically sending to the Division the information on the license, the record of conviction or court order revoking the license for failure to pay child support, and the receipt given for the license. The clerk of court or the child support enforcement agency must forward the required items unless the Commissioner has given the clerk of court or the child support enforcement agency approval to notify the Division electronically. If the clerk of court or the child support enforcement agency notifies the Division electronically, the clerk of court or the child support enforcement agency must destroy a license received after sending to the Division the required information. The clerk of court or the child support enforcement agency shall notify the Division within 30 days after entry of the conviction or court order revoking the license for failure to pay child support for which the license was received.

(b) Convictions, Court Orders of Drivers License Revocations, and PJCs. - The clerk of court shall send the Division a record of any of the following:

(1) A conviction of a violation of a law regulating the operation of a vehicle.

(2) A conviction for which the convicted person is placed on probation and a condition of probation is that the person not drive a motor vehicle for a period of time, stating the period of time for which the condition applies.

(3) A conviction of a felony in the commission of which a motor vehicle is used, when the judgment includes a finding that a motor vehicle was used in the commission of the felony.

(4) A conviction that requires revocation of the drivers license of the person convicted and is not otherwise reported under subdivision (1).

(4a) A court order revoking drivers license pursuant to G.S. 50-13.12.

(5) An order entering prayer for judgment continued in a case involving an alleged violation of a law regulating the operation of a vehicle.

The child support enforcement agency shall send the Division a record of any court order revoking drivers license pursuant to G.S. 110-142.2(a)(1).

With the approval of the Commissioner, the clerk of court or the child support enforcement agency may forward a record of conviction, court order revoking drivers license, or prayer for judgment continued to the Division by electronic data processing means.

(b1) In any case in which the Division, for any reason, does not receive a record of a conviction or a prayer for judgment continued until more than one year after the date it is entered, the Division may, in its discretion, substitute a period of probation for all or any part of a revocation or disqualification required because of the conviction or prayer for judgment continued.

(c) Repealed by Session Laws 1991, c. 726, s. 10.

(d) Scope. - This Article governs drivers license revocation and disqualification. A drivers license may not be revoked and a person may not be disqualified except in accordance with this Article.

(e) Special Information. - A judgment for a conviction for an offense for which special information is required under this subsection shall, when appropriate, include a finding of the special information. The convictions for which special information is required and the specific information required is as follows:

(1) Homicide. - If a conviction of homicide involves impaired driving, the judgment must indicate that fact.

(2) G.S. 20-138.1, Driving While Impaired. - If a conviction under G.S. 20-138.1 involves a commercial motor vehicle, the judgment must indicate that fact. If a conviction under G.S. 20-138.1 involves a commercial motor vehicle that

was transporting a hazardous substance required to be placarded, the judgment must indicate that fact.

(3) G.S. 20-138.2, Driving Commercial Motor Vehicle While Impaired. - If the commercial motor vehicle involved in an offense under G.S. 20-138.2 was transporting a hazardous material required to be placarded, a judgment for that offense must indicate that fact.

(4) G.S. 20-166, Hit and Run. - If a conviction under G.S. 20-166 involves a commercial motor vehicle, the judgment must indicate that fact. If a conviction under G.S. 20-166 involves a commercial motor vehicle that was transporting a hazardous substance required to be placarded, the judgment must indicate that fact.

(5) Felony Using Commercial Motor Vehicle. - If a conviction of a felony in which a commercial motor vehicle was used involves the manufacture, distribution, or dispensing of a controlled substance, or possession with intent to manufacture, distribute, or dispense a controlled substance, the judgment must indicate that fact. If a commercial motor vehicle used in a felony was transporting a hazardous substance required to be placarded, the judgment for that felony must indicate that fact. (1935, c. 52, s. 18; 1949, c. 373, ss. 3, 4; 1955, c. 1187, s. 14; 1959, c. 47; 1965, c. 38; 1973, c. 19; 1975, cc. 46, 445; c. 716, s. 5; c. 871, s. 1; 1979, c. 667, s. 41; 1981, c. 416; c. 839; 1983, c. 294, s. 5; c. 435, s. 19; 1985, c. 764, s. 18; 1985 (Reg. Sess., 1986), c. 852, s. 17; 1987, c. 581, s. 1; c. 658, s. 2; 1989, c. 771, s. 10; 1991, c. 726, s. 10; 1993, c. 533, s. 7; 1995, c. 538, s. 2(c).)

§ 20-24.1. Revocation for failure to appear or pay fine, penalty or costs for motor vehicle offenses.

(a) The Division must revoke the driver's license of a person upon receipt of notice from a court that the person was charged with a motor vehicle offense and he:

(1) failed to appear, after being notified to do so, when the case was called for a trial or hearing; or

(2) failed to pay a fine, penalty, or court costs ordered by the court.

Revocation orders entered under the authority of this section are effective on the sixtieth day after the order is mailed or personally delivered to the person.

(b)   A license revoked under this section remains revoked until the person whose license has been revoked:

(1)   disposes of the charge in the trial division in which he failed to appear when the case was last called for trial or hearing; or

(2)   demonstrates to the court that he is not the person charged with the offense; or

(3)   pays the penalty, fine, or costs ordered by the court; or

(4)   demonstrates to the court that his failure to pay the penalty, fine, or costs was not willful and that he is making a good faith effort to pay or that the penalty, fine, or costs should be remitted.

Upon receipt of notice from the court that the person has satisfied the conditions of this subsection applicable to his case, the Division must restore the person's license as provided in subsection (c). In addition, if the person whose license is revoked is not a resident of this State, the Division may notify the driver licensing agency in the person's state of residence that the person's license to drive in this State has been revoked.

(b1)   A defendant must be afforded an opportunity for a trial or a hearing within a reasonable time of the defendant's appearance. Upon motion of a defendant, the court must order that a hearing or a trial be heard within a reasonable time.

(c)   If the person satisfies the conditions of subsection (b) that are applicable to his case before the effective date of the revocation order, the revocation order and any entries on his driving record relating to it shall be deleted and the person does not have to pay the restoration fee set by G.S. 20-7(i1). For all other revocation orders issued pursuant to this section, G.S. 50-13.12 or G.S. 110-142.2, the person must pay the restoration fee and satisfy any other applicable requirements of this Article before the person may be relicensed.

(d)   To facilitate the prompt return of licenses and to prevent unjustified charges of driving while license revoked, the clerk of court, upon request, must give the person a copy of the notice it sends to the Division to indicate that the person has complied with the conditions of subsection (b) applicable to his case. If the person complies with the condition before the effective date of the revocation, the notice must indicate that the person is eligible to drive if he is otherwise validly licensed.

(e)   As used in this section and in G.S. 20-24.2, the word offense includes crimes and infractions created by this Chapter. (1985, c. 764, s. 19; 1985 (Reg. Sess., 1986), c. 852, ss. 4-6, 9, 17; 1987, c. 581, s. 4; 1991, c. 682, s. 4; 1993, c. 313, s. 1; 1995, c. 538, s. 2(d).)

§ 20-24.2. Court to report failure to appear or pay fine, penalty or costs.

(a)   The court must report to the Division the name of any person charged with a motor vehicle offense under this Chapter who:

(1)   Fails to appear to answer the charge as scheduled, unless within 20 days after the scheduled appearance, he either appears in court to answer the charge or disposes of the charge pursuant to G.S. 7A-146; or

(2)   Fails to pay a fine, penalty, or costs within 20 days of the date specified in the court's judgment.

(b)   The reporting requirement of this section and the revocation mandated by G.S. 20-24.1 do not apply to offenses in which an order of forfeiture of a cash bond is entered and reported to the Division pursuant to G.S. 20-24. If an order is sent to the Division by the clerk through clerical mistake or other inadvertence, the clerk's office that sent the report of noncompliance must withdraw the report and send notice to the Division which shall correct its records accordingly. (1985, c. 764, s. 3; 1985 (Reg. Sess., 1986), c. 852, s. 3; 1987, c. 581, s. 3; 1991, c. 682, s. 5.)

§ 20-25. Right of appeal to court.

Any person denied a license or whose license has been canceled, suspended or revoked by the Division, except where such cancellation is mandatory under the provisions of this Article, shall have a right to file a petition within 30 days thereafter for a hearing in the matter in the superior court of the county wherein such person shall reside, or to the resident judge of the district or judge holding the court of that district, or special or emergency judge holding a court in such district in which the violation was committed, and such court or judge is hereby vested with jurisdiction and it shall be its or his duty to set the matter for hearing upon 30 days' written notice to the Division, and thereupon to take testimony and examine into the facts of the case, and to determine whether the petitioner is entitled to a license or is subject to suspension, cancellation or revocation of license under the provisions of this Article. Provided, a judge of the district court shall have limited jurisdiction under this section to sign and enter a temporary restraining order only. (1935, c. 52, s. 19; 1975, c. 716, s. 5; 1987, c. 659.)

§ 20-26. Records; copies furnished; charge.

(a) The Division shall keep a record of all applications for a drivers license, all tests given an applicant for a drivers license, all applications for a drivers license that are denied, all drivers licenses issued, renewed, cancelled, or revoked, all disqualifications, all convictions affecting a drivers license, and all prayers for judgment continued that may lead to a license revocation. When the Division cancels or revokes a commercial drivers license or disqualifies a person, the Division shall update its records to reflect that action within 10 days after the cancellation, revocation, or disqualification becomes effective. When a person who is not a resident of this State is convicted of an offense or commits an act requiring revocation of the person's commercial drivers license or disqualification of the person, the Division shall notify the licensing authority of the person's state of residence.

The Division shall keep records of convictions occurring outside North Carolina for the offenses of exceeding a stated speed limit of 55 miles per hour or more by more than 15 miles per hour, driving while license suspended or revoked, careless and reckless driving, engaging in prearranged speed competition, engaging willfully in speed competition, hit-and-run driving resulting in damage to property, unlawfully passing a stopped school bus, illegal transportation of alcoholic beverages, and the offenses included in G.S. 20-17. The Division shall also keep records of convictions occurring outside North Carolina for any serious traffic violation that involves a commercial motor vehicle and is not otherwise required to be kept under this subsection.

(b) The Division shall furnish certified copies of license records required to be kept by subsection (a) of this section to State, county, municipal and court officials of this State for official use only, without charge. A certified copy of a driver's records kept pursuant to subsection (a) may be sent by the Police Information Network. In addition to the uses authorized by G.S. 8-35.1, a copy certified under the authority of this section is admissible as prima facie evidence of the status of the person's license. The Attorney General and the Commissioner of Motor Vehicles are authorized to promulgate such rules and regulations as may be necessary to implement the provision of this subsection.

(b1)   The registered or declared weight set forth on the vehicle registration card or a certified copy of the Division record sent by the Division of Criminal Information or otherwise is admissible in any judicial or administrative proceeding and shall be prima facie evidence of the registered or declared weight.

(c)   The Division shall furnish copies of license records required to be kept by subsection (a) of this section in accordance with G.S. 20-43.1 to other persons for uses other than official upon prepayment of the following fees:

(1)   Limited extract copy of license record, for period up to three years... $8.00

(2)   Complete extract copy of license record.. 8.00

(3)   Certified true copy of complete license record.................................. 11.00.

All fees received by the Division under this subsection shall be credited to the Highway Fund.

(d)   The charge for records provided pursuant to this section shall not be subject to the provisions of Chapter 132 of the General Statutes.

(e)   In the event of a mistake on the part of any person in ordering license records under subsection (c) of this section, the Commissioner may refund or credit to that person up to sixty-five percent (65%) of the amount paid for the license records.

(f)   On and after July 1, 1988, the Division shall expeditiously furnish to insurance agents, insurance companies, and to insurance support organizations as defined in G.S. 58-39-15(12), for the purpose of rating nonfleet private passenger motor vehicle insurance policies, through electronic data processing means or otherwise, copies of or information pertaining to license records that are required to be kept pursuant to subsection (a) of this section. (1935, c. 52, s. 20; 1961, c. 307; 1969, c. 783, s. 3; 1971, c. 486, s. 1; 1975, c. 716, s. 5; 1979, c. 667, s. 23; c. 903, ss. 9, 10; 1981, c. 145, s. 1; c. 412, s. 4; c. 690, s. 13; c. 747, s. 66; 1983, c. 435, s. 20; c. 761, s. 149; 1987, c. 869, s. 16; 1987 (Reg. Sess., 1988), c. 1112, ss. 14, 17; 1989, c. 771, ss. 9, 17, 18; 1991, c. 689, s. 330; c. 726, s. 11; 1997-443, s. 32.25(b); 2005-276, s. 44.1(e).)

§ 20-27. Availability of records.

(a)   All records of the Division pertaining to application and to drivers' licenses, except the confidential medical report referred to in G.S. 20-7, of the current or previous five years shall be open to public inspection in accordance with G.S. 20-43.1, at any reasonable time during office hours and copies shall be provided pursuant to the provisions of G.S. 20-26.

(b)   All records of the Division pertaining to chemical tests as provided in G.S. 20-16.2 shall be available to the courts as provided in G.S. 20-26(b). (1935, c. 52, s. 21; 1975, c. 716, s. 5; 1979, c. 667, s. 24; c. 903, s. 11; 1981, c. 145, s. 2; 1997-443, s. 32.25(c).)

§ 20-27.1. Unlawful for sex offender to drive commercial passenger vehicle or school bus without appropriate commercial license or while disqualified.

A person who drives a commercial passenger vehicle or a school bus and who does not have a valid commercial drivers license with a P or S endorsement because the person was convicted of a violation that requires registration under Article 27A of Chapter 14 of the General Statutes is guilty of a Class F felony. (2009-491, s. 4.)

§ 20-28. Unlawful to drive while license revoked, after notification, or while disqualified.

(a)   Driving While License Revoked. - Except as provided in subsection (a1) of this section, any person whose drivers license has been revoked who drives any motor vehicle upon the highways of the State while the license is revoked is guilty of a Class 3 misdemeanor unless the person's license was originally revoked for an impaired driving revocation, in which case the person is guilty of a Class 1 misdemeanor. Upon conviction, the person's license shall be revoked for an additional period of one year for the first offense, two years for the second offense, and permanently for a third or subsequent offense.

If the person's license was originally revoked for an impaired driving revocation, the court may order as a condition of probation that the offender abstain from alcohol consumption and verify compliance by use of a continuous alcohol monitoring system, of a type approved by the Division of Adult Correction of the Department of Public Safety, for a minimum period of 90 days.

The restoree of a revoked drivers license who operates a motor vehicle upon the highways of the State without maintaining financial responsibility as provided by law shall be punished as for driving without a license.

(a1) Driving Without Reclaiming License. - A person convicted under subsection (a) shall be punished as if the person had been convicted of driving without a license under G.S. 20-35 if the person demonstrates to the court that either subdivisions (1) and (2), or subdivision (3) of this subsection is true:

(1) At the time of the offense, the person's license was revoked solely under G.S. 20-16.5; and

(2) a. The offense occurred more than 45 days after the effective date of a revocation order issued under G.S. 20-16.5(f) and the period of revocation was 45 days as provided under subdivision (3) of that subsection; or

b. The offense occurred more than 30 days after the effective date of the revocation order issued under any other provision of G.S. 20-16.5; or

(3) At the time of the offense the person had met the requirements of G.S. 50-13.12, or G.S. 110-142.2 and was eligible for reinstatement of the person's drivers license privilege as provided therein.

In addition, a person punished under this subsection shall be treated for drivers license and insurance rating purposes as if the person had been convicted of driving without a license under G.S. 20-35, and the conviction report sent to the Division must indicate that the person is to be so treated.

(a2) Driving After Notification or Failure to Appear. - A person shall be guilty of a Class 1 misdemeanor if:

(1) The person operates a motor vehicle upon a highway while that person's license is revoked for an impaired drivers license revocation after the Division has sent notification in accordance with G.S. 20-48; or

(2) The person fails to appear for two years from the date of the charge after being charged with an implied-consent offense.

Upon conviction, the person's drivers license shall be revoked for an additional period of one year for the first offense, two years for the second offense, and permanently for a third or subsequent offense. The restoree of a revoked drivers license who operates a motor vehicle upon the highways of the State without maintaining financial responsibility as provided by law shall be punished as for driving without a license.

(b) Repealed by Session Laws 1993 (Reg. Sess., 1994), c. 761, s. 3.

(c) When Person May Apply for License. - A person whose license has been revoked may apply for a license as follows:

(1) If revoked under subsection (a) of this section for one year, the person may apply for a license after 90 days.

(2) If punished under subsection (a1) of this section and the original revocation was pursuant to G.S. 20-16.5, in order to obtain reinstatement of a drivers license, the person must obtain a substance abuse assessment and show proof of financial responsibility to the Division. If the assessment recommends education or treatment, the person must complete the education or treatment within the time limits specified by the Division.

(3) If revoked under subsection (a2) of this section for one year, the person may apply for a license after one year.

(4) If revoked under this section for two years, the person may apply for a license after one year.

(5) If revoked under this section permanently, the person may apply for a license after three years.

(c1) Upon the filing of an application the Division may, with or without a hearing, issue a new license upon satisfactory proof that the former licensee has not been convicted of a moving violation under this Chapter or the laws of another state, a violation of any provision of the alcoholic beverage laws of this State or another state, or a violation of any provisions of the drug laws of this State or another state when any of these violations occurred during the revocation period.

(c2) The Division may impose any restrictions or conditions on the new license that the Division considers appropriate for the balance of the revocation period. When the revocation period is permanent, the restrictions and conditions imposed by the Division may not exceed three years.

(c3) A person whose license is revoked for violation of subsection (a) of this section where the person's license was originally revoked for an impaired driving revocation, or a person whose license is revoked for a violation of subsection (a2) of this section, may only have the license conditionally restored by the Division pursuant to the provisions of subsection (c4) of this section.

(c4) For a conditional restoration under subsection (c3) of this section, the Division shall require at a minimum that the driver obtain a substance abuse assessment prior to issuance of a license and show proof of financial responsibility. If the substance abuse assessment recommends education or treatment, the person must complete the education or treatment within the time limits specified. If the assessment determines that the person abuses alcohol, the Division shall require the person to install and use an ignition interlock system on any vehicles that are to be driven by that person for the period of time that the conditional restoration is active.

(c5) For licenses conditionally restored pursuant to subsections (c3) and (c4) of this section, the Division shall cancel the license and impose the remaining revocation period if any of the following occur:

(1) The person violates any condition of the restoration.

(2) The person is convicted of any moving offense in this or another state.

(3) The person is convicted for a violation of the alcoholic beverage or controlled substance laws of this or any other state.

(d) Driving While Disqualified. - A person who was convicted of a violation that disqualified the person and required the person's drivers license to be revoked who drives a motor vehicle during the revocation period is punishable as provided in the other subsections of this section. A person who has been disqualified who drives a commercial motor vehicle during the disqualification period is guilty of a Class 1 misdemeanor and is disqualified for an additional period as follows:

(1) For a first offense of driving while disqualified, a person is disqualified for a period equal to the period for which the person was disqualified when the offense occurred.

(2) For a second offense of driving while disqualified, a person is disqualified for a period equal to two times the period for which the person was disqualified when the offense occurred.

(3) For a third offense of driving while disqualified, a person is disqualified for life.

The Division may reduce a disqualification for life under this subsection to 10 years in accordance with the guidelines adopted under G.S. 20-17.4(b). A person who drives a commercial motor vehicle while the person is disqualified and the person's drivers license is revoked is punishable for both driving while the person's license was revoked and driving while disqualified. (1935, c. 52, s. 22; 1945, c. 635; 1947, c. 1067, s. 16; 1955, c. 1020, s. 1; c. 1152, s. 18; c. 1187, s. 20; 1957, c. 1046; 1959, c. 515; 1967, c. 447; 1973, c. 47, s. 2; cc. 71, 1132; 1975, c. 716, s. 5; 1979, c 377, ss. 1, 2; c. 667, s. 41; 1981, c. 412, s. 4; c. 747, s. 66; 1983, c. 51; 1983 (Reg. Sess., 1984), c. 1101, s. 18A; 1989, c. 771, s. 4; 1991, c. 509, s. 2; c. 726, s. 12; 1993, c. 539, ss. 320-322; 1994, Ex. Sess., c. 24, s. 14(c); 1993 (Reg. Sess., 1994), c. 761, ss. 2, 3; 1995, c. 538, s. 2(e), (f); 2002-159, s. 6; 2006-253, s. 22.1; 2007-493, ss. 4, 19; 2012-146, s. 8; 2013-360, s. 18B.14(f).)

§ 20-28.1. Conviction of moving offense committed while driving during period of suspension or revocation of license.

(a) Upon receipt of notice of conviction of any person of a motor vehicle moving offense, except a conviction punishable under G.S. 20-28(a1), such offense having been committed while such person's driving privilege was in a state of suspension or revocation, the Division shall revoke such person's driving privilege for an additional period of time as set forth in subsection (b) hereof.

(b)   When a driving privilege is subject to revocation under this section, the additional period of revocation shall be as follows:

(1)   A first such revocation shall be for one year;

(2)   A second such revocation shall be for two years; and

(3)   A third or subsequent such revocation shall be permanent.

(c)   A person whose license has been revoked under this section for one year may apply for a license after 90 days. A person whose license has been revoked under this section for two years may apply for a license after 12 months. A person whose license has been revoked under this section permanently may apply for a license after three years. Upon the filing of an application, the Division may, with or without a hearing, issue a new license upon satisfactory proof that the former licensee has not been convicted of a moving violation under this Chapter or the laws of another state, or a violation of any provision of the alcoholic beverage laws of this State or another state, or a violation of any provision of the drug laws of this State or another state when any of these violations occurred during the revocation period. The Division may impose any restrictions or conditions on the new license that the Division considers appropriate for the balance of the revocation period. When the revocation period is permanent, the restrictions and conditions imposed by the Division may not exceed three years.

(d)   Repealed by Session Laws 1979, c. 378, s. 2. (1965, c. 286; 1969, c. 348; 1971, c. 163; 1973, c. 47, s. 2; 1975, c. 716, s. 5; 1979, c. 378, ss. 1, 2; 1981, c. 412, s. 4; c. 747, s. 66; 1991, c. 509, s. 1, c. 682, s. 6, c. 726, s. 22.1.)

§ 20-28.2. Forfeiture of motor vehicle for impaired driving after impaired driving license revocation; forfeiture for felony speeding to elude arrest.

(a)   Meaning of "Impaired Driving License Revocation". - The revocation of a person's drivers license is an impaired driving license revocation if the revocation is pursuant to:

(1) G.S. 20-13.2, 20-16(a)(8b), 20-16.2, 20-16.5, 20-17(a)(2), 20-17(a)(12), or 20-138.5; or

(2) G.S. 20-16(a)(7), 20-17(a)(1), 20-17(a)(3), 20-17(a)(9), or 20-17(a)(11), if the offense involves impaired driving; or

(3) The laws of another state and the offense for which the person's license is revoked prohibits substantially similar conduct which if committed in this State would result in a revocation listed in subdivisions (1) or (2).

(a1) Definitions. - As used in this section and in G.S. 20-28.3, 20-28.4, 20-28.5, 20-28.7, 20-28.8, 20-28.9, 20-54.1, and 20-141.5, the following terms mean:

(1) Fair Market Value. - The value of the seized motor vehicle, as determined in accordance with the schedule of values adopted by the Commissioner pursuant to G.S. 105-187.3.

(1a) Impaired Driving Acknowledgment. - A written document acknowledging that:

a. The motor vehicle was operated by a person charged with an offense involving impaired driving, and:

1. That person's drivers license was revoked as a result of a prior impaired drivers license revocation; or

2. That person did not have a valid drivers license, and did not have liability insurance.

b. If the motor vehicle is again operated by this particular person, and the person is charged with an offense involving impaired driving, then the vehicle is subject to impoundment and forfeiture if (i) the offense occurs while that person's drivers license is revoked, or (ii) the offense occurs while the person has no valid drivers license, and has no liability insurance.

c. A lack of knowledge or consent to the operation will not be a defense in the future, unless the motor vehicle owner has taken all reasonable precautions to prevent the use of the motor vehicle by this particular person and immediately reports, upon discovery, any unauthorized use to the appropriate law enforcement agency.

(2) Innocent Owner. - A motor vehicle owner:

a. Who, if the offense resulting in seizure was an impaired driving offense, did not know and had no reason to know that (i) the defendant's drivers license was revoked, or (ii) that the defendant did not have a valid drivers license, and that the defendant had no liability insurance; or

b. Who, if the offense resulting in seizure was an impaired driving offense, knew that (i) the defendant's drivers license was revoked, or (ii) that the defendant had no valid drivers license, and that the defendant had no liability insurance, but the defendant drove the vehicle without the person's expressed or implied permission, and the owner files a police report for unauthorized use of the motor vehicle and agrees to prosecute the unauthorized operator of the motor vehicle, or who, if the offense resulting in seizure was a felony speeding to elude arrest offense, did not give the defendant express or implied permission to drive the vehicle, and the owner files a police report for unauthorized use of the motor vehicle and agrees to prosecute the unauthorized operator of the motor vehicle; or

c. Whose vehicle was reported stolen; or

d. Repealed by Session Laws 1999-406, s. 17.

e. Who is (i) a rental car company as defined in G.S. 66-201(a) and the vehicle was driven by a person who is not listed as an authorized driver on the rental agreement as defined in G.S. 66-201; or (ii) a rental car company as defined in G.S. 66-201(a) and the vehicle was driven by a person who is listed as an authorized driver on the rental agreement as defined in G.S. 66-201 and if the offense resulting in seizure was an impaired driving offense, the rental car company has no actual knowledge of the revocation of the renter's drivers' license at the time the rental agreement is entered, or if the offense resulting in seizure was a felony speeding to elude arrest offense, the rental agreement expressly prohibits use of the vehicle while committing a felony; or

f. Who is in the business of leasing motor vehicles, who holds legal title to the motor vehicle as a lessor at the time of seizure and, if the offense resulting in seizure was an impaired driving offense, who has no actual knowledge of the revocation of the lessee's drivers license at the time the lease is entered.

(2a) Insurance Company. - Any insurance company that has coverage on or is otherwise liable for repairs or damages to the motor vehicle at the time of the seizure.

(2b) Insurance Proceeds. - Proceeds paid under an insurance policy for damage to a seized motor vehicle less any payments actually paid to valid lienholders and for towing and storage costs incurred for the motor vehicle after the time the motor vehicle became subject to seizure.

(3) Lienholder. - A person who holds a perfected security interest in a motor vehicle at the time of seizure.

(3a) Motor Vehicle Owner. - A person in whose name a registration card or certificate of title for a motor vehicle is issued at the time of seizure.

(4) Order of Forfeiture. - An order by the court which terminates the rights and ownership interest of a motor vehicle owner in a motor vehicle and any insurance proceeds or proceeds of sale in accordance with G.S. 20-28.2.

(5) Repealed by Session Laws 1998-182, s. 2.

(6) Registered Owner. - A person in whose name a registration card for a motor vehicle is issued at the time of seizure.

(7) Repealed by Session Laws 1998-182, s. 2.

(8) Speeding to Elude Arrest Acknowledgment. - A written document acknowledging that:

a. The motor vehicle was operated by a person charged with felony speeding to elude arrest pursuant to G.S. 20-141.5(b) or (b1).

b. If the motor vehicle is again operated by this particular person and the person is charged with felony speeding to elude arrest pursuant to G.S. 20-141.5(b) or (b1), then the vehicle is subject to impoundment and forfeiture.

c. A lack of knowledge or consent to the operation will not be a defense in the future unless the motor vehicle owner has taken all reasonable precautions to prevent the use of the motor vehicle by this particular person and immediately reports upon discovery any unauthorized use to the appropriate law enforcement agency.

(b) When Motor Vehicle Becomes Property Subject to Order of Forfeiture; Impaired Driving and Prior Revocation. - A judge may determine whether the vehicle driven by an impaired driver at the time of the offense becomes subject to an order of forfeiture. The determination may be made at any of the following times:

(1) A sentencing hearing for the underlying offense involving impaired driving.

(2) A separate hearing after conviction of the defendant.

(3) A forfeiture hearing held at least 60 days after the defendant failed to appear at the scheduled trial for the underlying offense, and the defendant's order of arrest for failing to appear has not been set aside.

The vehicle shall become subject to an order of forfeiture if the greater weight of the evidence shows that the defendant is guilty of an offense involving impaired driving, and that the defendant's license was revoked pursuant to an impaired driving license revocation as defined in subsection (a) of this section.

(b1) When a Motor Vehicle Becomes Property Subject to Order of Forfeiture; No License and No Insurance. - A judge may determine whether the vehicle driven by an impaired driver at the time of the offense becomes subject to an order of forfeiture. The determination may be made at any of the following times:

(1) A sentencing hearing for the underlying offense involving impaired driving.

(2) A separate hearing after conviction of the defendant.

(3) A forfeiture hearing held at least 60 days after the defendant failed to appear at the scheduled trial for the underlying offense, and the defendant's order of arrest for failing to appear has not been set aside.

The vehicle shall become subject to an order of forfeiture if the greater weight of the evidence shows that the defendant is guilty of an offense involving impaired driving, and: (i) the defendant was driving without a valid drivers license, and (ii) the defendant was not covered by an automobile liability policy.

(b2) When a Motor Vehicle Becomes Property Subject to Order of Forfeiture; Felony Speeding to Elude Arrest. - A judge may determine whether the vehicle driven at the time of the offense becomes subject to an order of forfeiture. The determination may be made at any of the following times:

(1) A sentencing hearing for the underlying felony speeding to elude arrest offense.

(2) A separate hearing after conviction of the defendant.

(3) A forfeiture hearing held at least 60 days after the defendant failed to appear at the scheduled trial for the underlying offense, and the defendant's order of arrest for failing to appear has not been set aside.

The vehicle shall become subject to an order of forfeiture if the greater weight of the evidence shows that the defendant is guilty of felony speeding to elude arrest pursuant to G.S. 20-141.5(b) or (b1).

(c) Duty of Prosecutor to Notify Possible Innocent Parties. - In any case in which a prosecutor determines that a motor vehicle driven by a defendant may be subject to forfeiture under this section and the motor vehicle has not been permanently released to a nondefendant vehicle owner pursuant to G.S. 20-28.3(e1), a defendant owner pursuant to G.S. 20-28.3(e2), or a lienholder, pursuant to G.S. 20-28.3(e3), the prosecutor shall notify the defendant, each motor vehicle owner, and each lienholder that the motor vehicle may be subject to forfeiture and that the defendant, motor vehicle owner, or the lienholder may intervene to protect that person's interest. The notice may be served by any means reasonably likely to provide actual notice, and shall be served at least 10 days before the hearing at which an order of forfeiture may be entered.

(c1) Motor Vehicles Involved in Accidents. - If a motor vehicle subject to forfeiture was damaged while the defendant operator was committing the underlying offense resulting in seizure, or was damaged incident to the seizure of the motor vehicle, the Division shall determine the name of any insurance companies that are the insurers of record with the Division for the motor vehicle at the time of the seizure or that may otherwise be liable for repair to the motor vehicle. In any case where a seized motor vehicle was involved in an accident, the Division shall notify the insurance companies that the claim for insurance proceeds for damage to the seized motor vehicle shall be paid to the clerk of superior court of the county where the motor vehicle driver was charged to be held and disbursed pursuant to further orders of the court. Any insurance company that receives written or other actual notice of seizure pursuant to this section shall not be relieved of any legal obligation under any contract of insurance unless the claim for property damage to the seized motor vehicle minus the policy owner's deductible is paid directly to the clerk of court. The insurance company paying insurance proceeds to the clerk of court pursuant to this section shall be immune from suit by the motor vehicle owner for any damages alleged to have occurred as a result of the motor vehicle seizure. The proceeds shall be held by the clerk. The clerk shall disburse the insurance proceeds pursuant to further orders of the court.

(d) Forfeiture Hearing. - Unless a motor vehicle that has been seized pursuant to G.S. 20-28.3 has been permanently released to an innocent owner pursuant to G.S. 20-28.3(e1), a defendant owner pursuant to G.S. 20-28.3(e2), or to a lienholder pursuant to G.S. 20-28.3(e3), the court shall conduct a hearing on the forfeiture of the motor vehicle. The hearing may be held at the sentencing hearing on the underlying offense resulting in seizure, at a separate hearing after conviction of the defendant, or at a separate forfeiture hearing held not less than 60 days after the defendant failed to appear at the scheduled trial for the underlying offense and the defendant's order of arrest for failing to appear has not been set aside. If at the forfeiture hearing, the judge determines that the motor vehicle is subject to forfeiture pursuant to this section and proper notice of the hearing has been given, the judge shall order the motor vehicle forfeited. If at the sentencing hearing or at a forfeiture hearing, the judge determines that the motor vehicle is subject to forfeiture pursuant to this section and proper notice of the hearing has been given, the judge shall order the motor vehicle forfeited unless another motor vehicle owner establishes, by the greater weight of the evidence, that such motor vehicle owner is an innocent owner as defined in this section, in which case the trial judge shall order the motor vehicle released to the innocent owner pursuant to the provisions of subsection (e) of this section. In any case where the motor vehicle is ordered forfeited, the judge shall:

(1) a. Authorize the sale of the motor vehicle at public sale or allow the county board of education to retain the motor vehicle for its own use pursuant to G.S. 20-28.5; or

b. Order the motor vehicle released to a lienholder pursuant to the provisions of subsection (f) of this section; and

(2) a. Order any proceeds of sale or insurance proceeds held by the clerk of court to be disbursed to the county board of education; and

b. Order any outstanding insurance claims be assigned to the county board of education in the event the motor vehicle has been damaged in an accident incident to the seizure of the motor vehicle.

If the judge determines that the motor vehicle is subject to forfeiture pursuant to this section, but that notice as required by subsection (c) has not been given, the judge shall continue the forfeiture proceeding until adequate notice has been given. In no circumstance shall the sentencing of the defendant be delayed as a result of the failure of the prosecutor to give adequate notice.

(e) Release of Vehicle to Innocent Motor Vehicle Owner. - At a forfeiture hearing, if a nondefendant motor vehicle owner establishes by the greater weight of the evidence that: (i) the motor vehicle was being driven by a person who was not the only motor vehicle owner or had no ownership interest in the motor vehicle at the time of the underlying offense and (ii) the petitioner is an "innocent owner", as defined by this section, a judge shall order the motor vehicle released to that owner, conditioned upon payment of all towing and storage charges incurred as a result of the seizure and impoundment of the motor vehicle.

Release to an innocent owner shall only be ordered upon satisfactory proof of:

(1) The identity of the person as a motor vehicle owner;

(2) The existence of financial responsibility to the extent required by Article 13 of this Chapter or by the laws of the state in which the vehicle is registered; and

(3) Repealed by Session Laws 1998-182, s. 2, effective December 1, 1998.

(4) The execution of:

a. An impaired driving acknowledgment as defined in subdivision (a1)(1a) of this section if the seizure was for an offense involving impaired driving; or

b. A speeding to elude arrest acknowledgment as defined in subdivision (a1)(8) of this section if the seizure was for violation of G.S. 20-141.5(b) or (b1).

If the nondefendant owner is a lessor, the release shall also be conditioned upon the lessor agreeing not to sell, give, or otherwise transfer possession of the forfeited motor vehicle to the defendant or any person acting on the defendant's behalf. A lessor who refuses to sell, give, or transfer possession of a seized motor vehicle to the defendant or any person acting on the behalf of the defendant shall not be liable for damages arising out of the refusal.

No motor vehicle subject to forfeiture under this section shall be released to a nondefendant motor vehicle owner if the records of the Division indicate the motor vehicle owner had previously signed an impaired driving acknowledgment or a speeding to elude arrest acknowledgment, as required by this section, and the same person was operating the motor vehicle at the time of the current seizure unless the innocent owner shows by the greater weight of the evidence that the motor vehicle owner has taken all reasonable precautions to prevent the use of the motor vehicle by this particular person and immediately reports, upon discovery, any unauthorized use to the appropriate law enforcement agency. A determination by the court at the forfeiture hearing held pursuant to subsection (d) of this section that the petitioner is not an innocent owner is a final judgment and is immediately appealable to the Court of Appeals.

(f) Release to Lienholder. - At a forfeiture hearing, the trial judge shall order a forfeited motor vehicle released to the lienholder upon payment of all towing and storage charges incurred as a result of the seizure of the motor vehicle if the judge determines, by the greater weight of the evidence, that:

(1) The lienholder's interest has been perfected and appears on the title to the forfeited vehicle;

(2) The lienholder agrees not to sell, give, or otherwise transfer possession of the forfeited motor vehicle to the defendant or to the motor vehicle owner who owned the motor vehicle immediately prior to forfeiture, or any person acting on the defendant's or motor vehicle owner's behalf;

(3) The forfeited motor vehicle had not previously been released to the lienholder;

(4) The owner is in default under the terms of the security instrument evidencing the interest of the lienholder and as a consequence of the default the lienholder is entitled to possession of the motor vehicle; and

(5) The lienholder agrees to sell the motor vehicle in accordance with the terms of its agreement and pursuant to the provisions of Part 6 of Article 9 of Chapter 25 of the General Statutes. Upon the sale of the motor vehicle, the

lienholder will pay to the clerk of court of the county in which the vehicle was forfeited all proceeds from the sale, less the amount of the lien in favor of the lienholder, and any towing and storage costs paid by the lienholder.

A lienholder who refuses to sell, give, or transfer possession of a forfeited motor vehicle to the defendant, the vehicle owner who owned the motor vehicle immediately prior to forfeiture, or any person acting on the behalf of the defendant or motor vehicle owner shall not be liable for damages arising out of such refusal. The defendant, the motor vehicle owner who owned the motor vehicle immediately prior to forfeiture, and any person acting on the defendant's or motor vehicle owner's behalf are prohibited from purchasing the motor vehicle at any sale conducted by the lienholder.

(g)   Repealed by Session Laws 1998-182, s. 2, effective December 1, 1998.

(h)   Any order issued pursuant to this section authorizing the release of a seized vehicle shall require the payment of all towing and storage charges incurred as a result of the seizure and impoundment of the motor vehicle. This requirement shall not be waived. (1983, c. 435, s. 21; 1983 (Reg. Sess., 1984), c. 1101, s. 19; 1989 (Reg. Sess., 1990), c. 1024, s. 6; 1997-379, s. 1.1; 1997-456, s. 30; 1998-182, s. 2; 1999-406, ss. 11, 12, 17; 2000-169, s. 28; 2001-362, s. 7; 2006-253, s. 31; 2007-493, ss. 7, 8, 21; 2013-243, s. 1; 2013-410, s. 18(a).)

§ 20-28.3. Seizure, impoundment, forfeiture of motor vehicles for offenses involving impaired driving while license revoked or without license and insurance, and for felony speeding to elude arrest.

(a)   Motor Vehicles Subject to Seizure for Impaired Driving Offenses. -

A motor vehicle that is driven by a person who is charged with an offense involving impaired driving is subject to seizure if:

(1)   At the time of the violation, the drivers license of the person driving the motor vehicle was revoked as a result of a prior impaired driving license revocation as defined in G.S. 20-28.2(a); or

(2)   At the time of the violation:

a.   The person was driving without a valid drivers license, and

b. The driver was not covered by an automobile liability policy.

For the purposes of this subsection, a person who has a complete defense, pursuant to G.S. 20-35, to a charge of driving without a drivers license, shall be considered to have had a valid drivers license at the time of the violation.

(a1) Motor Vehicles Subject to Seizure for Felony Speeding to Elude Arrest. - A motor vehicle is subject to seizure if it is driven by a person who is charged with the offense of felony speeding to elude arrest pursuant to G.S. 20-141.5(b) or (b1).

(b) Duty of Officer. - If the charging officer has probable cause to believe that a motor vehicle driven by the defendant may be subject to forfeiture under this section, the officer shall seize the motor vehicle and have it impounded. If the officer determines prior to seizure that the motor vehicle had been reported stolen, the officer shall not seize the motor vehicle pursuant to this section. If the officer determines prior to seizure that the motor vehicle was a rental vehicle driven by a person not listed as an authorized driver on the rental contract, the officer shall not seize the motor vehicle pursuant to this section, but shall make a reasonable effort to notify the owner of the rental vehicle that the vehicle was stopped and that the driver of the vehicle was not listed as an authorized driver on the rental contract. Probable cause may be based on the officer's personal knowledge, reliable information conveyed by another officer, records of the Division, or other reliable sources. The seizing officer shall notify the Division as soon as practical but no later than 24 hours after seizure of the motor vehicle of the seizure in accordance with procedures established by the Division.

(b1) Written Notification of Impoundment. - Within 48 hours of receipt within regular business hours of the notice of seizure, the Division shall issue written notification of impoundment to any lienholder of record and to any motor vehicle owner who was not operating the motor vehicle at the time of the offense. A notice of seizure received outside regular business hours shall be considered to have been received at the start of the next business day. The notification of impoundment shall be sent by first-class mail to the most recent address contained in the Division's records. If the motor vehicle is registered in another state, notice shall be sent to the address shown on the records of the state where the motor vehicle is registered. This written notification shall provide notice that the motor vehicle has been seized, state the reason for the seizure and the procedure for requesting release of the motor vehicle. Additionally, if the motor vehicle was damaged while the operator was committing an offense resulting in seizure or incident to the seizure, the Division shall issue written notification of the seizure to the owner's insurance company of record and to any other insurance companies that may be insuring other motor vehicles involved in the accident. The Division shall prohibit title to a seized motor vehicle from being transferred by a motor vehicle owner unless authorized by court order.

(b2)   Additional Notification to Lienholders. - In addition to providing written notification pursuant to subsection (b1) of this section, within eight hours of receipt within regular business hours of the notice of seizure, the Division shall notify by facsimile any lienholder of record that has provided the Division with a designated facsimile number for notification of impoundment. The facsimile notification of impoundment shall state that the vehicle has been seized, state the reason for the seizure, and notify the lienholder of the additional written notification that will be provided pursuant to subsection (b1) of this section. The Division shall establish procedures to allow a lienholder to provide one designated facsimile number for notification of impoundment for any vehicle for which the lienholder is a lienholder of record and shall maintain a centralized database of the provided facsimile numbers. The lienholder must provide a facsimile number at which the Division may give notification of impoundment at anytime.

(c)   Review by Magistrate. - Upon determining that there is probable cause for seizing a motor vehicle, the seizing officer shall present to a magistrate within the county where the driver was charged an affidavit of impoundment setting forth the basis upon which the motor vehicle has been or will be seized for forfeiture. The magistrate shall review the affidavit of impoundment and if the magistrate determines the requirements of this section have been met, shall order the motor vehicle held. The magistrate may request additional information and may hear from the defendant if the defendant is present. If the magistrate determines the requirements of this section have not been met, the magistrate shall order the motor vehicle released to a motor vehicle owner upon payment of towing and storage fees. If the motor vehicle has not yet been seized, and the magistrate determines that seizure is appropriate, the magistrate shall issue an order of seizure of the motor vehicle. The magistrate shall provide a copy of the order of seizure to the clerk of court. The clerk shall provide copies of the order of seizure to the district attorney and the attorney for the county board of education.

(c1)   Effecting an Order of Seizure. - An order of seizure shall be valid anywhere in the State. Any officer with territorial jurisdiction and who has subject matter jurisdiction for violations of this Chapter may use such force as may be reasonable to seize the motor vehicle and to enter upon the property of the defendant to accomplish the seizure. An officer who has probable cause to believe the motor vehicle is concealed or stored on private property of a person other than the defendant may obtain a search warrant to enter upon that property for the purpose of seizing the motor vehicle.

(d) Custody of Motor Vehicle. - Unless the motor vehicle is towed pursuant to a statewide or regional contract, or a contract with the county board of education, the seized motor vehicle shall be towed by a commercial towing company designated by the law enforcement agency that seized the motor vehicle. Seized motor vehicles not towed pursuant to a statewide or regional contract or a contract with a county board of education shall be retrieved from the commercial towing company within a reasonable time, not to exceed 10 days, by the county board of education or their agent who must pay towing and storage fees to the commercial towing company when the motor vehicle is retrieved. If either a statewide or regional contractor, or the county board of education, chooses to contract for local towing services, all towing companies on the towing list for each law enforcement agency with jurisdiction within the county shall be given written notice and an opportunity to submit proposals prior to a contract for local towing services being awarded. The seized motor vehicle is under the constructive possession of the county board of education for the county in which the operator of the vehicle is charged at the time the vehicle is delivered to a location designated by the county board of education or delivered to its agent pending release or sale, or in the event a statewide or regional contract is in place, under the constructive possession of the Department of Public Instruction, on behalf of the State at the time the vehicle is delivered to a location designated by the Department of Public Instruction or delivered to its agent pending release or sale. Absent a statewide or regional contract that provides otherwise, each county board of education may elect to have seized motor vehicles stored on property owned or leased by the county board of education and charge a reasonable fee for storage, not to exceed ten dollars ($10.00) per day. In the alternative, the county board of education may contract with a commercial towing and storage facility or other private entity for the towing, storage, and disposal of seized motor vehicles, and a storage fee of not more than ten dollars ($10.00) per day may be charged. Except for gross negligence or intentional misconduct, the county board of education, or any of its employees, shall not be liable to the owner or lienholder for damage to or loss of the motor vehicle or its contents, or to the owner of personal property in a seized vehicle, during the time the motor vehicle is being towed or stored pursuant to this subsection.

(e) Release of Motor Vehicle Pending Trial. - A motor vehicle owner, other than the driver at the time of the underlying offense resulting in the seizure, may apply to the clerk of superior court in the county where the charges are pending for pretrial release of the motor vehicle.

The clerk shall release the motor vehicle to a nondefendant motor vehicle owner conditioned upon payment of all towing and storage charges incurred as a result of seizure and impoundment of the motor vehicle under the following conditions:

(1) The motor vehicle has been seized for not less than 24 hours;

(2) Repealed by Session Laws 1998-182, s. 3, effective December 1, 1998.

(3) A bond in an amount equal to the fair market value of the motor vehicle as defined by G.S. 20-28.2 has been executed and is secured by a cash deposit in the full amount of the bond, by a recordable deed of trust to real property in the full amount of the bond, by a bail bond under G.S. 58-71-1(2), or by at least one solvent surety, payable to the county school fund and conditioned on return of the motor vehicle, in substantially the same condition as it was at the time of seizure and without any new or additional liens or encumbrances, on the day of any hearing scheduled and noticed by the district attorney under G.S. 20-28.2(c), unless the motor vehicle has been permanently released;

(4) Execution of either:

a. An impaired driving acknowledgment as described in G.S. 20-28.2(a1)(1a) if the seizure was for an offense involving impaired driving; or

b. A speeding to elude arrest acknowledgment as defined in G.S. 20-28.2(a1)(8) if the seizure was for violation of G.S. 20-141.5(b) or (b1).

(5) A check of the records of the Division indicates that the requesting motor vehicle owner has not previously executed an acknowledgment naming the operator of the seized motor vehicle; and

(6) A bond posted to secure the release of this motor vehicle under this subsection has not been previously ordered forfeited under G.S. 20-28.5.

In the event a nondefendant motor vehicle owner who obtains temporary possession of a seized motor vehicle pursuant to this subsection does not return the motor vehicle on the day of the forfeiture hearing as noticed by the district attorney under G.S. 20-28.2(c) or otherwise violates a condition of pretrial release of the seized motor vehicle as set forth in this subsection, the bond posted shall be ordered forfeited and an order of seizure shall be issued by the court. Additionally, a nondefendant motor vehicle owner or lienholder who willfully violates any condition of pretrial release may be held in civil or criminal contempt.

(e1) Pretrial Release of Motor Vehicle to Innocent Owner. - A nondefendant motor vehicle owner may file a petition with the clerk of court seeking a pretrial determination that the petitioner is an innocent owner. The clerk shall consider the petition and make a determination as soon as may be feasible. At any proceeding conducted pursuant to this subsection, the clerk is not required to determine the issue of forfeiture, only the issue of whether the petitioner is an innocent owner. If the clerk determines that the petitioner is an innocent owner, the clerk shall release the motor vehicle to the petitioner subject to the same conditions as if the petitioner were an innocent owner under G.S. 20-28.2(e). The clerk shall send a copy of the order authorizing or denying release of the vehicle to the district attorney and the attorney for the county board of education. An order issued under this subsection finding that the petitioner failed to establish that the petitioner is an innocent owner may be reconsidered by the court as part of the forfeiture hearing conducted pursuant to G.S. 20-28.2(d).

(e2) Pretrial Release of Motor Vehicle to Defendant Owner. -

(1) If the seizure was for an offense involving impaired driving, a defendant motor vehicle owner may file a petition with the clerk of court seeking a pretrial determination that the defendant's license was not revoked pursuant to an impaired driving license revocation as defined in G.S. 20-28.2(a). The clerk shall schedule a hearing before a judge of the division in which the underlying criminal charge is pending for a hearing to be held within 10 business days or as soon thereafter as may be feasible. Notice of the hearing shall be given to the defendant, the district attorney, and the attorney for the county board of education. The clerk shall forward a copy of the petition to the district attorney for the district attorney's review. If, based on available information, the district attorney determines that the defendant's motor vehicle is not subject to forfeiture, the district attorney may note the State's consent to the release of the motor vehicle on the petition and return the petition to the clerk of court who shall enter an order releasing the motor vehicle to the defendant upon payment of all towing and storage charges incurred as a result of the seizure and impoundment of the motor vehicle, subject to the satisfactory proof of the identity of the defendant as a motor vehicle owner and the existence of financial

responsibility to the extent required by Article 13 of this Chapter, and no hearing shall be held. The clerk shall send a copy of the order of release to the attorney for the county board of education. At any pretrial hearing conducted pursuant to this subdivision, the court is not required to determine the issue of the underlying offense of impaired driving only the existence of a prior drivers license revocation as an impaired driving license revocation. Accordingly, the State shall not be required to prove the underlying offense of impaired driving. An order issued under this subdivision finding that the defendant failed to establish that the defendant's license was not revoked pursuant to an impaired driving license revocation as defined in G.S. 20-28.2(a) may be reconsidered by the court as part of the forfeiture hearing conducted pursuant to G.S. 20-28.2(d).

(2) If the seizure was for a felony speeding to elude arrest offense, a defendant motor vehicle owner may apply to the clerk of superior court in the county where the charges are pending for pretrial release of the motor vehicle. The clerk shall release the motor vehicle to the defendant motor vehicle owner conditioned upon payment of all towing and storage charges incurred as a result of seizure and impoundment of the motor vehicle under the following conditions:

a. The motor vehicle has been seized for not less than 24 hours;

b. A bond in an amount equal to the fair market value of the motor vehicle as defined by G.S. 20-28.2 has been executed and is secured by a cash deposit in the full amount of the bond, by a recordable deed of trust to real property in the full amount of the bond, by a bail bond under G.S. 58-71-1(2), or by at least one solvent surety, payable to the county school fund and conditioned on return of the motor vehicle, in substantially the same condition as it was at the time of seizure and without any new or additional liens or encumbrances, on the day of any hearing scheduled and noticed by the district attorney under G.S. 20-28.2(c), unless the motor vehicle has been permanently released;

c. A bond posted to secure the release of this motor vehicle under this subdivision has not been previously ordered forfeited under G.S. 20-28.5.

In the event a defendant motor vehicle owner who obtains temporary possession of a seized motor vehicle pursuant to this subdivision does not return the motor vehicle on the day of the forfeiture hearing as noticed by the district attorney under G.S. 20-28.2(c) or otherwise violates a condition of pretrial release of the seized motor vehicle as set forth in this subdivision, the bond posted shall be ordered forfeited, and an order of seizure shall be issued by the court. Additionally, a defendant motor vehicle owner who willfully violates any condition of pretrial release may be held in civil or criminal contempt.

(e3) Pretrial Release of Motor Vehicle to Lienholder. -

(1) A lienholder may file a petition with the clerk of court requesting the court to order pretrial release of a seized motor vehicle. The lienholder shall serve a copy of the petition on all interested parties which shall include the registered owner, the titled owner, the district attorney, and the county board of education attorney. Upon 10 days' prior notice of the date, time, and location of the hearing sent by the lienholder to all interested parties, a judge, after a hearing, shall order a seized motor vehicle released to the lienholder conditioned upon payment of all towing and storage costs incurred as a result of the seizure and impoundment of the motor vehicle if the judge determines, by the greater weight of the evidence, that:

a. Default on the obligation secured by the motor vehicle has occurred;

b. As a consequence of default, the lienholder is entitled to possession of the motor vehicle;

c. The lienholder agrees to sell the motor vehicle in accordance with the terms of its agreement and pursuant to the provisions of Part 6 of Article 9 of Chapter 25 of the General Statutes. Upon sale of the motor vehicle, the lienholder will pay to the clerk of court of the county in which the driver was charged all proceeds from the sale, less the amount of the lien in favor of the lienholder, and any towing and storage costs paid by the lienholder;

d. The lienholder agrees not to sell, give, or otherwise transfer possession of the seized motor vehicle while the motor vehicle is subject to forfeiture, or the forfeited motor vehicle after the forfeiture hearing, to the defendant or the motor vehicle owner; and

e. The seized motor vehicle while the motor vehicle is subject to forfeiture, or the forfeited motor vehicle after the forfeiture hearing, had not previously been released to the lienholder as a result of a prior seizure involving the same defendant or motor vehicle owner.

(2) The clerk of superior court may order a seized vehicle released to the lienholder conditioned upon payment of all towing and storage costs incurred as a result of the seizure and impoundment of the motor vehicle at any time when

all interested parties have, in writing, waived any rights that they may have to notice and a hearing, and the lienholder has agreed to the provision of subdivision (1)d. above. A lienholder who refuses to sell, give, or transfer possession of a seized motor vehicle while the motor vehicle is subject to forfeiture, or a forfeited motor vehicle after the forfeiture hearing, to:

a. The defendant;

b. The motor vehicle owner who owned the motor vehicle immediately prior to seizure pending the forfeiture hearing, or to forfeiture after the forfeiture hearing; or

c. Any person acting on the behalf of the defendant or the motor vehicle owner,

shall not be liable for damages arising out of such refusal. However, any subsequent violation of the conditions of release by the lienholder shall be punishable by civil or criminal contempt.

(f),   (g) Repealed by Session Laws 1998-182, s. 3, effective December 1, 1998.

(h)   Insurance Proceeds. - In the event a motor vehicle is damaged incident to the conduct of the defendant which gave rise to the defendant's arrest and seizure of the motor vehicle pursuant to this section, the county board of education, or its authorized designee, is authorized to negotiate the county board of education's interest with the insurance company and to compromise and accept settlement of any claim for damages. Property insurance proceeds accruing to the defendant, or other owner of the seized motor vehicle, shall be paid by the responsible insurance company directly to the clerk of superior court in the county where the motor vehicle driver was charged. If the motor vehicle is declared a total loss by the insurance company liable for the damages to the motor vehicle, the clerk of superior court, upon application of the county board of education, shall enter an order that the motor vehicle be released to the insurance company upon payment into the court of all insurance proceeds for damage to the motor vehicle after payment of towing and storage costs and all valid liens. The clerk of superior court shall provide the Division with a certified copy of the order entered pursuant to this subsection, and the Division shall transfer title to the insurance company or to such other person or entity as may be designated by the insurance company. Insurance proceeds paid to the clerk of court pursuant to this subsection shall be subject to forfeiture pursuant to

G.S. 20-28.5 and shall be disbursed pursuant to further orders of the court. An affected motor vehicle owner or lienholder who objects to any agreed upon settlement under this subsection may file an independent claim with the insurance company for any additional monies believed owed. Notwithstanding any other provisions in this Chapter, nothing in this section or G.S. 20-28.2 shall require an insurance company to make payments in excess of those required pursuant to its policy of insurance on the seized motor vehicle.

(i) Expedited Sale of Seized Motor Vehicles in Certain Cases. - In order to avoid additional liability for towing and storage costs pending resolution of the criminal proceedings of the defendant, the county board of education may, after expiration of 90 days from the date of seizure, sell any motor vehicle having a fair market value of one thousand five hundred dollars ($1,500) or less. The county board of education may also sell a motor vehicle, regardless of the fair market value, any time the outstanding towing and storage costs exceed eighty-five percent (85%) of the fair market value of the vehicle, or with the consent of all the motor vehicle owners. Any sale conducted pursuant to this subsection shall be conducted in accordance with the provisions of G.S. 20-28.5(a), and the proceeds of the sale, after the payment of outstanding towing and storage costs or reimbursement of towing and storage costs paid by a person other than the defendant, shall be deposited with the clerk of superior court. If an order of forfeiture is entered by the court, the court shall order the proceeds held by the clerk to be disbursed as provided in G.S. 20-28.5(b). If the court determines that the motor vehicle is not subject to forfeiture, the court shall order the proceeds held by the clerk to be disbursed first to pay the sale, towing, and storage costs, second to pay outstanding liens on the motor vehicle, and the balance to be paid to the motor vehicle owners.

(j) Retrieval of Certain Personal Property. - At reasonable times, the entity charged with storing the motor vehicle may permit owners of personal property not affixed to the motor vehicle to retrieve those items from the motor vehicle, provided satisfactory proof of ownership of the motor vehicle or the items of personal property is presented to the storing entity.

(k) County Board of Education Right to Appear and Participate in Proceedings. - The attorney for the county board of education shall be given notice of all proceedings regarding offenses related to a motor vehicle subject to forfeiture under this section. However, the notice requirement under this subsection does not apply to proceedings conducted under G.S. 20-28.3(e1). The attorney for the county board of education shall also have the right to appear and to be heard on all issues relating to the seizure, possession, release, forfeiture, sale, and other matters related to the seized vehicle under this section. With the prior consent of the county board of education, the district attorney may delegate to the attorney for the county board of education any or all of the duties of the district attorney under this section. Clerks of superior court, law enforcement agencies, and all other agencies with information relevant to the seizure, impoundment, release, or forfeiture of motor vehicles are authorized and directed to provide county boards of education with access to that information and to do so by electronic means when existing technology makes this type of transmission possible.

(l) Payment of Fees Upon Conviction. - If the driver of a motor vehicle seized pursuant to this section is convicted of the underlying offense resulting in the seizure of a motor vehicle pursuant to this section, the defendant shall be ordered to pay as restitution to the county board of education, the motor vehicle owner, or the lienholder the cost paid or owing for the towing, storage, and sale of the motor vehicle to the extent the costs were not covered by the proceeds from the forfeiture and sale of the motor vehicle. If the underlying offense resulting in the seizure is felony speeding to elude arrest pursuant to G.S. 20-141.5(b) or (b1) and the defendant's conviction is for misdemeanor speeding to elude arrest pursuant to G.S. 20-141.5(a), whether or not the reduced charge is by plea agreement, the defendant shall be ordered to pay as restitution to the county board of education, the motor vehicle owner, or the lienholder the cost paid or owing for the towing and storage of the motor vehicle. In addition, a civil judgment for the costs under this section in favor of the party to whom the restitution is owed shall be docketed by the clerk of superior court. If the defendant is sentenced to an active term of imprisonment, the civil judgment shall become effective and be docketed when the defendant's conviction becomes final. If the defendant is placed on probation, the civil judgment in the amount found by a judge during the probation revocation or termination hearing to be due shall become effective and be docketed by the clerk when the defendant's probation is revoked or terminated.

(m) Trial Priority. - District court trials of offenses involving forfeitures of motor vehicles pursuant to G.S. 20-28.2 shall be scheduled on the arresting officer's next court date or within 30 days of the offense, whichever comes first.

Once scheduled, the case shall not be continued unless all of the following conditions are met:

(1) A written motion for continuance is filed with notice given to the opposing party prior to the motion being heard.

(2) The judge makes a finding of a "compelling reason" for the continuance.

(3) The motion and finding are attached to the court case record.

Upon a determination of guilt, the issue of vehicle forfeiture shall be heard by the judge immediately, or as soon thereafter as feasible, and the judge shall issue the appropriate orders pursuant to G.S. 20-28.2(d).

Should a defendant appeal the conviction to superior court, any party who has not previously been heard on a petition for pretrial release under subsection (e1) or (e3) of this section or any party whose motor vehicle has not been the subject of a forfeiture hearing held pursuant to G.S. 20-28.2(d) may be heard on a petition for pretrial release pursuant to subsection (e1) or (e3) of this section. The provisions of subsection (e) of this section shall also apply to seized motor vehicles pending trial in superior court. Where a motor vehicle was released pursuant to subsection (e) of this section pending trial in district court, the release of the motor vehicle continues, and the terms and conditions of the original bond remain the same as those required for the initial release of the motor vehicle under subsection (e) of this section, pending the resolution of the underlying offense involving impaired driving in superior court.

(n) Any order issued pursuant to this section authorizing the release of a seized vehicle shall require the payment of all towing and storage charges incurred as a result of the seizure and impoundment of the motor vehicle. This requirement shall not be waived. (1997-379, s. 1.2; 1997-456, s. 31; 1998-182, s. 3; 1998-217, s. 62(a)-(c); 2000-169, s. 29; 2001-362, ss. 1, 2, 3, 4, 5, 6; 2001-487, s. 9; 2006-253, s. 32; 2013-243, s. 2.)

§ 20-28.4. Release of impounded motor vehicles by judge.

(a) Release Upon Conclusion of Trial. - If the driver of a motor vehicle seized pursuant to G.S. 20-28.3:

(1) Is subsequently not convicted of the underlying offense resulting in seizure due to dismissal or a finding of not guilty; or

(2) The judge at a forfeiture hearing conducted pursuant to G.S. 20-28.2(d) finds that the criteria for forfeiture have not otherwise been met; and

(3) The vehicle has not previously been released to a lienholder pursuant to G.S. 20-28.3(e3),

the seized motor vehicle or insurance proceeds held by the clerk of court pursuant to G.S. 20-28.2(c1) or G.S. 20-28.3(h) shall be released to the motor vehicle owner conditioned upon payment of towing and storage costs. The court shall not waive the payment of towing and storage costs. The court shall include in its order notice to the owner of the seized motor vehicle still being held, that within 30 days of the date of the court's order, the owner must make payment of the outstanding towing and storage costs for the motor vehicle and retrieve the motor vehicle, or give notice to Division of Motor Vehicles requesting a judicial hearing on the validity of any mechanics' lien on the motor vehicle for towing and storage costs.

(b) Notwithstanding G.S. 44A-2(d), if the owner of the seized motor vehicle does not obtain release of the vehicle within 30 days from the date of the court's order, the possessor of the seized motor vehicle has a mechanics' lien on the seized motor vehicle for the full amount of the towing and storage charges incurred since the motor vehicle was seized and may dispose of the seized motor vehicle pursuant to Article 1 of Chapter 44A of the General Statutes. Notice of the right to a judicial hearing on the validity of the mechanics' lien given to the owner of the motor vehicle in open court in accordance with subsection (a) of this section or delivery to the owner of the vehicle of a copy of the court's order entered in accordance with subsection (a) of this section shall satisfy the notice requirement of G.S. 44A-4(b). (1997-379, s. 1.3; 1998-182, s. 4; 2001-362, s. 8; 2004-128, s. 4; 2013-243, s. 3.)

§ 20-28.5. Forfeiture of impounded motor vehicle or funds.

(a) Sale. - A motor vehicle ordered forfeited and sold or a seized motor vehicle authorized to be sold pursuant to G.S. 20-28.3(i), shall be sold at a public sale conducted in accordance with the provisions of Article 12 of Chapter 160A of the General Statutes, applicable to sales authorized pursuant to G.S. 160A-266(a)(2), (3), or (4), subject to the notice requirements of this subsection, and shall be conducted by the county board of education or a person acting on its behalf. Notice of sale, including the date, time, location, and manner of sale, shall be given by first-class mail to all motor vehicle owners of the vehicle to be sold at the address shown by the records of the Division. Written notice of sale shall also be given to all lienholders on file with the Division. Notice of sale shall be given to the Division in accordance with the procedures established by the Division. Notices required to be given under this subsection shall be mailed at least 10 days prior to the date of sale. A lienholder shall be permitted to purchase the motor vehicle at any such sale by bidding in the amount of its lien, if that should be the highest bid, without being required to tender any additional funds, other than the towing and storage fees. The county board of education, or its agent, shall not sell, give, or otherwise transfer possession of the forfeited motor vehicle to the defendant, the motor vehicle owner who owned the motor vehicle immediately prior to forfeiture, or any person acting on the defendant's or motor vehicle owner's behalf.

(b) Proceeds of Sale. - Proceeds of any sale conducted under this section, G.S. 20-28.2(f)(5), or G.S. 20-28.3(e3)(3), shall first be applied to the cost of sale and then to satisfy towing and storage costs. The balance of the proceeds of sale, if any, shall be used to satisfy any other existing liens of record that were properly recorded prior to the date of initial seizure of the vehicle. Any remaining balance shall be paid to the county school fund in the county in which the motor vehicle was ordered forfeited. If there is more than one school board in the county, then the net proceeds of sale, after reimbursement to the county board of education of reasonable administrative costs incurred in connection with the forfeiture and sale of the motor vehicle, shall be distributed in the same manner as fines and other forfeitures. The sale of a motor vehicle pursuant to this section shall be deemed to extinguish all existing liens on the motor vehicle and the motor vehicle shall be transferred free and clear of any liens.

(c) Retention of Motor Vehicle. - A board of education may, at its option, retain any forfeited motor vehicle for its use upon payment of towing and storage costs. If the motor vehicle is retained, any valid lien of record at the time of the initial seizure of the motor vehicle shall be satisfied by the county board of education relieving the motor vehicle owner of all liability for the obligation secured by the motor vehicle. If there is more than one school board in the county, and the motor vehicle is retained by a board of education, then the fair market value of the motor vehicle, less the costs for towing, storage, reasonable administrative costs, and liens paid, shall be used to determine and pay the share due each of the school boards in the same manner as fines and other forfeitures.

(d) Repealed by Session Laws 1998-182, s. 5.

(e) Order of Forfeiture; Appeals. - An order of forfeiture is stayed pending appeal of a conviction for an offense that is the basis for the order. When the conviction of an offense that is the basis for an order of forfeiture is appealed from district court, the issue of forfeiture shall be heard in superior court de novo. Appeal from a final order of forfeiture shall be to the Court of Appeals. (1997-379, s. 1.4; 1998-182, s. 5; 1998-217, s. 62(d); 1999-456, s. 11.)

§ 20-28.6: Repealed by Session Laws 1998-182, s. 6 effective December 1, 1998, and applicable to offenses committed, contracts entered, and motor vehicles seized on or after that date.

§ 20-28.7. Responsibility of Division of Motor Vehicles.

The Division shall establish procedures by rule to provide for the orderly seizure, forfeiture, sale, and transfer of motor vehicles pursuant to the provisions of G.S. 20-28.2, 20-28.3, 20-28.4, and 20-28.5. (1997-379, s. 1.6; 1998-182, s. 7.)

§ 20-28.8. Reports to the Division.

In any case in which a vehicle has been seized pursuant to G.S. 20-28.3, in addition to any other information that must be reported pursuant to this Chapter, the clerk of superior court shall report to the Division by electronic means the execution of an impaired driving acknowledgment as defined in G.S. 20-28.2(a1)(1a), a speeding to elude arrest acknowledgment as defined in G.S. 20-28.2(a1)(8), the entry of an order of forfeiture as defined in G.S. 20-28.2(a1)(4), and the entry of an order of release as defined in G.S. 20-28.3 and G.S. 20-28.4. Each report shall include any of the following information that has not previously been reported to the Division in the case: the name, address, and drivers license number of the defendant; the name, address, and drivers license number of the nondefendant motor vehicle owner, if known; and the make, model, year, vehicle identification number, state of registration, and vehicle registration plate number of the seized vehicle, if known. (1998-182, s. 8; 2013-243, s. 4.)

§ 20-28.9. Authority for the Department of Public Instruction to administer a statewide or regional towing, storage, and sales program for driving while impaired vehicles forfeited.

(a)   The Department of Public Instruction is authorized to enter into a contract for a statewide service or contracts for regional services to tow, store, process, maintain, and sell motor vehicles seized pursuant to G.S. 20-28.3. All motor vehicles seized under G.S. 20-28.3 shall be subject to contracts entered into pursuant to this section. Contracts shall be let by the Department of Public Instruction in accordance with the provisions of Article 3 of Chapter 143 of the General Statutes. All contracts shall ensure the safety of the motor vehicles while held and any funds arising from the sale of any seized motor vehicle. The contract shall require the contractor to maintain and make available to the agency a computerized up-to-date inventory of all motor vehicles held under the contract, together with an accounting of all accrued charges, the status of the vehicle, and the county school fund to which the proceeds of sale are to be paid. The contract shall provide that the contractor shall pay the towing and storage charges owed on a seized vehicle to a commercial towing company at the time the seized vehicle is obtained from the commercial towing company, with the contractor being reimbursed this expense when the vehicle is released or sold. The Department shall not enter into any contract under this section under which the State will be obligated to pay a deficiency arising from the sale of any forfeited motor vehicle.

(b)   The Department, through its contractor or contractors designated in accordance with subsection (a) of this section, may charge a reasonable fee for storage not to exceed ten dollars ($10.00) per day for the storage of seized vehicles pursuant to G.S. 20-28.3.

(c)   In order to help defray the administrative costs associated with the administration of this section, the Department shall collect a ten dollar ($10.00) administrative fee from a person to whom a seized vehicle is released at the time the motor vehicle is released and shall collect a ten dollar ($10.00) administrative fee out of the proceeds of the sale of any forfeited motor vehicle. The funds collected under this subsection shall be paid to the General Fund. (1998-182, s. 8.)

§ 20-29. Surrender of license.

Any person operating or in charge of a motor vehicle, when requested by an officer in uniform, or, in the event of accident in which the vehicle which he is operating or in charge of shall be involved, when requested by any other person, who shall refuse to write his name for the purpose of identification or to give his name and address and the name and address of the owner of such vehicle, or who shall give a false name or address, or who shall refuse, on demand of such officer or such other person, to produce his license and exhibit same to such officer or such other person for the purpose of examination, or who shall refuse to surrender his license on demand of the Division, or fail to produce same when requested by a court of this State, shall be guilty of a Class 2 misdemeanor. Pickup notices for drivers' licenses or revocation or suspension of license notices and orders or demands issued by the Division for the surrender of such licenses may be served and executed by patrolmen or other peace officers or may be served in accordance with G.S. 20-48. Patrolmen and peace officers, while serving and executing such notices, orders and demands, shall have all the power and authority possessed by peace officers when serving the executing warrants charging violations of the criminal laws of the State. (1935, c. 52, s. 23; 1949, c. 583, s. 7; 1975, c. 716, s. 5; 1979, c. 667, s. 25; 1981, c. 938, s. 1; 1993, c. 539, s. 323; 1994, Ex. Sess., c. 24, s. 14(c).)

§ 20-29.1. Commissioner may require reexamination; issuance of limited or restricted licenses.

The Commissioner of Motor Vehicles, having good and sufficient cause to believe that a licensed operator is incompetent or otherwise not qualified to be licensed, may, upon written notice of at least five days to such licensee, require him to submit to a reexamination to determine his competency to operate a motor vehicle. Upon the conclusion of such examination, the Commissioner shall take such action as may be appropriate, and may suspend or revoke the license of such person or permit him to retain such license, or may issue a license subject to restrictions or upon failure of such reexamination may cancel the license of such person until he passes a reexamination. Refusal or neglect of the licensee to submit to such reexamination shall be grounds for the cancellation of the license of the person failing to be reexamined, and the license so canceled shall remain canceled until such person satisfactorily complies with the reexamination requirements of the Commissioner. The Commissioner may, in his discretion and upon the written application of any person qualified to receive a driver's license, issue to such person a driver's license restricting or limiting the licensee to the operation of a single prescribed motor vehicle or to the operation of a particular class or type of motor vehicle. Such a limitation or restriction shall be noted on the face of the license, and it shall be unlawful for the holder of such limited or restricted license to operate any motor vehicle or class of motor vehicle not specified by such restricted or limited license, and the operation by such licensee of motor vehicles not specified by such license shall be deemed the equivalent of operating a motor vehicle without any driver's license. Any such restricted or limited licensee may at any time surrender such restricted or limited license and apply for and receive an unrestricted driver's license upon meeting the requirements therefor. (1943, c. 787, s. 2; 1949, c. 1121; 1971, c. 546; 1979, c. 667, ss. 26, 41.)

§ 20-30. Violations of license, learner's permit, or special identification card provisions.

It shall be unlawful for any person to commit any of the following acts:

(1)   To display or cause to be displayed or to have in possession a driver's license, learner's permit, or special identification card, knowing the same to be fictitious or to have been canceled, revoked, suspended or altered.

(2)   To counterfeit, sell, lend to, or knowingly permit the use of, by one not entitled thereto, a driver's license, learner's permit, or special identification card.

(3)   To display or to represent as one's own a drivers license, learner's permit, or special identification card not issued to the person so displaying same.

(4)   To fail or refuse to surrender to the Division upon demand any driver's license, learner's permit, or special identification card that has been suspended, canceled or revoked as provided by law.

(5)   To use a false or fictitious name or give a false or fictitious address in any application for a driver's license, learner's permit, or special identification card, or any renewal or duplicate thereof, or knowingly to make a false statement or knowingly conceal a material fact or otherwise commit a fraud in any such application, or for any person to procure, or knowingly permit or allow another to commit any of the foregoing acts. Any license, learner's permit, or special identification card procured as aforesaid shall be void from the issuance thereof, and any moneys paid therefor shall be forfeited to the State. Any person

violating the provisions of this subdivision shall be guilty of a Class 1 misdemeanor.

(6) To make a color photocopy or otherwise make a color reproduction of a drivers license, learner's permit, or special identification card which has been color-photocopied or otherwise reproduced in color, unless such color photocopy or other color reproduction was authorized by the Commissioner. It shall be lawful to make a black and white photocopy of a drivers license, learner's permit, or special identification card or otherwise make a black and white reproduction of a drivers license, learner's permit, or special identification card.

(7) To sell or offer for sale any reproduction or facsimile or simulation of a driver's license, learner's permit, or special identification card. The provisions of this subdivision shall not apply to agents or employees of the Division while acting in the course and scope of their employment. Any person, firm or corporation violating the provisions of this subsection shall be guilty of a Class I felony.

(8) To possess more than one commercial drivers license or to possess a commercial drivers license and a regular drivers license. Any commercial drivers license other than the one most recently issued is subject to immediate seizure by any law enforcement officer or judicial official. Any regular drivers license possessed at the same time as a commercial drivers license is subject to immediate seizure by any law enforcement officer or judicial official.

(9) To present, display, or use a drivers license, learner's permit, or special identification card that contains a false or fictitious name in the commission or attempted commission of a felony. Any person violating the provisions of this subdivision shall be guilty of a Class I felony. (1935, c. 52, s. 24; 1951, c. 542, s. 4; 1967, c. 1098, s. 1; 1973, c. 18, s. 2; 1975, c. 716, s. 5; 1979, c. 415; c. 667, ss. 27, 41; 1979, 2nd Sess., c. 1316, s. 22; 1989, c. 771, s. 8; 1991, c. 726, s. 13; 1991 (Reg. Sess., 1992), c. 1007, s. 29; 1993, c. 539, s. 1247; 1994, Ex. Sess., c. 24, s. 14(c); 1999-299, s. 1; 2001-461, s. 1.1; 2001-487, s. 50(b); 2011-381, s. 4.)

§ 20-31. Making false affidavits perjury.

Any person who shall make any false affidavit, or shall knowingly swear or affirm falsely, to any matter or thing required by the terms of this Article to be sworn to or affirmed shall be guilty of a Class I felony. (1935, c. 52, s. 25; 1993, c. 539, s. 1249; 1994, Ex. Sess., c. 24, s. 14(c).)

§ 20-32. Unlawful to permit unlicensed minor to drive motor vehicle.

It shall be unlawful for any person to cause or knowingly permit any minor under the age of 18 years to drive a motor vehicle upon a highway as an operator, unless such minor shall have first obtained a license to so drive a motor vehicle under the provisions of this Article. (1935, c. 52, s. 26; 1973, c. 684.)

§ 20-33. Repealed by Session Laws 1979, c. 667, s. 28.

§ 20-34. Unlawful to permit violations of this Article.

No person shall authorize or knowingly permit a motor vehicle owned by him or under his control to be driven by any person who has no legal right to do so or in violation of any of the provisions of this Article. (1935, c. 52, s. 28.)

§ 20-34.1. Violations for wrongful issuance of a drivers license or a special identification card.

(a) An employee of the Division or of an agent of the Division who does any of the following commits a Class I felony:

(1) Charges or accepts any money or other thing of value, except the required fee, for the issuance of a drivers license or a special identification card.

(2) Knowing it is false, accepts false proof of identification submitted for a drivers license or a special identification card.

(3) Knowing it is false, enters false information concerning a drivers license or a special identification card in the records of the Division.

(b) Defenses Precluded. - The fact that the Division does not issue a license or a special identification card after an employee or an agent of the Division charges or accepts money or another thing of value for its issuance is not a defense to a criminal action under this section. It is not a defense to a criminal action under this section to show that the person who received or was intended to receive the license or special identification card was eligible for it.

(c) Dismissal. - An employee of the Division who violates this section shall be dismissed from employment and may not hold any public office or public employment in this State for five years after the violation. If a person who violates this section is an employee of the agent of the Division, the Division shall cancel the contract of the agent unless the agent dismisses that person. A person dismissed by an agent because of a violation of this section may not hold any public office or public employment in this State for five years after the violation. (1951, c. 211; 1975, c. 716, s. 5; 1979, c. 667, s. 41; 1993, c. 533, s. 8; 1994, Ex. Sess., c. 14, s. 30; c. 24, s. 14(c).)

§ 20-35. Penalties for violating Article; defense to driving without a license.

(a) Penalty. - Except as otherwise provided in subsection (a1) or (a2) of this section, a violation of this Article is a Class 2 misdemeanor unless a statute in the Article sets a different punishment for the violation. If a statute in this Article sets a different punishment for a violation of the Article, the different punishment applies.

(a1) The following offenses are Class 3 misdemeanors:

(1) Failure to obtain a license before driving a motor vehicle, in violation of G.S. 20-7(a).

(2) Failure to comply with license restrictions, in violation of G.S. 20-7(e).

(3) Permitting a motor vehicle owned by the person to be operated by an unlicensed person, in violation of G.S. 20-34.

(a2) A person who does any of the following is responsible for an infraction:

(1) Fails to carry a valid license while driving a motor vehicle, in violation of G.S. 20-7(a).

(2) Operates a motor vehicle with an expired license, in violation of G.S. 20-7(f).

(3) Fails to notify the Division of an address change for a drivers license within 60 days after the change occurs, in violation of G.S. 20-7.1.

(b) Repealed by Session Laws 1993 (Reg. Sess., 1994), c. 761, s. 4.

(c) Defenses. - A person may not be found responsible for failing to carry a regular drivers license if, when tried for that offense, the person produces in court a regular drivers license issued to the person that was valid when the person was charged with the offense. A person may not be found responsible for driving a motor vehicle with an expired drivers license if, when tried for that offense, the person shows all the following:

(1) That, at the time of the offense, the person had an expired license.

(2) The person renewed the expired license within 30 days after it expired and now has a drivers license.

(3) The person could not have been charged with driving without a license if the person had the renewed license when charged with the offense. (1935, c. 52, s. 29; 1991, c. 726, s. 14; 1993, c. 539, s. 324; 1994, Ex. Sess., c. 24, s. 14(c); 1993 (Reg. Sess., 1994), c. 761, s. 4; 2013-360, s. 18B.14(g); 2013-385, s. 4.)

§ 20-36. Ten-year-old convictions not considered.

Except for offenses occurring in a commercial motor vehicle, offenses by the holder of a commercial drivers license involving a noncommercial motor vehicle, or a second failure to submit to a chemical test when charged with an implied-consent offense, as defined in G.S. 20-16.2, that occurred while the person was driving a commercial motor vehicle, no conviction of any other violation of the motor vehicle laws shall be considered by the Division in determining whether any person's driving privilege shall be suspended or revoked or in determining the appropriate period of suspension or revocation after 10 years has elapsed from the date of that conviction. (1971, c. 15; 1975, c. 716, s. 5; 1998-182, s. 22; 2005-349, s. 7; 2009-416, s. 4.)

§ 20-37. Limitations on issuance of licenses.

There shall be no driver's license issued within this State other than that provided for in this Article, nor shall there be any other examination required: Provided, however, that cities and towns shall have the power to license, regulate and control drivers and operators of taxicabs within the city or town limits and to regulate and control operators of taxicabs operating between the city or town to points, not incorporated, within a radius of five miles of said city or town. (1935, c. 52, s. 34; 1943, c. 639, s. 2; 1979, c. 667, s. 41.)

§ 20-37.01. Drivers License Technology Fund.

The Drivers License Technology Fund is established in the Department of Transportation as a nonreverting, interest-bearing special revenue account. The revenue in the Fund at the end of a fiscal year does not revert, and earnings on the Fund shall be credited to the Fund annually. All money collected by the Commissioner pursuant to G.S. 20-37.02 shall be remitted to the State Treasurer and held in the Fund. Money held in the Fund shall be used to supplement funds otherwise available to the Division for information technology and office automation needs. The Commissioner shall report by February 1 and August 1 of each year to the Joint Legislative Commission on Governmental Operations, the chairs of the Senate and House of Representatives Appropriation Committees, and the chairs of the Senate and House of Representatives Appropriations Subcommittees on Transportation on all money collected and deposited in the Fund and on the proposed expenditure of funds collected during the preceding six months. (2001-461, s. 4; 2001-487, s. 42(c).)

§ 20-37.02. Verification of drivers license information.

(a)   The Commissioner shall establish and operate an electronic system that can be used to verify drivers licenses and identification cards issued by the

Division and the dates of birth on these documents in order to facilitate access to drivers license information by retailers and persons holding ABC permits to prevent the utilization of fictitious identification for the purpose of underage purchases of certain age-restricted products or to commit certain crimes.

(b) The electronic system established and operated by the Commissioner pursuant to subsection (a) of this section shall allow a retailer, as defined in G.S. 105-164.3(14), a person who holds an ABC permit, as defined in G.S. 18B-101(2), or an agent of the retailer or a person holding an ABC permit, to verify the validity of a drivers license or identification card issued by the Division and the date of birth of the person issued the drivers license or identification card. The Commissioner shall make drivers license and identification card information available in a read-only format, and the information to be made available shall not exceed the information contained on the face of the drivers license. The Division shall not keep a record of the inquiry. The retailer or a person holding an ABC permit may retain such information as is necessary to provide evidence that the person's drivers license or identification card was validated or that the person's age was verified. A retailer or permittee shall agree to comply with the requirements of this section prior to using the system.

(c) Except for purposes allowed in this section, a person using the electronic system established in accordance with subsection (a) of this section shall not collect or retain any information obtained through the use of the electronic system, nor transfer or make accessible to a third party any information obtained through an inquiry permitted under this section. A violation of the provisions of this subsection shall be punished as a Class 2 misdemeanor.

(d) A retailer or permittee using the electronic system established pursuant to this section shall be responsible for the costs of the equipment and communication lines approved by the Division needed by the retailer or permittee to access the system.

(e) The establishment and operation of an electronic system pursuant to this section may be funded through grants received from the State, the federal government, a private entity, or any other funding source made available to the Drivers License Technology Fund. All funds obtained through grants to the Fund shall be remitted to the State Treasurer to be held in the Drivers License Technology Fund established in G.S. 20-37.01. (2001-461, s. 4.)

Article 2A.

Afflicted, Disabled or Handicapped Persons.

§ 20-37.1: Repealed by Session Laws 1989, c. 157, s. 1.

§§ 20-37.2 through 20-37.4: Repealed by Session Laws 1991, c. 411, s. 5.

§ 20-37.5. Definitions.

Unless the context requires otherwise, the following definitions apply throughout this Article to the defined words and phrases and their cognates:

(1)   "Distinguishing license plate" means a license plate that displays the International Symbol of Access using the same color, size of plate, and size of letters or numbers as a regular plate.

(2)   "Handicapped" shall mean a person with a mobility impairment who, as determined by a licensed physician:

a.   Cannot walk 200 feet without stopping to rest;

b.   Cannot walk without the use of, or assistance from, a brace, cane, crutch, another person, prosthetic device, wheelchair, or other assistive device;

c.   Is restricted by lung disease to such an extent that the person's forced (respiratory) expiratory volume of one second, when measured by spirometry, is less than one liter, or the arterial oxygen tension is less than 60 mm/hg on room air at rest;

d.   Uses portable oxygen;

e. Has a cardiac condition to the extent that the person's functional limitations are classified in severity as Class III or Class IV according to standards set by the American Heart Association;

f. Is severely limited in their ability to walk due to an arthritic, neurological, or orthopedic condition; or

g. Is totally blind or whose vision with glasses is so defective as to prevent the performance of ordinary activity for which eyesight is essential, as certified by a licensed ophthalmologist, optometrist, or the Division of Services for the Blind.

(3) "International Symbol of Access" means the symbol adopted by Rehabilitation International in 1969 at its Eleventh World Congress on Rehabilitation of the Disabled.

(4) "Removable windshield placard" means a two-sided, hooked placard which includes on each side:

a. The International Symbol of Access, which is at least three inches in height, centered on the placard, and is white on a blue shield;

b. An identification number;

c. An expiration date that is visible from at least 20 feet and the month and year of expiration; and

d. The seal or other identification of the issuing authority. (1967, c. 296, s. 5; 1977, c. 340, s. 1; 1991, c. 411, s. 1; 2009-493, s. 1.)

§ 20-37.6. Parking privileges for handicapped drivers and passengers.

(a) General Parking. - Any vehicle that is driven by or is transporting a person who is handicapped and that displays a distinguishing license plate, a removable windshield placard, or a temporary removable windshield placard may be parked for unlimited periods in parking zones restricted as to the length of time parking is permitted. This provision has no application to those zones or during times in which the stopping, parking, or standing of all vehicles is prohibited or which are reserved for special types of vehicles. Any qualifying vehicle may park in spaces designated as restricted to vehicles driven by or transporting the handicapped.

(b)   Handicapped Car Owners; Distinguishing License Plates. - If the handicapped person is a registered owner of a vehicle, the owner may apply for and display a distinguishing license plate. This license plate shall be issued for the normal fee applicable to standard license plates. Any vehicle owner who qualifies for a distinguishing license plate may also receive one removable windshield placard.

(c)   Handicapped Drivers and Passengers; Distinguishing Placards. - Handicapped Drivers and Passengers; Distinguishing Placards. - A handicapped person may apply for the issuance of a removable windshield placard or a temporary removable windshield placard. Upon request, one additional placard may be issued to applicants who do not have a distinguishing license plate. Any organization which, as determined and certified by the State Vocational Rehabilitation Agency, regularly transports handicapped persons may also apply. These organizations may receive one removable windshield placard for each transporting vehicle. When the removable windshield or temporary removable windshield placard is properly displayed, all parking rights and privileges extended to vehicles displaying a distinguishing license plate issued pursuant to subsection (b) shall apply. The removable windshield placard or the temporary removable windshield placard shall be displayed so that it may be viewed from the front and rear of the vehicle by hanging it from the front windshield rearview mirror of a vehicle using a parking space allowed for handicapped persons. When there is no inside rearview mirror, or when the placard cannot reasonably be hung from the rearview mirror by the handicapped person, the placard shall be displayed on the driver's side of the dashboard. A removable windshield placard placed on a motorized wheelchair or similar vehicle shall be displayed in a clearly visible location. The Division shall establish procedures for the issuance of the placards and may charge a fee sufficient to pay the actual cost of issuance, but in no event less than five dollars ($5.00) per placard. The Division shall issue a placard registration card with each placard issued to a handicapped person. The registration card shall bear the name of the person to whom the placard is issued, the person's address, the placard number, and an expiration date. The registration card shall be in the vehicle in which the placard is being used, and the person to whom the placard is issued shall be the operator or a passenger in the vehicle in which the placard is displayed.

(c1)   Application and Renewal; Physician's Certification. - The initial application for a distinguishing license plate, removable windshield placard, or temporary removable windshield placard shall be accompanied by a certification of a licensed physician, ophthalmologist, or optometrist or of the Division of Services for the Blind that the applicant is handicapped. The application for a temporary removable windshield placard shall contain additional certification to include the period of time the certifying authority determines the applicant will have the disability. Distinguishing license plates shall be renewed annually, but subsequent applications shall not require a medical certification that the applicant is handicapped. Removable windshield placards shall be renewed every five years, and the renewal shall require a medical recertification that the person is handicapped. Temporary removable windshield placards shall expire no later than six months after issuance.

(c2)   Existing Placards; Expiration; Exchange for New Placards. - All existing placards shall expire on January 1, 1992. No person shall be convicted of parking in violation of this Article by reason of an expired placard if the defendant produces in court, at the time of trial on the illegal parking charge, an expired placard and a renewed placard issued within 30 days of the expiration date of the expired placard and which would have been a defense to the charge had it been issued prior to the time of the alleged offense. Existing placards issued on or after July 1, 1989, may be exchanged without charge for the new placards.

(c3)   It shall be unlawful to sell a distinguishing license plate, a removable windshield placard, or a temporary removable windshield placard issued pursuant to this section. A violation of this subsection shall be a Class 2 misdemeanor and may be punished pursuant to G.S. 20-176(c) and (c1).

(d)   Designation of Parking Spaces. - Designation of parking spaces for handicapped persons on streets and public vehicular areas shall comply with G.S. 136-30. A sign designating a parking space for handicapped persons shall state the maximum penalty for parking in the space in violation of the law.

(d1)   Repealed by Session Laws 1991, c. 530, s. 4.

(e)   Enforcement of Handicapped Parking Privileges. - It shall be unlawful:

(1)   To park or leave standing any vehicle in a space designated with a sign pursuant to subsection (d) of this section for handicapped persons when the vehicle does not display the distinguishing license plate, removable windshield

placard, or temporary removable windshield placard as provided in this section, or a disabled veteran registration plate issued under G.S. 20-79.4;

(2)   For any person not qualifying for the rights and privileges extended to handicapped persons under this section to exercise or attempt to exercise such rights or privileges by the unauthorized use of a distinguishing license plate, removable windshield placard, or temporary removable windshield placard issued pursuant to the provisions of this section;

(3)   To park or leave standing any vehicle so as to obstruct a curb ramp or curb cut for handicapped persons as provided for by the North Carolina Building Code or as designated in G.S. 136-44.14;

(4)   For those responsible for designating parking spaces for the handicapped to erect or otherwise use signs not conforming to G.S. 20-37.6(d) for this purpose.

This section is enforceable in all public vehicular areas.

(f)   Penalties for Violation. -

(1)   A violation of G.S. 20-37.6(e)(1), (2) or (3) is an infraction which carries a penalty of at least one hundred dollars ($100.00) but not more than two hundred fifty dollars ($250.00) and whenever evidence shall be presented in any court of the fact that any automobile, truck, or other vehicle was found to be parked in a properly designated handicapped parking space in violation of the provisions of this section, it shall be prima facie evidence in any court in the State of North Carolina that the vehicle was parked and left in the space by the person, firm, or corporation in whose name the vehicle is registered and licensed according to the records of the Division. No evidence tendered or presented under this authorization shall be admissible or competent in any respect in any court or tribunal except in cases concerned solely with a violation of this section.

(2)   A violation of G.S. 20-37.6(e)(4) is an infraction which carries a penalty of at least one hundred dollars ($100.00) but not more than two hundred fifty dollars ($250.00) and whenever evidence shall be presented in any court of the fact that a nonconforming sign is being used it shall be prima facie evidence in any court in the State of North Carolina that the person, firm, or corporation with ownership of the property where the nonconforming sign is located is responsible for violation of this section. Building inspectors and others

responsible for North Carolina State Building Code violations specified in G.S. 143-138(h) where such signs are required by the Handicapped Section of the North Carolina State Building Code, may cause a citation to be issued for this violation and may also initiate any appropriate action or proceeding to correct such violation.

(3)   A law-enforcement officer, including a company police officer commissioned by the Attorney General under Chapter 74E of the General Statutes, or a campus police officer commissioned by the Attorney General under Chapter 74G of the General Statutes, may cause a vehicle parked in violation of this section to be towed. The officer is a legal possessor as provided in G.S. 20-161(d)(2). The officer shall not be held to answer in any civil or criminal action to any owner, lienholder or other person legally entitled to the possession of any motor vehicle removed from a space pursuant to this section, except where the motor vehicle is willfully, maliciously, or negligently damaged in the removal from the space to a place of storage.

(4)   Notwithstanding any other provision of the General Statutes, the provisions of this section relative to handicapped parking shall be enforced by State, county, city and other municipal authorities in their respective jurisdictions whether on public or private property in the same manner as is used to enforce other parking laws and ordinances by said agencies. (1971, c. 374, s. 1; 1973, cc. 126, 1384; 1977, c. 340, s. 2; 1979, c. 632; 1981, c. 682, s. 7; 1983, c. 326, ss. 1, 2; 1985, c. 249; c. 586; c. 764, s. 24; 1985 (Reg. Sess., 1986), c. 852, s. 17; 1987, c. 843; 1989, c. 760, s. 3; 1989 (Reg. Sess., 1990), c. 1052, ss. 1-3.1; 1991, c. 411, s. 2; c. 530, s. 4; c. 672, s. 5; c. 726, s. 23; c. 761, s. 5; 1991 (Reg. Sess., 1992), c. 1007, s. 30; c. 1043, s. 4; 1993, c. 373, s. 1; 1994, Ex. Sess., c. 14, s. 31; 1999-265, s. 1; 2005-231, s. 11; 2009-493, s. 2.)

§ 20-37.6A. Parking privileges for out-of-state handicapped drivers and passengers.

Any vehicle displaying an out-of-State handicapped license plate, placard, or other evidence of handicap issued by the appropriate authority of the appropriate jurisdiction may park in any space reserved for the handicapped pursuant to G.S. 20-37.6. (1981, c. 48; 1991, c. 411, s. 3; 1991 (Reg. Sess., 1992), c. 1007, s. 31.)

Article 2B.

Special Identification Cards for Nonoperators.

§ 20-37.7. Special identification card.

(a) Eligibility. - A person who is a resident of this State is eligible for a special identification card.

(b) Application. - To obtain a special identification card from the Division, a person must complete the application form used to obtain a drivers license.

(b1) Search National Sex Offender Public Registry. - The Division shall not issue a special identification card to an applicant who has resided in this State for less than 12 months until the Division has searched the National Sex Offender Public Registry to determine if the person is currently registered as a sex offender in another state.

(1) If the Division finds that the person is currently registered as a sex offender in another state, the Division shall not issue a special identification card to the person until the person submits proof of registration pursuant to Article 27A of Chapter 14 of the General Statutes issued by the sheriff of the county where the person resides.

(2) If the person does not appear on the National Sex Offender Public Registry, the Division shall issue a special identification card but shall require the person to sign an affidavit acknowledging that the person has been notified that if the person is a sex offender, then the person is required to register pursuant to Article 27A of Chapter 14 of the General Statutes.

(3) If the Division is unable to access all states' information contained in the National Sex Offender Public Registry, but the person is otherwise qualified to obtain a special identification card, then the Division shall issue the card but shall first require the person to sign an affidavit stating that: (i) the person does not appear on the National Sex Offender Public Registry and (ii) acknowledging that the person has been notified that if the person is a sex offender, then the person is required to register pursuant to Article 27A of Chapter 14 of the General Statutes. The Division shall search the National Sex Offender Public Registry for the person within a reasonable time after access to the Registry is restored. If the person does appear in the National Sex Offender Public

Registry, the person is in violation of G.S. 20-37.8, and the Division shall promptly notify the sheriff of the county where the person resides of the offense.

(4) Any person denied a special identification card by the Division pursuant to this subsection shall have a right to file a petition within 30 days thereafter for a hearing in the matter in the superior court of the county wherein such person shall reside, or to the resident judge of the district or judge holding the court of that district, or special or emergency judge holding a court in such district, and such court or judge is hereby vested with jurisdiction, and it shall be its or his duty to set the matter for hearing upon 30 days' written notice to the Division, and thereupon to take testimony and examine into the facts of the case and to determine whether the petitioner is entitled to a special identification card under the provisions of this subsection and whether the petitioner is in violation of G.S. 20-37.8.

(c) (Effective until July 1, 2014) Format. - A special identification card shall be similar in size, shape, and design to a drivers license, but shall clearly state that it does not entitle the person to whom it is issued to operate a motor vehicle. A special identification card issued to an applicant must have the same background color that a drivers license issued to the applicant would have.

(c) (Effective July 1, 2014) Format. - A special identification card shall include a color photograph of the special identification card holder and be similar in size, shape, and design to a drivers license, but shall clearly state that it does not entitle the person to whom it is issued to operate a motor vehicle. A special identification card issued to an applicant must have the same background color that a drivers license issued to the applicant would have.

(d) Expiration and Fee. - A special identification card issued to a person for the first time under this section expires when a drivers license issued on the same day to that person would expire. A special identification card renewed under this section expires when a drivers license renewed by the card holder on the same day would expire.

The fee for a special identification card is the same as the fee set in G.S. 20-14 for a duplicate license. The fee does not apply to a special identification card issued to a resident of this State as follows:

(1) The applicant is legally blind.

(2) The applicant is at least 70 years old.

(3) The applicant or who has been issued a drivers license but the drivers license is cancelled under G.S. 20-15, in accordance with G.S. 20-9(e) and (g), as a result of a physical or mental disability or disease.

(4) The applicant is homeless. To obtain a special identification card without paying a fee, a homeless person must present a letter to the Division from the director of a facility that provides care or shelter to homeless persons verifying that the person is homeless.

(5) The applicant is registered to vote in this State and does not have photo identification acceptable under G.S. 163-166.13. To obtain a special identification card without paying a fee, a registered voter shall sign a declaration stating the registered voter is registered and does not have other photo identification acceptable under G.S. 163-166.13. The Division shall verify that voter registration prior to issuing the special identification card. Any declaration shall prominently include the penalty under G.S. 163-275(13) for falsely making the declaration.

(6) The applicant is appearing before the Division for the purpose of registering to vote in accordance with G.S. 163-82.19 and does not have other photo identification acceptable under G.S. 163-166.13. To obtain a special identification card without paying a fee, that applicant shall sign a declaration stating that applicant is registering to vote and does not have other photo identification acceptable under G.S. 163-166.13. Any declaration shall prominently include the penalty under G.S. 163-275(13) for falsely making the declaration.

(d1) (Effective July 1, 2014) For a person who has a physician's letter certifying that a severe disability causes the person to be homebound, the Division shall adopt rules allowing for application for or renewal of a special photo identification card under this section by means other than a personal appearance.

(e) Offense. - Any fraud or misrepresentation in the application for or use of a special identification card issued under this section is a Class 2 misdemeanor.

(f) Records. - The Division shall maintain a record of all recipients of a special identification card.

(g) No State Liability. - The fact of issuance of a special identification card pursuant to this section shall not place upon the State of North Carolina or any agency thereof any liability for the misuse thereof and the acceptance thereof as valid identification is a matter left entirely to the discretion of any person to whom such card is presented.

(h) Advertising. - The Division may utilize the various communications media throughout the State to inform North Carolina residents of the provisions of this section. (1973, c. 438, s. 1; 1975, c. 716, s. 5; 1979, c. 469, c. 667, s. 30; 1981, c. 673, ss. 1, 2; c. 690, s. 12; 1981 (Reg. Sess., 1982), c. 1257, s. 3; 1983, c. 443, s. 2; 1983 (Reg. Sess., 1984), c. 1062, s. 7; 1985, c. 141, s. 5; 1991, c. 689, s. 328; 1993, c. 368, s. 3; c. 490, ss. 1, 2; c. 539, s. 325; c. 553, s. 77; 1994, Ex. Sess., c. 24, s. 14(c); 1993 (Reg. Sess., 1994), c. 750, s. 2; 2006-247, s. 19(d); 2009-493, s. 3; 2013-233, ss. 1, 2; 2013-381, s. 3.1.)

§ 20-37.8. Fraudulent use prohibited.

(a) It shall be unlawful for any person to use a false or fictitious name or give a false or fictitious address in any application for a special identification card or knowingly to make a false statement or knowingly conceal a material fact or otherwise commit a fraud in any such application or to obtain or possess more than one such card for a fraudulent purpose or knowingly to permit or allow another to commit any of the foregoing acts.

(b) It shall be unlawful for any person to present, display, or use a special identification card which contains a false or fictitious name in the commission or attempted commission of a felony.

(c) A violation of subsection (a) of this section shall constitute a Class 2 misdemeanor. A violation of subsection (b) of this section shall constitute a Class I felony. (1979, c. 603, s. 1; 1993, c. 539, s. 326; 1994, Ex. Sess., c. 24, s. 14(c); 1999-299, s. 2.)

§ 20-37.9. Notice of change of address or name.

(a) Address. - A person whose address changes from the address stated on a special identification card must notify the Division of the change within 60 days after the change occurs. If the person's address changed because the person moved, the person must obtain a new special identification card within that time limit stating the new address. A person who does not move but whose address changes due to governmental action may not be charged with violating this subsection.

(b) Name. - A person whose name changes from the name stated on a special identification card must notify the Division of the change within 60 days after the change occurs and obtain a new special identification card stating the new name.

(c) Fee. - G.S. 20-37.7 sets the fee for a special identification card. (1981, c. 521, s. 2; 1991, c. 689, s. 329; 1997-122, s. 6.)

Article 2C.

Commercial Driver License.

§ 20-37.10. Title of Article.

This Article may be cited as the Commercial Driver License Act. (1989, c. 771, s. 2.)

§ 20-37.11. Purpose.

The purpose of this Article is to implement the federal Commercial Motor Vehicle Safety Act of 1986, 49 U.S.C. Chapter 36, and reduce or prevent commercial motor vehicle accidents, fatalities, and injuries by:

(1) Permitting commercial drivers to hold one license;

(2) Disqualifying commercial drivers who have committed certain serious traffic violations, or other specified offenses; and

(3) Strengthening commercial driver licensing and testing standards.

To the extent that this Article conflicts with general driver licensing provisions, this Article prevails. Where this Article is silent, the general driver licensing provisions apply. (1989, c. 771, s. 2.)

§ 20-37.12. Commercial drivers license required.

(a) On or after April 1, 1992, no person shall operate a commercial motor vehicle on the highways of this State unless he has first been issued and is in immediate possession of a commercial drivers license with applicable endorsements valid for the vehicle he is driving; provided, a person may operate a commercial motor vehicle after being issued and while in possession of a commercial driver learner's permit and while accompanied by the holder of a commercial drivers license valid for the vehicle being driven.

(b) The out-of-service criteria as referred to in 49 C.F.R. Subchapter B apply to a person who drives a commercial motor vehicle. No person shall drive a commercial motor vehicle on the highways of this State in violation of an out-of-service order.

(c) Repealed by Session Laws 1991, c. 726, s. 15.

(d) Any person who is not a resident of this State, who has been issued a commercial drivers license by his state of residence, or who holds any license recognized by the federal government that grants the privilege of driving a commercial motor vehicle, who has that license in his immediate possession, whose privilege to drive any motor vehicle is not suspended, revoked, or cancelled, and who has not been disqualified from driving a commercial motor vehicle shall be permitted without further examination or licensure by the Division to drive a commercial motor vehicle in this State.

(e) G.S. 20-7 sets the time period in which a new resident of North Carolina must obtain a license from the Division. The Commissioner may establish by rule the conditions under which the test requirements for a commercial drivers license may be waived for a new resident who is licensed in another state.

(f) A person shall not be convicted of failing to carry a commercial drivers license if, by the date the person is required to appear in court for the violation, the person produces to the court a commercial drivers license issued to the person that was valid on the date of the offense. (1989, c. 771, s. 2; 1991, c. 726, s. 15; 1997-122, s. 5; 1998-149, s. 4; 2003-397, s. 3; 2009-416, s. 5.)

§ 20-37.13. Commercial drivers license qualification standards.

(a) No person shall be issued a commercial drivers license unless the person:

(1) Is a resident of this State;

(2) Is 21 years of age;

(3) Has passed a knowledge test and a skills test for driving a commercial motor vehicle that comply with minimum federal standards established by federal regulation enumerated in 49 C.F.R., Part 383, Subparts F, G and H; and

(4) Has satisfied all other requirements of the Commercial Motor Vehicle Safety Act in addition to other requirements of this Chapter or federal regulation.

For the purpose of skills testing and determining commercial drivers license classification, only the manufacturer's GVWR shall be used.

The tests shall be prescribed and conducted by the Division. Provided, a person who is at least 18 years of age may be issued a commercial drivers license if the person is exempt from, or not subject to, the age requirements of the federal Motor Carrier Safety Regulations contained in 49 C.F.R., Part 391, as adopted by the Division.

(b) The Division may permit a person, including an agency of this or another state, an employer, a private driver training facility, or an agency of local government, to administer the skills test specified by this section, provided:

(1) The test is the same as that administered by the Division; and

(2) The third party has entered into an agreement with the Division which complies with the requirements of 49 C.F.R. § 383.75. The Division may charge a fee to applicants for third-party testing authority in order to investigate the applicants' qualifications and to monitor their program as required by federal law.

(b1) The Division shall allow a third party to administer a skills test for driving a commercial motor vehicle pursuant to subsection (b) of this section any day of the week.

(c) Prior to October 1, 1992, the Division may waive the skills test for applicants licensed at the time they apply for a commercial drivers license if:

(1) For an application submitted by April 1, 1992, the applicant has not, and certifies that he or she has not, at any time during the two years immediately preceding the date of application done any of the following and for an application submitted after April 1, 1992, the applicant has not, and certifies that he or she has not, at any time during the two years preceding April 1, 1992:

a. Had more than one drivers license, except during the 10-day period beginning on the date he or she is issued a drivers license, or unless, prior to December 31, 1989, he or she was required to have more than one license by a State law enacted prior to June 1, 1986;

b. Had any drivers license or driving privilege suspended, revoked, or cancelled;

c. Had any convictions involving any kind of motor vehicle for the offenses listed in G.S. 20-17 or had any convictions for the offenses listed in G.S. 20-17.4;

d. Been convicted of a violation of State or local laws relating to motor vehicle traffic control, other than a parking violation, which violation arose in connection with any reportable traffic accident; or

e. Refused to take a chemical test when charged with an implied consent offense, as defined in G.S. 20-16.2; and

(2) The applicant certifies, and provides satisfactory evidence, that he or she is regularly employed in a job requiring the operation of a commercial motor vehicle, and he or she either:

a. Has previously taken and successfully completed a skills test that was administered by a state with a classified licensing and testing system and the test was behind the wheel in a vehicle representative of the class and, if applicable, the type of commercial motor vehicle for which the applicant seeks to be licensed; or

b. Has operated for the relevant two-year period under subpart (1)a. of this subsection, a vehicle representative of the class and, if applicable, the type of commercial motor vehicle for which the applicant seeks to be licensed.

(c1) The Division may waive the skills test for any qualified military applicant at the time the applicant applies for a commercial drivers license if the applicant is currently licensed at the time of application and meets all of the following:

(1) The applicant has passed all required written knowledge exams.

(2) The applicant has not, and certifies that the applicant has not, at any time during the two years immediately preceding the date of application done any of the following:

a. Had any drivers license or driving privilege suspended, revoked, or cancelled.

b. Had any convictions involving any kind of motor vehicle for the offenses listed in G.S. 20-17 or had any convictions for the offenses listed in G.S. 20-17.4.

c. Been convicted of a violation of military, State, or local laws relating to motor vehicle traffic control, other than a parking violation, which violation arose in connection with any reportable traffic accident.

d. Refused to take a chemical test when charged with an implied consent offense, as defined in G.S. 20-16.2.

e. Had more than one drivers license, except for a drivers license issued by the military.

(3) The applicant certifies, and provides satisfactory evidence on the date of application, that the applicant is a retired, discharged, or current member of an active or reserve component of the Armed Forces of the United States and is regularly employed or was regularly employed within the 90-day period immediately preceding the date of application in a military position requiring the operation of a commercial motor vehicle, and the applicant meets either of the following requirements:

a. Repealed by Session Laws 2013-201, s. 1, effective June 26, 2013.

b. Has operated for the two-year period immediately preceding the date of application a vehicle representative of the class and, if applicable, the type of commercial motor vehicle for which the applicant seeks to be licensed, and has taken and successfully completed a skills test administered by the military.

c. For an applicant who is a retired or discharged member of an active or reserve component of the Armed Forces of the United States, the applicant (i) has operated for the two-year period immediately preceding the date of retirement or discharge a vehicle representative of the class and, if applicable, the type of commercial motor vehicle for which the applicant seeks to be licensed, and has taken and successfully completed a skills test administered by the military, (ii) has retired or received either an honorable or general discharge, and (iii) has retired or been discharged from the Armed Forces within the 90-day period immediately preceding the date of application.

(d) A commercial drivers license or learner's permit shall not be issued to a person while the person is subject to a disqualification from driving a commercial motor vehicle, or while the person's drivers license is suspended, revoked, or cancelled in any state; nor shall a commercial drivers license be issued unless the person who has applied for the license first surrenders all other drivers licenses issued by the Division or by another state. If a person surrenders a drivers license issued by another state, the Division must return the license to the issuing state for cancellation.

(e) A commercial driver learner's permit may be issued to an individual who holds a regular Class C drivers license and has passed the knowledge test for the class and type of commercial motor vehicle the individual will be driving. The permit is valid for a period not to exceed six months and may be renewed or reissued only once within a two-year period. The fee for a commercial driver learner's permit is the same as the fee set by G.S. 20-7 for a regular learner's permit. G.S. 20-7(m) governs the issuance of a restricted instruction permit for a prospective school bus driver.

(f) Notwithstanding subsection (e) of this section, a commercial driver learner's permit with a P or S endorsement shall not be issued to any person who is required to register under Article 27A of Chapter 14 of the General Statutes. (1989, c. 771, s. 2; 1991, c. 726, s. 16; 1991 (Reg. Sess., 1992), c.

916, s. 1; 2005-349, s. 8; 2009-274, s. 4; 2009-491, s. 5; 2009-494, s. 1; 2011-183, s. 22; 2013-195, s. 1; 2013-201, s. 1.)

§ 20-37.14. Nonresident commercial driver license.

The Division may issue a nonresident commercial driver license (NRCDL) to a resident of a foreign jurisdiction if the United States Secretary of Transportation has determined that the commercial motor vehicle testing and licensing standards in the foreign jurisdiction do not meet the testing standards established in 49 C.F.R., Part 383. The word "Nonresident" must appear on the face of the NRCDL. An applicant must surrender any NRCDL issued by another state. Prior to issuing a NRCDL, the Division shall establish the practical capability of revoking, suspending, or cancelling the NRCDL and disqualifying that person with the same conditions applicable to the commercial driver license issued to a resident of this State. (1989, c. 771, s. 2.)

§ 20-37.14A. Prohibit issuance or renewal of certain categories of commercial drivers licenses to sex offenders.

(a) Effective December 1, 2009, the Division shall not issue or renew a commercial drivers license with a P or S endorsement to any person who is required to register under Article 27A of Chapter 14 of the General Statutes.

(b) The Division shall not issue a commercial drivers license with a P or S endorsement to an applicant until the Division has searched both the statewide registry and the National Sex Offender Public Registry to determine if the person is currently registered as a sex offender in North Carolina or another state.

(1) If the Division finds that the person is currently registered as a sex offender in either North Carolina or another state, the Division, in compliance with subsection (a) of this section, shall not issue a commercial drivers license with a P or S endorsement to the person.

(2) If the Division is unable to access either the statewide registry or all of the states' information contained in the National Sex Offender Public Registry, but the person is otherwise qualified to obtain a commercial drivers license with

a P or S endorsement, then the Division shall issue the commercial drivers license with the P or S endorsement but shall first require the person to sign an affidavit stating that the person does not appear on either the statewide registry or the National Sex Offender Public Registry. The Division shall search the statewide registry and the National Sex Offender Public Registry for the person within a reasonable time after access to the statewide registry or the National Sex Offender Public Registry is restored. If the person does appear in either registry, the person is in violation of this section, and the Division shall immediately cancel the commercial drivers license and shall promptly notify the sheriff of the county where the person resides of the offense.

(3) Any person denied a commercial license with a P or S endorsement or who is disqualified from driving a commercial motor vehicle that requires a commercial drivers license with a P or S endorsement by the Division pursuant to this subsection shall have a right to file a petition within 30 days thereafter for a hearing in the matter, in the superior court of the county where the person resides, or to the resident judge of the district or judge holding the court of that district, or special or emergency judge holding a court in such district. The court or judge is vested with jurisdiction to hear the petition, and it shall be the duty of the judge or court to set the matter for hearing upon 30 days' written notice to the Division, and thereupon to take testimony and examine into the facts of the case and to determine whether the petitioner is entitled to a commercial drivers license with a P or S endorsement under the provisions of this subsection.

(c) Any person who makes a false affidavit, or who knowingly swears or affirms falsely, to any matter or thing required by the terms of this section to be affirmed to or sworn is guilty of a Class I felony. (2009-491, s. 6.)

§ 20-37.15. Application for commercial drivers license.

(a) An application for a commercial drivers license must include the information required by G.S. 20-7 for a regular drivers license and a consent to release driving record information.

(a1) The application must be accompanied by a nonrefundable application fee of thirty dollars ($30.00). This fee does not apply in any of the following circumstances:

(1) When an individual surrenders a commercial driver learner's permit issued by the Division when submitting the application.

(2) When the application is to renew a commercial drivers license issued by the Division.

This fee shall entitle the applicant to three attempts to pass the written knowledge test without payment of a new fee. No application fee shall be charged to an applicant eligible for a waiver under G.S. 20-37.13(c).

(b) When the holder of a commercial drivers license changes his name or residence address, an application for a duplicate shall be made as provided in G.S. 20-7.1 and a fee paid as provided in G.S. 20-14. (1989, c. 771, s. 2; 1991, c. 726, s. 17; 1993 (Reg. Sess., 1994), c. 750, s. 3; 2005-276, s. 44.1(f).)

§ 20-37.16. Content of license; classifications and endorsements; fees.

(a) A commercial drivers license must be marked "Commercial Drivers License" or "CDL" and must contain the information required by G.S. 20-7 for a regular drivers license.

(b) The classes of commercial drivers licenses are:

(1) Class A CDL - A Class A commercial drivers license authorizes the holder to drive any Class A motor vehicle.

(2) Class B CDL - A Class B commercial drivers license authorizes the holder to drive any Class B motor vehicle.

(3) Class C CDL - A Class C commercial drivers license authorizes the holder to drive any Class C motor vehicle.

(c) Endorsements. - The endorsements required to drive certain motor vehicles are as follows:

Endorsement   Vehicles That Can Be Driven

H   Vehicles, regardless of size or class, except tank vehicles, when transporting hazardous materials that require the vehicle to be placarded

M	Motorcycles
N	Tank vehicles not carrying hazardous materials
P	Vehicles carrying passengers
S	School bus
T	Double trailers
X	Tank vehicles carrying hazardous materials.

To qualify for any of the above endorsements, an applicant shall pass a knowledge test. To obtain an H or an X endorsement, an applicant must take a test. This requirement applies when a person first obtains an H or an X endorsement and each time a person renews an H or an X endorsement. An applicant who has an H or an X endorsement issued by another state who applies for an H or an X endorsement must take a test unless the person has passed a test that covers the information set out in 49 C.F.R. § 383.121 within the preceding two years.

(c1) Expired.

(c2) (For contingent effective date, see Editor's note) Expiration of H and X Endorsements. - Hazardous materials endorsements shall be renewed every five years or less so that individuals subject to a Transportation Security Administration security screening required pursuant to 49 C.F.R. § 383.141 may receive the screening and be authorized to renew the endorsements of H or X to transport hazardous materials. Notwithstanding G.S. 20-7(f), a commercial drivers license that contains an H or X endorsement as defined in subsection (c) of this section shall expire on the date of expiration of the licensee's security threat assessment conducted by the Transportation Security Administration of the United States Department of Homeland Security. When the commercial drivers license also contains an S endorsement and the licensee is certified to drive a school bus in this State, the commercial drivers license shall expire as provided in G.S. 20-7(f). The H and X endorsements on a commercial drivers license shall expire when the commercial drivers license expires.

(d) The fee for a Class A, B, or C commercial drivers license is fifteen dollars ($15.00) for each year of the period for which the license is issued. The fee for each endorsement is three dollars ($3.00) for each year of the period for which the endorsement is issued. The fees required under this section do not apply to employees of the Driver License Section of the Division who are designated by the Commissioner.

(e)   The requirements for a commercial drivers license do not apply to vehicles used for personal use such as recreational vehicles. A commercial drivers license is also waived for the following classes of vehicles as permitted by regulation of the United States Department of Transportation:

(1)   Vehicles owned or operated by the Department of Defense, including the National Guard, while they are driven by active duty military personnel, or members of the National Guard when on active duty, in the pursuit of military purposes.

(2)   Any vehicle when used as firefighting or emergency equipment for the purpose of preserving life or property or to execute emergency governmental functions.

(3)   A farm vehicle that meets all of the following criteria:

a.   Is controlled and operated by the farmer or the farmer's employee and used exclusively for farm use.

b.   Is used to transport either agricultural products, farm machinery, or farm supplies, both to or from a farm.

c.   Is not used in the operations of a for-hire motor carrier.

d.   Is used within 150 miles of the farmer's farm.

A farm vehicle includes a forestry vehicle that meets the listed criteria when applied to the forestry operation.

(f)   For the purposes of this section, the term "school bus" has the same meaning as in 49 C.F.R. § 383.5. (1989, c. 771, s. 2; 1991, c. 726, s. 18; 1993, c. 368, s. 4; 1993 (Reg. Sess., 1994), c. 750, ss. 4, 6; 1995 (Reg. Sess., 1996), c. 695, s. 1; c. 756, s. 5; 1998-149, s. 5; 2003-397, ss. 4, 5; 2005-276, s. 44.1(g); 2005-349, s. 9; 2011-228, s. 1; 2012-85, s. 3.)

§ 20-37.17. Record check and notification of license issuance.

Before issuing a commercial driver license, the Division shall obtain driving record information from the Commercial Driver License Information System (CDLIS), the National Driver Register, and from each state in which the person has been licensed.

Within 10 days after issuing a commercial driver license, the Division shall notify CDLIS of the issuance of the commercial driver license, providing all information necessary to ensure identification of the person. (1989, c. 771, s. 2.)

§ 20-37.18. Notification required by driver.

(a) Any driver holding a commercial driver license issued by this State who is convicted of violating any State law or local ordinance relating to motor vehicle traffic control in any other state, other than parking violations, shall notify the Division in the manner specified by the Division within 30 days of the date of the conviction.

(b) Any driver holding a commercial driver license issued by this State who is convicted of violating any State law or local ordinance relating to motor vehicle traffic control in this or any other state, other than parking violations, shall notify his employer in writing of the conviction within 30 days of the date of conviction.

(c) Any driver whose commercial driver license is suspended, revoked, or cancelled by any state, or who loses the privilege to drive a commercial motor vehicle in any state for any period, including being disqualified from driving a commercial motor vehicle, or who is subject to an out-of-service order, shall notify his employer of that fact before the end of the business day following the day the driver received notice of that fact.

(d) Any person who applies to be a commercial motor vehicle driver shall provide the employer, at the time of the application, with the following information for the 10 years preceding the date of application:

(1) A list of the names and addresses of the applicant's previous employers for which the applicant was a driver of a commercial motor vehicle;

(2) The dates between which the applicant drove for each employer; and

(3) The reason for leaving that employer.

The applicant shall certify that all information furnished is true and complete. Any employer may require an applicant to provide additional information. (1989, c. 771, s. 2.)

§ 20-37.19. Employer responsibilities.

(a) Each employer shall require the applicant to provide the information specified in G.S. 20-37.18(c).

(b) No employer shall knowingly allow, permit, or authorize a driver to drive a commercial motor vehicle during any period:

(1) In which the driver has had his commercial driver license suspended, revoked, or cancelled by any state, is currently disqualified from driving a commercial vehicle, or is subject to an out-of-service order in any state; or

(2) In which the driver has more than one driver license; [or]

(3) In which the driver, the commercial motor vehicle being operated, or the motor carrier operation, is subject to an out-of-service order.

(c) The employer of any employee or applicant who tests positive or of any employee who refuses to participate in a drug or alcohol test required under 49 C.F.R. Part 382 and 49 C.F.R. Part 655 must notify the Division in writing within five business days following the employer's receipt of confirmation of a positive drug or alcohol test or of the employee's refusal to participate in the test. The notification must include the driver's name, address, drivers license number, social security number, and results of the drug or alcohol test or documentation from the employer of the refusal by the employee to take the test. (1989, c. 771, s. 2; 2005-156, s. 1; 2007-492, s. 2; 2009-416, s. 6.)

§ 20-37.20. Notification of traffic convictions.

(a) Out-of-state Resident. - Within 10 days after receiving a report of the conviction of any nonresident holder of a commercial driver license for any violation of State law or local ordinance relating to motor vehicle traffic control, other than parking violations, committed in a commercial vehicle, the Division shall notify the driver licensing authority in the licensing state of the conviction.

(b) (For effective date, see note) Foreign Diplomat. - The Division must notify the United States Department of State within 15 days after it receives one or more of the following reports for a holder of a drivers license issued by the United States Department of State:

(1) A report of a conviction for a violation of State law or local ordinance relating to motor vehicle traffic control, other than parking violations.

(2) A report of a civil revocation order. (1989, c. 771, s. 2; 2001-498, s. 7; 2002-159, s. 31; 2006-209, s. 7.)

§ 20-37.20A. Driving record notation for testing positive in a drug or alcohol test.

Upon receipt of notice pursuant to G.S. 20-37.19(c) of positive result in an alcohol or drug test of a person holding a commercial drivers license, and subject to any appeal of the disqualification pursuant to G.S. 20-37.20B, the Division shall place a notation on the driving record of the driver. A notation of a disqualification pursuant to G.S. 20-17.4(l) shall be retained on the record of a person for a period of three years following the end of any disqualification of that person. (2005-156, s. 3; 2008-175, s. 2.)

§ 20-37.20B. Appeal of disqualification for testing positive in a drug or alcohol test.

Following receipt of notice pursuant to G.S. 20-37.19(c) of a positive test in an alcohol or drug test, the Division shall notify the driver of the pending disqualification of the driver to operate a commercial vehicle and the driver's right to a hearing if requested within 20 days of the date of the notice. If the Division receives no request for a hearing, the disqualification shall become effective at the end of the 20-day period. If the driver requests a hearing, the disqualification shall be stayed pending outcome of the hearing. The hearing shall take place at the offices of the Division of Motor Vehicles in Raleigh. The hearing shall be limited to issues of testing procedure and protocol. A copy of a positive test result accompanied by certification by the testing officer of the accuracy of the laboratory protocols that resulted in the test result shall be prima facie evidence of a confirmed positive test result. The decision of the Division hearing officer may be appealed in accordance with the procedure of G.S. 20-19(c6). (2005-156, s. 4.)

§ 20-37.21. Penalties.

(a) Any person who drives a commercial motor vehicle in violation of G.S. 20-37.12 shall be guilty of a Class 3 misdemeanor and, upon conviction, shall be fined not less than two hundred fifty dollars ($250.00) for a first offense and not less than five hundred dollars ($500.00) for a second or subsequent offense. In addition, the person shall be subject to a civil penalty pursuant to the provisions of 49 C.F.R. § 383.53(b).

(b) Any person who violates G.S. 20-37.18 shall have committed an infraction and, upon being found responsible, shall pay a penalty of not less than one hundred dollars ($100.00) nor more than five hundred dollars ($500.00).

(c) Any employer who violates G.S. 20-37.19 shall have committed an infraction and, upon being found responsible, shall pay a penalty of not less than five hundred dollars ($500.00) nor more than one thousand dollars ($1,000). In addition, upon conviction, the employer shall be subject to a civil penalty of not less than two thousand seven hundred fifty dollars ($2,750) nor more than eleven thousand dollars ($11,000).

(d) An employer who knowingly allows, requires, permits, or otherwise authorizes an employee to violate any railroad grade requirements contained in G.S. 20-142.1 through G.S. 20-142.5 shall pay a civil penalty of not more than ten thousand dollars ($10,000). (1989, c. 771, s. 2; 1993, c. 539, s. 327; 1994, Ex. Sess., c. 24, s. 14(c); 2005-349, s. 10; 2009-416, s. 7.)

§ 20-37.22. Rule making authority.

The Division may adopt any rules necessary to carry out the provisions of this Article. (1989, c. 771, s. 2.)

§ 20-37.23. Authority to enter agreements.

The Commissioner shall have the authority to execute or make agreements, arrangements, or declarations to carry out the provisions of this Article. (1989, c. 771, s. 2.)

§ 20-38: Repealed by Session Laws 1973, c. 1330, s. 39.

Article 2D.

Implied-Consent Offense Procedures.

§ 20-38.1. Applicability.

The procedures set forth in this Article shall be followed for the investigation and processing of an implied-consent offense as defined in G.S. 20-16.2. The trial procedures shall apply to any implied-consent offense litigated in the District Court Division. (2006-253, s. 5.)

§ 20-38.2. Investigation.

A law enforcement officer who is investigating an implied-consent offense or a vehicle crash that occurred in the officer's territorial jurisdiction is authorized to investigate and seek evidence of the driver's impairment anywhere in-state or out-of-state, and to make arrests at any place within the State. (2006-253, s. 5.)

§ 20-38.3. Police processing duties.

Upon the arrest of a person, with or without a warrant, but not necessarily in the order listed, a law enforcement officer:

(1) Shall inform the person arrested of the charges or a cause for the arrest.

(2) May take the person arrested to any place within the State for one or more chemical analyses at the request of any law enforcement officer and for any evaluation by a law enforcement officer, medical professional, or other person to determine the extent or cause of the person's impairment.

(3) May take the person arrested to some other place within the State for the purpose of having the person identified, to complete a crash report, or for any other lawful purpose.

(4) May take photographs and fingerprints in accordance with G.S. 15A-502.

(5) Shall take the person arrested before a judicial official for an initial appearance after completion of all investigatory procedures, crash reports, chemical analyses, and other procedures provided for in this section. (2006-253, s. 5.)

§ 20-38.4. Initial appearance.

(a) Appearance Before a Magistrate. - Except as modified in this Article, a magistrate shall follow the procedures set forth in Article 24 of Chapter 15A of the General Statutes.

(1) A magistrate may hold an initial appearance at any place within the county and shall, to the extent practicable, be available at locations other than the courthouse when it will expedite the initial appearance.

(2) In determining whether there is probable cause to believe a person is impaired, the magistrate may review all alcohol screening tests, chemical analyses, receive testimony from any law enforcement officer concerning impairment and the circumstances of the arrest, and observe the person arrested.

(3) If there is a finding of probable cause, the magistrate shall consider whether the person is impaired to the extent that the provisions of G.S. 15A-534.2 should be imposed.

(4) The magistrate shall also:

a. Inform the person in writing of the established procedure to have others appear at the jail to observe his condition or to administer an additional chemical analysis if the person is unable to make bond; and

b. Require the person who is unable to make bond to list all persons he wishes to contact and telephone numbers on a form that sets forth the procedure for contacting the persons listed. A copy of this form shall be filed with the case file.

(b) The Administrative Office of the Courts shall adopt forms to implement this Article. (2006-253, s. 5.)

§ 20-38.5. Facilities.

(a) The Chief District Court Judge, the Department of Health and Human Services, the district attorney, and the sheriff shall:

(1) Establish a written procedure for attorneys and witnesses to have access to the chemical analysis room.

(2) Approve the location of written notice of implied-consent rights in the chemical analysis room in accordance with G.S. 20-16.2.

(3) Approve a procedure for access to a person arrested for an implied-consent offense by family and friends or a qualified person contacted by the arrested person to obtain blood or urine when the arrested person is held in custody and unable to obtain pretrial release from jail.

(b) Signs shall be posted explaining to the public the procedure for obtaining access to the room where the chemical analysis of the breath is administered and to any person arrested for an implied-consent offense. The initial signs shall be provided by the Department of Transportation, without costs. The signs shall thereafter be maintained by the county for all county buildings and the county courthouse.

(c)   If the instrument for performing a chemical analysis of the breath is located in a State or municipal building, then the head of the highway patrol for the county, the chief of police for the city or that person's designee shall be substituted for the sheriff when determining signs and access to the chemical analysis room. The signs shall be maintained by the owner of the building. When a breath testing instrument is in a motor vehicle or at a temporary location, the Department of Health and Human Services shall alone perform the functions listed in subdivisions (a)(1) and (a)(2) of this section. (2006-253, s. 5.)

§ 20-38.6. Motions and district court procedure.

(a)   The defendant may move to suppress evidence or dismiss charges only prior to trial, except the defendant may move to dismiss the charges for insufficient evidence at the close of the State's evidence and at the close of all of the evidence without prior notice. If, during the course of the trial, the defendant discovers facts not previously known, a motion to suppress or dismiss may be made during the trial.

(b)   Upon a motion to suppress or dismiss the charges, other than at the close of the State's evidence or at the close of all the evidence, the State shall be granted reasonable time to procure witnesses or evidence and to conduct research required to defend against the motion.

(c)   The judge shall summarily grant the motion to suppress evidence if the State stipulates that the evidence sought to be suppressed will not be offered in evidence in any criminal action or proceeding against the defendant.

(d)   The judge may summarily deny the motion to suppress evidence if the defendant failed to make the motion pretrial when all material facts were known to the defendant.

(e)   If the motion is not determined summarily, the judge shall make the determination after a hearing and finding of facts. Testimony at the hearing shall be under oath.

(f) The judge shall set forth in writing the findings of fact and conclusions of law and preliminarily indicate whether the motion should be granted or denied. If the judge preliminarily indicates the motion should be granted, the judge shall not enter a final judgment on the motion until after the State has appealed to superior court or has indicated it does not intend to appeal. (2006-253, s. 5.)

§ 20-38.7. Appeal to superior court.

(a) The State may appeal to superior court any district court preliminary determination granting a motion to suppress or dismiss. If there is a dispute about the findings of fact, the superior court shall not be bound by the findings of the district court but shall determine the matter de novo. Any further appeal shall be governed by Article 90 of Chapter 15A of the General Statutes.

(b) The defendant may not appeal a denial of a pretrial motion to suppress or to dismiss but may appeal upon conviction as provided by law.

(c) Notwithstanding the provisions of G.S. 15A-1431, for any implied-consent offense that is first tried in district court and that is appealed to superior court by the defendant for a trial de novo as a result of a conviction, the sentence imposed by the district court is vacated upon giving notice of appeal. The case shall only be remanded back to district court with the consent of the prosecutor and the superior court. When an appeal is withdrawn or a case is remanded back to district court, the district court shall hold a new sentencing hearing and shall consider any new convictions.

(d) Following a new sentencing hearing in district court pursuant to subsection (c) of this section, a defendant has a right of appeal to the superior court only if:

(1) The sentence is based upon additional facts considered by the district court that were not considered in the previously vacated sentence, and

(2) The defendant would be entitled to a jury determination of those facts pursuant to G.S. 20-179.

A defendant who has a right of appeal under this subsection, gives notice of appeal, and subsequently withdraws the appeal shall have the sentence imposed by the district court reinstated by the district court as a final judgment that is not subject to further appeal. (2006-253, s. 5; 2007-493, s. 9; 2008-187, s. 10.)

Article 3.

Motor Vehicle Act of 1937.

Part 1. General Provisions.

§ 20-38.100: Reserved for future codification purposes.

Part 2. Authority and Duties of Commissioner and Division.

§ 20-39. Administering and enforcing laws; rules and regulations; agents, etc.; seal; fees.

(a)   The Commissioner is hereby vested with the power and is charged with the duty of administering and enforcing the provisions of this Article and of all laws regulating the operation of vehicles or the use of the highways, the enforcement or administration of which is now or hereafter vested in the Division.

(b)   The Commissioner is hereby authorized to adopt and enforce such rules and regulations as may be necessary to carry out the provisions of this Article and any other laws the enforcement and administration of which are vested in the Division.

(c)   The Commissioner is authorized to designate and appoint such agents, field deputies, and clerks as may be necessary to carry out the provisions of this Article.

(d)   The Commissioner shall adopt an official seal for the use of the Division.

(e)   The Commissioner is authorized to cooperate with and provide assistance to the Environmental Management Commission, or appropriate local government officials, and to develop, adopt, and ensure enforcement of necessary rules and regulations, regarding programs of motor vehicle emissions inspection/maintenance required for areas in which ambient air pollutant concentrations exceed National Ambient Air Quality Standards.

(f) The Commissioner is authorized to charge and collect the following fees for the verification of equipment to be used on motor vehicles or to be sold in North Carolina, when that approval is required pursuant to this Chapter:

(1) When a federal standard has been established, the fee shall be equal to the cost of verifying compliance with the applicable federal standard; or.

(2) When no federal standard has been established, the fee shall be equal to the cost of verifying compliance with the applicable State standard. Any motor vehicle manufacturer or distributor who is required to certify his products under the National Traffic and Motor Vehicle Safety Act of 1966, as from time to time amended, may satisfy the provisions of this section by submitting an annual written certification to the Commissioner attesting to the compliance of his vehicles with applicable federal requirements. Failure to comply with the certification requirement or failure to meet the federal standards will subject the manufacturer or distributor to the fee requirements of this subsection.

(g), (h) Repealed by Session Laws 2001-424, s. 6.14(e).

(i) Notwithstanding the requirements of G.S. 20-7.1 and G.S. 20-67(a), the Commissioner may correct the address records of drivers license and registration plate holders as shown in the files of the Division to that shown on notices and renewal cards returned to the Division with new addresses provided by the United States Postal Service. (1937, c. 407, s. 4; 1975, c. 716, s. 5; 1979, 2nd Sess., c. 1180, s. 1; 1983, c. 223; c. 629, s. 2; c. 768, ss. 25.1, 25.2; 1985, c. 767, ss. 1, 2; 1987, c. 552; 1991, c. 53, s. 1; c. 654, s. 1; 1993, c. 539, s. 328; 1994, Ex. Sess., c. 24, s. 14(c); 1995, c. 507, s. 6.2(b); 1996, 2nd Ex. Sess., c. 18, s. 23(a); 1997-256, s. 8; 1997-347, s. 4; 1997-401, s. 4; 1997-418, s. 3; 1997-443, s. 20.10(a), (b); 2001-424, ss. 6.14(e), 6.14(f).)

§ 20-39.1. Publicly owned vehicles to be marked; private license plates on publicly owned vehicles.

(a) Except as otherwise provided in this section, the executive head of every department of State government and every county, institution, or agency of the State shall mark every motor vehicle owned by the State, county, institution, or agency with a statement that the vehicle belongs to the State, county, institution, or agency. The requirements of this subsection are complied with if:

(1) The vehicle has imprinted on the license plate, above the license number, the words "State Owned" and the vehicle has affixed to the front the words "State Owned";

(2) In the case of a county, the vehicle has painted or affixed on its side a circle not less than eight inches in diameter showing a replica of the seal of the county; or

(3) In the case of vehicles assigned to members of the Council of State, the vehicle has imprinted on the license plate the license number assigned to the appropriate member of the Council of State pursuant to G.S. 20-79.5(a); a member of the Council of State shall not be assessed any registration fee if the member elects to have a State-owned motor vehicle assigned to the member designated by the official plate number.

(b) A motor vehicle used by any State or county officer or official for transporting, apprehending, or arresting persons charged with violations of the laws of the United States or the laws of this State is not required to be marked as provided in subsection (a) of this section. The Commissioner may lawfully provide private license plates to local, State, or federal departments or agencies for use on publicly owned or leased vehicles used for those purposes. Private license plates issued under this subsection shall be issued on an annual basis and the records of issuance shall be maintained in accordance with the provisions of G.S. 20-56.

(c) A motor vehicle used by a county for transporting day or residential facility clients of area mental health, developmental disabilities, and substance abuse authorities established under Article 4 of Chapter 122C of the General Statutes is not required to be marked as provided in subsection (a) of this section. The Commissioner may lawfully provide private license plates to counties for use on publicly owned or leased vehicles used for that purpose. Private license plates issued under this subsection shall be issued on an annual basis and the records of issuance shall be maintained in accordance with the provisions of G.S. 20-56.

(d) For purposes of this section, the term "private license plate" refers to a license plate that would normally be issued to a private party and therefore lacks any markings indicating that it has been assigned to a publicly owned vehicle. "Confidential" license plates are a specialized form of private license plate for which a confidential registration has been authorized under subsection (e) of this section. "Fictitious" license plates are a specialized form of private license plate for which a fictitious registration has been issued under subsection (f) or (g) of this section.

(e) Upon approval and request of the Director of the State Bureau of Investigation, the Commissioner shall issue confidential license plates to local, State, or federal law enforcement agencies, the Department of Public Safety, agents of the Internal Revenue Service, and agents of the Department of Defense in accordance with the provisions of this subsection. Applicants in these categories shall provide satisfactory evidence to the Director of the State Bureau of Investigation of the following:

(1) The confidential license plate requested is to be used on a publicly owned or leased vehicle that is primarily used for transporting, apprehending, or arresting persons charged with violations of the laws of the United States or the State of North Carolina;

(2) The use of a confidential license plate is necessary to protect the personal safety of an officer or for placement on a vehicle used primarily for surveillance or undercover operations; and

(3) The application contains an original signature of the head of the requesting agency or department or, in the case of a federal agency, the signature of the senior ranking officer for that agency in this State.

Confidential license plates issued under this subsection shall be issued on an annual basis and the Division shall maintain a separate registration file for vehicles bearing confidential license plates. That file shall be confidential for the use of the Division and is not a public record within the meaning of Chapter 132 of the General Statutes. Upon the annual renewal of the registration of a vehicle for which a confidential status has been established under this section, the registration shall lose its confidential status unless the agency or department supplies the Director of the State Bureau of Investigation with information demonstrating that an officer's personal safety remains at risk or that the vehicle is still primarily used for surveillance or undercover operations at the time of renewal.

(f) The Commissioner may to the extent necessary provide law enforcement officers of the Division on special undercover assignments with motor vehicle operator's licenses and motor vehicle license plates under assumed names, using false or fictitious addresses. The Commissioner shall be responsible for the request for issuance and use of such licenses and license plates, and may direct the immediate return of any license or license plate issued pursuant to this subsection.

(g) The Commissioner may, upon the request of the Director of the State Bureau of Investigation and to the extent necessary, lawfully provide local, State, and federal law enforcement officers on special undercover assignments and to agents of the Department of Defense with motor vehicle drivers licenses and motor vehicle license plates under assumed names, using false or fictitious addresses. Fictitious license plates shall only be used on publicly owned or leased vehicles. A request for fictitious licenses and license plates by a local, State or federal law enforcement agency or department or by the Department of Defense shall be made in writing to the Director of the State Bureau of Investigation and shall contain an original signature of the head of the requesting agency or department or, in the case of a federal agency, the signature of the senior ranking officer for that agency in this State.

Prior to the issuance of any fictitious license or license plate, the Director of the State Bureau of Investigation shall make a specific written finding that the request is justified and necessary. The Director shall maintain a record of all such licenses, license plates, assumed names, false or fictitious addresses, and law enforcement officers using the licenses or license plates. That record shall be confidential and is not a public record within the meaning of Chapter 132 of the General Statutes. The Director shall request the immediate return of any license or registration that is no longer necessary.

Licenses and license plates provided under this subsection shall expire six months after initial issuance unless the Director of the State Bureau of Investigation has approved an extension in writing. The head of the local, State, or federal law enforcement agency or the Department of Defense shall be responsible for the use of the licenses and license plates and shall return them immediately to the Director for cancellation upon either (i) their expiration, (ii) request of the Director of the State Bureau of Investigation, or (iii) request of the Commissioner. Failure to return a license or license plate issued pursuant to this subsection shall be punished as a Class 2 misdemeanor. At no time shall the number of valid licenses issued under this subsection exceed two hundred nor shall the number of valid license plates issued under this subsection exceed one hundred twenty-five unless the Director determines that exceptional circumstances justify exceeding those amounts. However, fictitious licenses and license plates issued to special agents of the State Bureau of Investigation, State alcohol law enforcement agents, and the Department of Defense shall not be counted against the limitation on the total number of fictitious licenses and plates established by this subsection and shall be renewable annually.

(h)   No private, confidential, or fictitious license plates issued under this section shall be used on privately owned vehicles under any circumstances.

(i)   The Commissioner shall administer the issuance of private plates for publicly owned vehicles under the provisions of this section to ensure strict compliance with those provisions. The Division shall report to the Joint Legislative Commission on Governmental Operations by January 1 and July 1 of each year on the total number of private plates issued to each agency, and the total number of fictitious licenses and plates issued by the Division. (2001-424, s. 6.14(a); 2001-424, s. 6.14(b); 2001-487, ss. 53, 54; 2003-152, ss. 3, 4; 2003-284, ss. 6.5(a), (b); 2004-124, s. 6.5(a), (b); 2005-276, s. 6.18(a); 2011-145, s. 19.1(g).)

§ 20-40. Offices of Division.

The Commissioner shall maintain an office in Raleigh, North Carolina, and in such places in the State as he shall deem necessary to properly carry out the provisions of this Article. (1937, c. 407, s. 5.)

§ 20-41. Commissioner to provide forms required.

The Commissioner shall provide suitable forms for applications, certificates of title and registration cards, registration number plates and all other forms requisite for the purpose of this Article, and shall prepay all transportation charges thereon. (1937, c. 407, s. 6.)

§ 20-42. Authority to administer oaths and certify copies of records.

(a) Officers and employees of the Division designated by the Commissioner are, for the purpose of administering the motor vehicle laws, authorized to administer oaths and acknowledge signatures, and shall charge for the acknowledgment of signatures a fee according to the following schedule:

(1) One signature $2.00

(2) Two signatures 3.00

(3) Three or more signatures 4.00

Funds received under the provisions of this subsection shall be used to defray a part of the costs of distribution of license plates, registration certificates and certificates of title issued by the Division.

(b) The Commissioner and officers of the Division designated by the Commissioner may prepare under the seal of the Division and deliver upon request a certified copy of any document of the Division for a fee. The fee for a document, other than an accident report under G.S. 20-166.1, is ten dollars ($10.00). The fee for an accident report is five dollars ($5.00). A certified copy shall be admissible in any proceeding in any court in like manner as the original thereof, without further certification. The certification fee does not apply to a document furnished for official use to a judicial official or to an official of the federal government, a state government, or a local government. (1937, c. 407, s. 7; 1955, c. 480; 1961, c. 861, s. 1; 1967, c. 691, s. 41; c. 1172; 1971, c. 749; 1975, c. 716, s. 5; 1977, c. 785; 1979, c. 801, s. 7; 1981, c. 690, ss. 22, 23; 1991, c. 689, s. 331; 1995, c. 191, s. 8; 2005-276, s. 44.1(h).)

§ 20-43. Records of Division.

(a) All records of the Division, other than those declared by law to be confidential for the use of the Division, shall be open to public inspection during office hours in accordance with G.S. 20-43.1. A signature recorded in any format by the Division for a drivers license or a special identification card is confidential and shall not be released except for law enforcement purposes. A photographic image recorded in any format by the Division for a drivers license or a special identification card is confidential and shall not be released except for law enforcement purposes or to the Office of the State Controller for the purposes of G.S. 143B-426.38A.

(b) The Commissioner, upon receipt of notification from another state or foreign country that a certificate of title issued by the Division has been surrendered by the owner in conformity with the laws of such other state or foreign country, may cancel and destroy such record of certificate of title. (1937, c. 407, s. 8; 1947, c. 219, s. 1; 1971, c. 1070, s. 1; 1975, c. 716, s. 5; 1995, c. 195, s. 1; 1997-443, s. 32.25(d); 2013-360, s. 7.10(b).)

§ 20-43.1. Disclosure of personal information in motor vehicle records.

(a) The Division shall disclose personal information contained in motor vehicle records in accordance with the federal Driver's Privacy Protection Act of 1994, as amended, 18 U.S.C. §§ 2721, et seq.

(b) As authorized in 18 U.S.C. § 2721, the Division shall not disclose personal information for the purposes specified in 18 U.S.C. § 2721(b)(11).

(c) The Division shall not disclose personal information for the purposes specified in 18 U.S.C. § 2721(b)(12) unless the Division receives prior written permission from the person about whom the information is requested.

(d) As authorized in 18 U.S.C. § 2721, the Division may disclose personal information to federally designated organ procurement organizations and eye banks operating in this State for the purpose of identifying individuals who have indicated an intent to be an organ donor. Personal information authorized under this subsection is limited to the individual's first, middle, and last name, date of birth, address, sex, county of residence, and drivers license number. Employees of the Division who provide access to or disclosure of information in good-faith compliance with this subsection are not liable in damages for access to or disclosure of the information.

(e) As authorized in 18 U.S.C. § 2721, the Division may also provide copies of partial crash report data collected pursuant to G.S. 20-166.1, partial driver license data kept pursuant to G.S. 20-26(a), and partial vehicle registration application data collected pursuant to G.S. 20-52 in bulk form to persons, private companies, or other entities, for uses other than official, upon payment of a fee of three cents (3¢) per individual record. The Division shall not furnish such data except upon execution by the recipient of a written agreement to comply with the Driver's Privacy Protection Act of 1994, as amended, 18 U.S.C.

§§ 2721, et seq. The information released to persons, private companies, or other entities, for uses other than official, pursuant to this subsection, shall not be a public record pursuant to Chapter 132 of the General Statutes. (1997-443, s. 32.25(a); 1999-237, s. 27.9(b); 2004-189, s. 2; 2011-145, s. 31.29.)

§ 20-43.2. Internet access to organ donation records by organ procurement organizations.

(a) The Department of Transportation, Division of Motor Vehicles, shall establish and maintain a statewide, online Organ Donor Registry Internet site (hereafter "Donor Registry"). The purpose of the Donor Registry is to enable federally designated organ procurement organizations and eye banks to have access 24 hours per day, seven days per week to obtain relevant information on the Donor Registry to determine, at or near death of the donor or a prospective donor, whether the donor or prospective donor has made, amended, or revoked an anatomical gift through a symbol on the donor's or prospective donor's drivers license, special identification card, or other manner. The data available on the Donor Registry shall be limited to the individual's first, middle, and last name, date of birth, address, sex, county of residence, and drivers license number. The Division of Motor Vehicles shall ensure that only federally designated organ procurement organizations and eye banks operating in this State have access to the Donor Registry in read-only format. The Division of Motor Vehicles shall enable federally designated organ procurement organizations and eye banks operating in this State to have online access in read-only format to the Donor Registry through a unique identifier and password issued to the organ procurement organization or eye bank by the Division of Motor Vehicles. Employees of the Division who provide access to or disclosure of information in good-faith compliance with this section are not liable in damages for access to or disclosure of the information.

(b) When accessing and using information obtained from the Donor Registry, federally designated organ procurement organizations and eye banks shall comply with the requirements of Part 3A of Article 16 of Chapter 130A of the General Statutes.

(c) Personally identifiable information on a donor registry about a donor or prospective donor may not be used or disclosed without the express consent of the donor, prospective donor, or person that made the anatomical gift for any purpose other than to determine, at or near death of the donor or prospective donor, whether the donor or prospective donor has made, amended, or revoked an anatomical gift.

(d) This section does not prohibit any person from creating or maintaining a donor registry that is not established by or under contract with the State. Any such registry must comply with subsections (b) and (c) of this section. (2004-189, s. 1; 2007-538, s. 2.)

§ 20-43.3. Reserved for future codification purposes.

§ 20-43.4. Current list of licensed drivers to be provided to jury commissions.

(a) The Commissioner of Motor Vehicles shall provide to each county jury commission an alphabetical list of all persons that the Commissioner has determined are residents of the county, who will be 18 years of age or older as of the first day of January of the following year, and licensed to drive a motor vehicle as of July 1 of each odd-numbered year, provided that if an annual master jury list is being prepared under G.S. 9-2(a), the list to be provided to the county jury commission shall be updated and provided annually.

(b) The list shall include those persons whose license to drive has been suspended, and those former licensees whose license has been canceled, except that the list shall not include the name of any formerly licensed driver whose license is expired and has not been renewed for eight years or more. The list shall contain the address and zip code of each driver, plus the driver's date of birth, sex, social security number, and drivers license number, and may be in either printed or computerized form, as requested by each county. Before providing the list to the county jury commission, the Commissioner shall have computer-matched the list with the voter registration list of the State Board of Elections to eliminate duplicates. The Commissioner shall also remove from the list the names of those residents of the county who are (i) issued a drivers license of limited duration under G.S. 20-7(s), (ii) issued a drivers license of regular duration under G.S. 20-7(f) and who hold a valid permanent resident card issued by the United States, or (iii) who are recently deceased, which names shall be supplied to the Commissioner by the State Registrar under G.S. 130A-121(b). The Commissioner shall include in the list provided to the county jury commission names of registered voters who do not have drivers licenses, and shall indicate the licensed or formerly licensed drivers who are also registered voters, the licensed or formerly licensed drivers who are not registered voters, and the registered voters who are not licensed or formerly licensed drivers.

(c) The list so provided shall be used solely for jury selection and election records purposes and no other. Information provided by the Commissioner to county jury commissions and the State Board of Elections under this section shall remain confidential, shall continue to be subject to the disclosure restriction provisions of G.S. 20-43.1, and shall not be a public record for purposes of Chapter 132 of the General Statutes. (1981, c. 720, s. 2; 1983, c. 197, ss. 1, 1.1; c. 754; c. 768, s. 25.3; 2003-226, s. 7(c); 2007-512, s. 3; 2012-180, s. 11.5.)

§ 20-44. Authority to grant or refuse applications.

The Division shall examine and determine the genuineness, regularity and legality of every application for registration of a vehicle and for a certificate of title therefor, and of any other application lawfully made in the Division, and may in all cases make investigation as may be deemed necessary or require additional information, and shall reject any such application if not satisfied of the genuineness, regularity, or legality thereof or the truth of any statement contained therein, or for any other reason, when authorized by law. (1937, c. 407, s. 9; 1975, c. 716, s. 5.)

§ 20-45. Seizure of documents and plates.

(a) The Division is hereby authorized to take possession of any certificate of title, registration card, permit, license, or registration plate issued by it upon expiration, revocation, cancellation, or suspension thereof, or which is fictitious, or which has been unlawfully or erroneously issued, or which has been unlawfully used.

(b) The Division may give notice to the owner, licensee or lessee of its authority to take possession of any certificate of title, registration card, permit, license, or registration plate issued by it and require that person to surrender it to the Commissioner or his officers or agents. Any person who fails to surrender the certificate of title, registration card, permit, license, or registration plate or any duplicate thereof, upon personal service of notice or within 10 days after receipt of notice by mail as provided in G.S. 20-48, shall be guilty of a Class 2 misdemeanor.

(c) Any sworn law enforcement officer with jurisdiction, including a member of the State Highway Patrol, is authorized to seize the certificate of title, registration card, permit, license, or registration plate, if the officer has electronic or other notification from the Division that the item has been revoked or cancelled, or otherwise has probable cause to believe that the item has been revoked or cancelled under any law or statute, including G.S. 20-309(e). If a criminal proceeding relating to a certificate of title, registration card, permit, or license is pending, the law enforcement officer in possession of that item shall retain the item pending the entry of a final judgment by a court with jurisdiction. If there is no criminal proceeding pending, the law enforcement officer shall deliver the item to the Division.

(d) Any law enforcement officer who seizes a registration plate pursuant to this section shall report the seizure to the Division within 48 hours of the seizure and shall return the registration plate, but not a fictitious registration plate, to the Division within 10 business days of the seizure. (1937, c. 407, s. 10; 1975, c. 716, s. 5; 1981, c. 938, s. 2; 1993, c. 539, s. 329; 1994, Ex. Sess., c. 24, s. 14(c); 2005-357, s. 1; 2006-105, ss. 2.1, 2.2; 2006-264, s. 98.1.)

§ 20-46. Repealed by Session Laws 1979, c. 99.

§ 20-47. Division may summon witnesses and take testimony.

(a) The Commissioner and officers of the Division designated by him shall have authority to summon witnesses to give testimony under oath or to give written deposition upon any matter under the jurisdiction of the Division. Such summons may require the production of relevant books, papers, or records.

(b) Every such summons shall be served at least five days before the return date, either by personal service made by any person over 18 years of age or by registered mail, but return acknowledgment is required to prove such latter service. Failure to obey such a summons so served shall constitute a Class 2 misdemeanor. The fees for the attendance and travel of witnesses shall be the same as for witnesses before the superior court.

(c)   The superior court shall have jurisdiction, upon application by the Commissioner, to enforce all lawful orders of the Commissioner under this section. (1937, c. 407, s. 12; 1975, c. 716, s. 5; 1993, c. 539, s. 330; 1994, Ex. Sess., c. 24, s. 14(c).)

§ 20-48. Giving of notice.

(a)   Whenever the Division is authorized or required to give any notice under this Chapter or other law regulating the operation of vehicles, unless a different method of giving such notice is otherwise expressly prescribed, such notice shall be given either by personal delivery thereof to the person to be so notified or by deposit in the United States mail of such notice in an envelope with postage prepaid, addressed to such person at his address as shown by the records of the Division. The giving of notice by mail is complete upon the expiration of four days after such deposit of such notice. Proof of the giving of notice in either such manner may be made by a notation in the records of the Division that the notice was sent to a particular address and the purpose of the notice. A certified copy of the Division's records may be sent by the Police Information Network, facsimile, or other electronic means. A copy of the Division's records sent under the authority of this section is admissible as evidence in any court or administrative agency and is sufficient evidence to discharge the burden of the person presenting the record that notice was sent to the person named in the record, at the address indicated in the record, and for the purpose indicated in the record. There is no requirement that the actual notice or letter be produced.

(b)   Notwithstanding any other provision of this Chapter at any time notice is now required by registered mail with return receipt requested, certified mail with return receipt requested may be used in lieu thereof and shall constitute valid notice to the same extent and degree as notice by registered mail with return receipt requested.

(c)   The Commissioner shall appoint such agents of the Division as may be needed to serve revocation notices required by this Chapter. The fee for service of a notice shall be fifty dollars ($50.00). (1937, c. 407, s. 13; 1955, c. 1187, s.

21; 1971, c. 1231, s. 1; 1975, c. 326, s. 3; c. 716, s. 5; 1983, c. 761, s. 148; 1985, c. 479, s. 171; 2006-253, s. 21.)

§ 20-49. Police authority of Division.

The Commissioner and such officers and inspectors of the Division as he shall designate and all members of the Highway Patrol and law enforcement officers of the Department of Public Safety shall have the power:

(1)   Of peace officers for the purpose of enforcing the provisions of this Article and of any other law regulating the operation of vehicles or the use of the highways.

(2)   To make arrests upon view and without warrant for any violation committed in their presence of any of the provisions of this Article or other laws regulating the operation of vehicles or the use of the highways.

(3)   At all time to direct all traffic in conformance with law, and in the event of a fire or other emergency or to expedite traffic or to insure safety, to direct traffic as conditions may require, notwithstanding the provisions of law.

(4)   When on duty, upon reasonable belief that any vehicle is being operated in violation of any provision of this Article or of any other law regulating the operation of vehicles to require the driver thereof to stop and exhibit his driver's license and the registration card issued for the vehicle, and submit to an inspection of such vehicle, the registration plates and registration card thereon or to an inspection and test of the equipment of such vehicle.

(5)   To inspect any vehicle of a type required to be registered hereunder in any public garage or repair shop or in any place where such vehicles are held for sale or wrecking, for the purpose of locating stolen vehicles and investigating the title and registration thereof.

(6)   To serve all warrants relating to the enforcement of the laws regulating the operation of vehicles or the use of the highways.

(7)   To investigate traffic accidents and secure testimony of witnesses or of persons involved.

(8) To investigate reported thefts of motor vehicles, trailers and semitrailers and make arrest for thefts thereof.

(9) For the purpose of determining compliance with the provisions of this Chapter, to inspect all files and records of the persons hereinafter designated and required to be kept under the provisions of this Chapter or of the registrations of the Division:

a. Persons dealing in or selling and buying new, used or junked motor vehicles and motor vehicle parts; and

b. Persons operating garages or other places where motor vehicles are repaired, dismantled, or stored. (1937, c. 407, s. 14; 1955, c. 554, s. 1; 1975, c. 716, s. 5; 1979, c. 93; 2002-159, s. 31.5(b); 2002-190, s. 5; 2011-145, s. 19.1(g).)

§ 20-49.1. Supplemental police authority of Division officers.

(a) In addition to the law enforcement authority granted in G.S. 20-49 or elsewhere, the Commissioner and the officers and inspectors of the Division whom the Commissioner designates have the authority to enforce criminal laws under any of the following circumstances:

(1) When they have probable cause to believe that a person has committed a criminal act in their presence and at the time of the violation they are engaged in the enforcement of laws otherwise within their jurisdiction.

(2) When they are asked to provide temporary assistance by the head of a State or local law enforcement agency or his designee and the request is within the scope of the agency's subject matter jurisdiction.

While acting pursuant to this subsection, the Division officers shall have the same powers vested in law enforcement officers by statute or common law. When acting pursuant to subdivision (2) of this subsection, the Division officers shall not be considered an officer, employee, or agent of the State or local law enforcement agency or designee asking for temporary assistance. Nothing in this section shall be construed to expand the Division officers' authority to initiate or conduct an independent investigation into violations of criminal laws outside the scope of their subject matter or territorial jurisdiction.

(b) In addition to the law enforcement authority granted in G.S. 20-49 or elsewhere, the Commissioner and the officers and inspectors of the Division whom the Commissioner designates have the authority to investigate drivers license fraud and identity thefts related to drivers license fraud and to make arrests for these offenses. (2004-148, s. 1.)

§ 20-49.2. Supplemental authority of State Highway Patrol Motor Carrier Enforcement officers.

In addition to law enforcement authority granted in G.S. 20-49 or elsewhere, all sworn Motor Carrier Enforcement officers of the State Highway Patrol shall have the authority to enforce criminal laws under the following circumstances:

(1) When they have probable cause to believe that a person has committed a criminal act in their presence and at the time of the violation they are engaged in the enforcement of laws otherwise within their jurisdiction.

(2) When they are asked to provide temporary assistance by the head of a State or local law enforcement agency or his designee and the request is within the scope of the agency's subject matter jurisdiction.

While acting pursuant to this section, they shall have the same powers invested in law enforcement officers by statute or common law. When acting pursuant to subdivision (2) of this section, they shall not be considered an officer, employee, or agent for the State or local law enforcement agency or designee asking for temporary assistance. Nothing in this statute shall be construed to expand their authority to initiate or conduct an independent investigation into violations of criminal laws outside the scope of their subject matter or territorial jurisdiction. (2004-148, s. 2.)

§ 20-49.3. Bureau of License and Theft; custody of seized vehicles.

(a) Vehicles Seized by the Division of Motor Vehicles. - Notwithstanding any other provision of law, the Division of Motor Vehicles, Bureau of License and Theft, may retain any vehicle seized by the Division of Motor Vehicles, Bureau of License and Theft, in the course of any investigation authorized by the provisions of G.S. 20-49 or G.S. 20-49.1 and forfeited to the Division by a court of competent jurisdiction.

(b)   Vehicles Seized by the United States Government. - Notwithstanding any other provision of law, the Division may accept custody and ownership of any vehicle seized by the United States Government, forfeited by a court of competent jurisdiction, and turned over to the Division.

(c)   Use of Vehicles. - All vehicles forfeited to, or accepted by, the Division pursuant to this section shall be used by the Bureau of License and Theft to conduct undercover operations and inspection station compliance checks throughout the State.

(d)   Disposition of Seized Vehicles. - Upon determination by the Commissioner of Motor Vehicles that a vehicle transferred pursuant to the provisions of this section is of no further use to the agency for use in official investigations, the vehicle shall be sold as surplus property in the same manner as other vehicles owned by the law enforcement agency and the proceeds from the sale after deducting the cost of sale shall be paid to the treasurer or proper officer authorized to receive fines and forfeitures to be used for the school fund of the county in the county in which the vehicle was seized, provided, that any vehicle transferred to any law enforcement agency under the provisions of this Article that has been modified to increase speed shall be used in the performance of official duties only and not for resale, transfer, or disposition other than as junk. The Division shall also reimburse the appropriate county school fund for any diminution in value of any vehicle seized under subsection (a) of this section during its period of use by the Division. Any vehicle seized outside of this State shall be sold as surplus property in the same manner as other vehicles owned by the law enforcement agency and the proceeds from the sale after deducting the cost of sale shall be paid to the treasurer and placed in the Civil Fines and Forfeitures Fund established pursuant to G.S. 115C-457.1. (2009-495, s. 1.)

Part 3. Registration and Certificates of Titles of Motor Vehicles.

§ 20-50. Owner to secure registration and certificate of title; temporary registration markers.

(a)   A vehicle intended to be operated upon any highway of this State must be registered with the Division in accordance with G.S. 20-52, and the owner of the vehicle must comply with G.S. 20-52 before operating the vehicle. A vehicle that is leased to an individual who is a resident of this State is a vehicle intended to be operated upon a highway of this State.

The Commissioner of Motor Vehicles or the Commissioner's duly authorized agent is empowered to grant a special one-way trip permit to move a vehicle without license upon good cause being shown. When the owner of a vehicle leases the vehicle to a carrier of passengers or property and the vehicle is actually used by the carrier in the operation of its business, the license plates may be obtained by the lessee, upon written consent of the owner, after the certificate of title has been obtained by the owner. When the owner of a vehicle leases the vehicle to a farmer and the vehicle is actually used by the farmer in the operation of a farm, the license plates may be obtained by the farmer at the applicable farmer rate, upon written consent of the owner, after the certificate of title has been obtained by the owner. The lessee shall make application on an appropriate form furnished by the Division and file such evidence of the lease as the Division may require.

(b)   The Division may issue a temporary license plate for a vehicle. A temporary license plate is valid for the period set by the Division. The period may not be less than 10 days nor more than 60 days.

A person may obtain a temporary license plate for a vehicle by filing an application with the Division and paying the required fee. An application must be filed on a form provided by the Division.

The fee for a temporary license plate that is valid for 10 days is five dollars ($5.00). The fee for a temporary license plate that is valid for more than 10 days is the amount that would be required with an application for a license plate for the vehicle. If a person obtains for a vehicle a temporary license plate that is valid for more than 10 days and files an application for a license plate for that vehicle before the temporary license plate expires, the person is not required to pay the fee that would otherwise be required for the license plate.

A temporary license plate is subject to the following limitations and conditions:

(1)   It may be issued only upon proper proof that the applicant has met the applicable financial responsibility requirements.

(2)   It expires on midnight of the day set for expiration.

(3) It may be used only on the vehicle for which issued and may not be transferred, loaned, or assigned to another.

(4) If it is lost or stolen, the person who applied for it must notify the Division.

(5) It may not be issued by a dealer.

(6) The provisions of G.S. 20-63, 20-71, 20-110 and 20-111 that apply to license plates apply to temporary license plates insofar as possible. (1937, c. 407, s. 15; 1943, c. 648; 1945, c. 956, s. 3; 1947, c. 219, s. 2; 1953, c. 831, s. 3; 1957, c. 246, s. 2; 1961, c. 360, s. 1; 1963, c. 552, s. 1; 1973, c. 919; 1975, c. 462; c. 716, s. 5; c. 767, s. 1; 1995, c. 394, s. 1; 1999-438, s. 26; 2005-276, s. 44.1(i).)

§ 20-50.1. Repealed by Session Laws 1979, c. 574, s. 5.

§ 20-50.2: Repealed by Session Laws 1991, c. 624, s. 4.

§ 20-50.3: Repealed by Session Laws 2005-294, s. 10, effective July 1, 2013, and applicable to combined tax and registration notices issued on or after that date. See Editor's note.

§ 20-50.4. Division to refuse to register vehicles on which county and municipal taxes and fees are not paid and when there is a failure to meet court-ordered child support obligations.

(a) Property Taxes Paid with Registration. - The Division shall refuse to register a vehicle on which county and municipal taxes and fees have not been paid.

(b) Delinquent Child Support Obligations. - Upon receiving a report from a child support enforcement agency that sanctions pursuant to G.S. 110-

142.2(a)(3) have been imposed, the Division shall refuse to register a vehicle for the owner named in the report until the Division receives certification pursuant to G.S. 110-142.2 that the payments are no longer considered delinquent. (1991, c. 624, s. 5; 1995, c. 538, s. 2(g); 1995 (Reg. Sess., 1996), c. 741, ss. 1, 2; 2005-294, s. 11; 2006-259, s. 31.5; 2007-527, s. 22(b); 2008-134, s. 65; 2011-330, s. 42(a); 2012-79, s. 3.6; 2013-414, s. 70(d).)

§ 20-51. Exempt from registration.

The following shall be exempt from the requirement of registration and certificate of title:

(1)   Any such vehicle driven or moved upon a highway in conformance with the provisions of this Article relating to manufacturers, dealers, or nonresidents.

(2)   Any such vehicle which is driven or moved upon a highway only for the purpose of crossing such highway from one property to another.

(3)   Any implement of husbandry, farm tractor, road construction or maintenance machinery or other vehicle which is not self-propelled that was designed for use in work off the highway and which is operated on the highway for the purpose of going to and from such nonhighway projects.

(4)   Any vehicle owned and operated by the government of the United States.

(5)   Farm tractors equipped with rubber tires and trailers or semitrailers when attached thereto and when used by a farmer, his tenant, agent, or employee in transporting his own farm implements, farm supplies, or farm products from place to place on the same farm, from one farm to another, from farm to market, or from market to farm. This exemption shall extend also to any tractor, implement of husbandry, and trailer or semitrailer while on any trip within a radius of 10 miles from the point of loading, provided that the vehicle does not exceed a speed of 35 miles per hour. This section shall not be construed as granting any exemption to farm tractors, implements of husbandry, and trailers or semitrailers which are operated on a for-hire basis, whether money or some other thing of value is paid or given for the use of such tractors, implements of husbandry, and trailers or semitrailers.

(6) Any trailer or semitrailer attached to and drawn by a properly licensed motor vehicle when used by a farmer, his tenant, agent, or employee in transporting unginned cotton, peanuts, soybeans, corn, hay, tobacco, silage, cucumbers, potatoes, all vegetables, fruits, greenhouse and nursery plants and flowers, Christmas trees, livestock, live poultry, animal waste, pesticides, seeds, fertilizers or chemicals purchased or owned by the farmer or tenant for personal use in implementing husbandry, irrigation pipes, loaders, or equipment owned by the farmer or tenant from place to place on the same farm, from one farm to another, from farm to gin, from farm to dryer, or from farm to market, and when not operated on a for-hire basis. The term "transporting" as used herein shall include the actual hauling of said products and all unloaded travel in connection therewith.

(7) Those small farm trailers known generally as tobacco-handling trailers, tobacco trucks or tobacco trailers when used by a farmer, his tenant, agent or employee, when transporting or otherwise handling tobacco in connection with the pulling, tying or curing thereof.

(8) Any vehicle which is driven or moved upon a highway only for the purpose of crossing or traveling upon such highway from one side to the other provided the owner or lessee of the vehicle owns the fee or a leasehold in all the land along both sides of the highway at the place or crossing.

(9) Mopeds as defined in G.S. 20-4.01(27)d1.

(10) Devices which are designed for towing private passenger motor vehicles or vehicles not exceeding 5,000 pounds gross weight. These devices are known generally as "tow dollies." A tow dolly is a two-wheeled device without motive power designed for towing disabled motor vehicles and is drawn by a motor vehicle in the same manner as a trailer.

(11) Devices generally called converter gear or dollies consisting of a tongue attached to either a single or tandem axle upon which is mounted a fifth wheel and which is used to convert a semitrailer to a full trailer for the purpose of being drawn behind a truck tractor and semitrailer.

(12) Motorized wheelchairs or similar vehicles not exceeding 1,000 pounds gross weight when used for pedestrian purposes by a handicapped person with a mobility impairment as defined in G.S. 20-37.5.

(13) Any vehicle registered in another state and operated temporarily within this State by a public utility, a governmental or cooperative provider of utility services, or a contractor for one of these entities for the purpose of restoring utility services in an emergency outage.

(14) Electric personal assistive mobility devices as defined in G.S. 20-4.01(7a).

(15) Any vehicle that meets all of the following:

a. Is designed for use in work off the highway.

b. Is used for agricultural quarantine programs under the supervision of the Department of Agriculture and Consumer Services.

c. Is driven or moved on the highway for the purpose of going to and from nonhighway projects.

d. Is identified in a manner approved by the Division of Motor Vehicles.

e. Is operated by a person who possesses an identification card issued by the Department of Agriculture and Consumer Services.

(16) A vehicle that meets all of the following conditions is exempt from the requirement of registration and certificate of title. The provisions of G.S. 105-449.117 continue to apply to the vehicle and to the person in whose name the vehicle would be registered.

a. Is an agricultural spreader vehicle. An "agricultural spreader vehicle" is a vehicle that is designed for off-highway use on a farm to spread fertilizer, seed, lime, or other agricultural products on a field.

b. Is driven on the highway only for the purpose of going from the location of its supply source for fertilizer or other products to and from a farm.

c. Does not exceed a speed of 35 miles per hour.

d. Does not drive outside a radius of 50 miles from the location of its supply source for fertilizer and other products.

e. Is driven by a person who has a license appropriate for the class of the vehicle.

f. Is insured under a motor vehicle liability policy in the amount required under G.S. 20-309.

g. Displays a valid federal safety inspection decal if the vehicle has a gross vehicle weight rating of at least 10,001 pounds.

(17) A header trailer when transported to or from a dealer, or after a sale or repairs, to the farm or another dealership. (1937, c. 407, s. 16; 1943, c. 500; 1949, c. 429; 1951, c. 705, s. 2; 1953, c. 826, ss. 2, 3; c. 1316, s. 1; 1961, cc. 334, 817; 1963, c. 145; 1965, c. 1146; 1971, c. 107; 1973, cc. 478, 757, 964; 1979, c. 574, s. 6; 1981 (Reg. Sess., 1982), c. 1286; 1983, cc. 288, 732; 1987, c. 608; 1989, c. 157, s. 2; 1991, c. 411, s. 4; 1995, c. 50, s. 4; 1999-281, s. 2; 2002-98, s. 4; 2002-150, s. 1; 2006-135, s. 2; 2007-194, s. 1; 2007-527, s. 41; 2012-78, ss. 2, 3.)

§ 20-52. Application for registration and certificate of title.

(a) An owner of a vehicle subject to registration must apply to the Division for a certificate of title, a registration plate, and a registration card for the vehicle. To apply, an owner must complete an application provided by the Division. The application must request all of the following information and may request other information the Division considers necessary:

(1) The owner's name.

(1a) If the owner is an individual, the following information:

a. The owner's mailing address and residence address.

b. One of the following at the option of the applicant:

1. The owner's North Carolina drivers license number or North Carolina special identification card number.

2. The owner's home state drivers license number or home state special identification card number and valid active duty military identification card

number or military dependent identification card number if the owner is a person or the spouse or dependent child of a person on active duty in the Armed Forces of the United States who is stationed in this State or deployed outside this State from a home base in this State. The owner's inability to provide a photocopy or reproduction of a military or military dependent identification card pursuant to any prohibition of the United States government or any agency thereof against the making of such photocopy or reproduction shall not operate to prevent the owner from making an application for registration and certificate of title pursuant to this subdivision.

3. The owner's home state drivers license number or home state special identification card number and proof of enrollment in a school in this State if the owner is a permanent resident of another state but is currently enrolled in a school in this State.

4. The owner's home state drivers license number or home state special identification card number if the owner provides a signed affidavit certifying that the owner intends to principally garage the vehicle in this State and provides the address where the vehicle is or will be principally garaged. For purposes of this section, "principally garage" means the vehicle is garaged for six or more months of the year on property in this State which is owned, leased, or otherwise lawfully occupied by the owner of the vehicle.

5. The owner's home state drivers license number or home state special identification card number, provided that the application is made pursuant to a court authorized sale or a sale authorized by G.S. 44A-4 for the purpose of issuing a title to be registered in another state or country.

6. The co-owner's home state drivers license number or home state special identification card number if at least one co-owner provides a North Carolina drivers license number or North Carolina special identification number.

7. The owner's home state drivers license number or special identification card number if the application is for a motor home or house car, as defined in G.S. 20-4.01(27)d2., or for a house trailer, as defined in G.S. 20-4.01(14).

(1b) If the owner is a firm, partnership, a corporation, or another entity, the address of the entity.

(2) A description of the vehicle, including the following:

a. The make, model, type of body, and vehicle identification number of the vehicle.

b. Whether the vehicle is new or used and, if a new vehicle, the date the manufacturer or dealer sold the vehicle to the owner and the date the manufacturer or dealer delivered the vehicle to the owner.

(3) A statement of the owner's title and of all liens upon the vehicle, including the names and addresses of all lienholders in the order of their priority, and the date and nature of each lien.

(4) A statement that the owner is an eligible risk for insurance coverage as defined in G.S. 58-37-1(4a).

(5) For registration and certificate of title for a nonfleet private passenger motor vehicle, a statement that providing incorrect or false and misleading information as to the owner's status as an eligible risk can result in criminal prosecution and the denial of insurance coverage for any loss of the owner under any insurance policies for which application is made if the owner provides false and misleading information as to eligible risk status.

(6) For registration and certificate of title for a nonfleet private passenger motor vehicle, a statement that the owner will inform the insurer before the next policy renewal if the owner ceases to be an eligible risk.

(a1) An owner who would otherwise be capable of attaining a drivers license or special identification card from this State or any other state, except for a medical or physical condition that can be documented to, and verified by, the Division, shall be issued a registration plate and certificate of title if the owner provides a signed affidavit certifying that the owner intends to principally garage the vehicle in this State and provides the address where the vehicle is or will be principally garaged.

(b) When such application refers to a new vehicle purchased from a manufacturer or dealer, such application shall be accompanied with a manufacturer's certificate of origin that is properly assigned to the applicant. If the new vehicle is acquired from a dealer or person located in another jurisdiction other than a manufacturer, the application shall be accompanied with such evidence of ownership as is required by the laws of that jurisdiction duly assigned by the disposer to the purchaser, or, if no such evidence of ownership be required by the laws of such other jurisdiction, a notarized bill of sale from the disposer. (1937, c. 407, s. 17; 1961, c. 835, ss. 2, 3; 1975, c. 716, s. 5; 1991, c. 183, s. 2; 1993 (Reg. Sess., 1994), c. 750, s. 5; 2007-164, s. 4; 2007-209, ss. 1, 2; 2007-443, s. 6; 2007-481, ss. 4-7; 2008-124, s. 4.1; 2009-274, s. 4.)

§ 20-52.1. Manufacturer's certificate of transfer of new motor vehicle.

(a) Any manufacturer transferring a new motor vehicle to another shall, at the time of the transfer, supply the transferee with a manufacturer's certificate of origin assigned to the transferee.

(b) Any dealer transferring a new vehicle to another dealer shall, at the time of transfer, give such transferee the proper manufacturer's certificate assigned to the transferee.

(c) Upon sale of a new vehicle by a dealer to a consumer-purchaser, the dealer shall execute in the presence of a person authorized to administer oaths an assignment of the manufacturer's certificate of origin for the vehicle, including in such assignment the name and address of the transferee and no title to a new motor vehicle acquired by a dealer under the provisions of subsections (a) and (b) of this section shall pass or vest until such assignment is executed and the motor vehicle delivered to the transferee.

Any dealer transferring title to, or an interest in, a new vehicle shall deliver the manufacturer's certificate of origin duly assigned in accordance with the foregoing provision to the transferee at the time of delivering the vehicle, except that where a security interest is obtained in the motor vehicle from the transferee in payment of the purchase price or otherwise, the transferor shall deliver the manufacturer's certificate of origin to the lienholder and the lienholder shall forthwith forward the manufacturer's certificate of origin together with the transferee's application for certificate of title and necessary fees to the Division. Any person who delivers or accepts a manufacturer's certificate of origin assigned in blank shall be guilty of a Class 2 misdemeanor, unless done in accordance with subsection (d) of this section.

(d) When a manufacturer's statement of origin or an existing certificate of title on a motor vehicle is unavailable, a motor vehicle dealer licensed under Article 12 of this Chapter may also transfer title to another by certifying in writing in a sworn statement to the Division that all prior perfected liens on the vehicle have been paid and that the motor vehicle dealer, despite having used reasonable diligence, is unable to obtain the vehicle's statement of origin or certificate of title. The Division is authorized to develop a form for this purpose. The filing of a false sworn certification with the Division pursuant to this subsection shall constitute a Class H felony. The dealer shall hold harmless the consumer-purchaser from any damages arising from the use of the procedure authorized by this subsection. (1961, c. 835, s. 4; 1967, c. 863; 1975, c. 716, s. 5; 1993, c. 539, s. 331; 1994, Ex. Sess., c. 24, s. 14(c); 2000-182, s. 1.)

§ 20-53. Application for specially constructed, reconstructed, or foreign vehicle.

(a) In the event the vehicle to be registered is a specially constructed, reconstructed, or foreign vehicle, such fact shall be stated in the application, and with reference to every foreign vehicle which has been registered outside of this State, the owner shall surrender to the Division all registration cards, certificates of title or notarized copies of original titles on vehicles 35 model years old and older, or other evidence of such foreign registration as may be in his possession or under his control, except as provided in subsection (b) hereof. After initial review, the Division shall return to the owner any original titles presented on vehicles 35 model years old and older appropriately marked indicating that the title has been previously submitted.

(b) Where, in the course of interstate operation of a vehicle registered in another state, it is desirable to retain registration of said vehicle in such other state, such applicant need not surrender, but shall submit for inspection said evidence of such foreign registration, and the Division in its discretion, and upon a proper showing, shall register said vehicle in this State but shall not issue a certificate of title for such vehicle.

(c), (d) Repealed by Session Laws 1965, c. 734, s. 2.

(e) No title shall be issued to an initial applicant for (i) out-of-state vehicles that are 35 model years old or older or (ii) a specially constructed vehicle prior to the completion of a vehicle verification conducted by the License and Theft Bureau of the Division of Motor Vehicles. These verifications shall be conducted as soon as practical. For an out-of-state vehicle that is 35 model years old or older, this inspection shall consist of verifying the public vehicle identification number to ensure that it matches the vehicle and ownership documents. No covert vehicle identification numbers are to be examined on an out-of-state vehicle 35 model years or older unless the inspector develops probable cause to believe that the ownership documents or public vehicle identification number presented does not match the vehicle being examined. However, upon such application and the submission of any required documentation, the Division shall be authorized to register the vehicle pending the completion of the verification of the vehicle. The registration shall be valid for one year but shall not be renewed unless and until the vehicle examination has been completed.

If an inspection and verification is not conducted by the License and Theft Bureau of the Division of Motor Vehicles within 15 days after receiving a request for such and the inspector has no probable cause to believe that the ownership documents or public vehicle identification number presented does not match the vehicle being examined, the vehicle shall be deemed to have satisfied all inspection and verification requirements and title shall issue to the owner within 15 days thereafter. If an inspection and verification is timely performed and the vehicle passes the inspection and verification, title shall issue to the owner within 15 days of the date of the inspection.

(f)   If a vehicle owner desires a vehicle title classification change, he or she may, upon proper application, be eligible for a reclassification. (1937, c. 407, s. 18; 1949, c. 675; 1953, c. 853; 1957, c. 1355; 1965, c. 734, s. 2; 1975, c. 716, s. 5; 2009-405, s. 5; 2013-349, s. 1.)

§ 20-53.1. Specially constructed vehicle certificate of title and registration.

(a)   Specially constructed vehicles shall be titled in the following manner:

(1)   Replica vehicles shall be titled as the year, make, and model of the vehicle intended to be replicated. A label of "Replica" shall be applied to the title and registration card. All replica vehicle titles shall be labeled "Specially Constructed Vehicle."

(2)   The model year of a street rod vehicle shall continue to be recognized as the manufacturer's assigned model year. The manufacturer's name shall continue to be used as the make with a label of "Street Rod" applied to the title and registration card. All street rod vehicle titles shall be labeled "Specially Constructed Vehicle."

(3) Custom-built vehicles shall be titled and registered showing the make as "Custom-built," and the year the vehicle was built shall be the vehicle model year. All custom-built vehicle titles shall be labeled "Specially Constructed Vehicle."

(b) Inoperable vehicles may be titled, but no registration may be issued until such time as the License and Theft Bureau inspects the vehicle to ensure it is substantially assembled. Once a vehicle has been verified as substantially assembled pursuant to an inspection by the License and Theft Bureau, the Commissioner shall title the vehicle by classifying it in the proper category and collecting all highway use taxes applicable to the value of the car at the time the vehicle is retitled to a proper classification, as described in this section.

(c) Motor vehicle certificates of title and registration cards issued pursuant to this section shall be labeled in accordance with this section. As used in this section, "labeled" means that the title and registration card shall contain a designation that discloses if the vehicle is classified as any of the following:

(1) Specially constructed vehicle.

(2) Inoperable vehicle. (2009-405, s. 2.)

§ 20-53.2: Reserved for future codification purposes.

§ 20-53.3. Appeal of specially constructed vehicle classification determination to Vehicle Classification Review Committee.

(a) Any person aggrieved by the Division's determination of the appropriate vehicle classification for a specially constructed vehicle may request review of that determination by the Vehicle Classification Review Committee. This review shall be initiated by completing a Vehicle Classification Review Request and returning the request to the Division. The Vehicle Classification Review Request shall be made on a form provided by the Division. The decision of the Review Committee may be appealed to the Commissioner of Motor Vehicles.

(b) The Vehicle Classification Review Committee shall consist of five members as follows:

(1) Two members shall be personnel of the License and Theft Bureau of the Division of Motor Vehicles appointed by the Commissioner.

(2) One member shall be a member of the public with expertise in antique or specially constructed vehicles appointed by the Commissioner from a list of nominees provided by the Antique Automobile Club of America.

(3) One member shall be a member of the public with expertise in antique or specially constructed vehicles appointed by the Commissioner from a list of nominees provided by the Specialty Equipment Market Association.

(4) One member shall be a member of the public with expertise in antique or specially constructed vehicles appointed by the Commissioner from a list of nominees provided by the National Corvette Restorers Society.

(c) Members of the Vehicle Classification Review Committee shall serve staggered two-year terms. Initial appointments shall be made on or before October 1, 2009. The initial appointment of one of the members from the License and Theft Bureau and the member nominated by the Antique Automobile Club of America shall be for one year. The initial appointments of the remaining members shall be for two years. At the expiration of these initial terms, appointments shall be for two years. A member of the Committee may be removed at any time by unanimous vote of the remaining four members. Vacancies shall be filled in the manner set out in subsection (b) of this section. (2009-405, s. 6.)

§ 20-54. Authority for refusing registration or certificate of title.

The Division shall refuse registration or issuance of a certificate of title or any transfer of registration upon any of the following grounds:

(1) The application contains a false or fraudulent statement, the applicant has failed to furnish required information or reasonable additional information requested by the Division, or the applicant is not entitled to the issuance of a certificate of title or registration of the vehicle under this Article.

(2) The vehicle is mechanically unfit or unsafe to be operated or moved upon the highways.

(3) The Division has reasonable ground to believe that the vehicle is a stolen or embezzled vehicle, or that the granting of registration or the issuance of a certificate of title would constitute a fraud against the rightful owner or another person who has a valid lien against the vehicle.

(4) The registration of the vehicle stands suspended or revoked for any reason as provided in the motor vehicle laws of this State, except in such cases to abide by the ignition interlock installation requirements of G.S. 20-17.8.

(5) The required fee has not been paid, including any additional registration fees or taxes due pursuant to G.S. 20-91(c).

(6) The vehicle is not in compliance with the inspection requirements of Part 2 of Article 3A of this Chapter or a civil penalty assessed as a result of the failure of the vehicle to comply with that Part has not been paid.

(7) The Division has been notified that the motor vehicle has been seized by a law enforcement officer and is subject to forfeiture pursuant to G.S. 20-28.2, et seq., or any other statute. However, the Division shall not prevent the renewal of existing registration prior to an order of forfeiture.

(8) The vehicle is a golf cart or utility vehicle.

(9) The applicant motor carrier is subject to an order issued by the Federal Motor Carrier Safety Administration or the Division to cease all operations based on a finding that the continued operations of the motor carrier pose an "imminent hazard" as defined in 49 C.F.R. § 386.72(b)(1).

(10) The North Carolina Turnpike Authority has notified the Division that the owner of the vehicle has not paid the amount of tolls, fees, and civil penalties the owner owes the Authority for use of a Turnpike project.

(11) The Division has been notified pursuant to G.S. 20-217(g2) that the owner of the vehicle has failed to pay any fine imposed pursuant to G.S. 20-217. (1937, c. 407, s. 19; 1975, c. 716, s. 5; 1993 (Reg. Sess., 1994), c. 754, s. 7; 1998-182, s. 9; 2001-356, s. 3; 2002-152, s. 1; 2007-164, s. 5; 2008-225, s. 7; 2009-319, s. 1; 2013-293, s. 4.)

§ 20-54.1. Forfeiture of right of registration.

(a) Upon receipt of notice of conviction of a violation of an offense involving impaired driving while the person's license is revoked as a result of a prior impaired driving license revocation as defined in G.S. 20-28.2, the Division shall revoke the registration of all motor vehicles registered in the convicted person's name and shall not register a motor vehicle in the convicted person's name until the convicted person's license is restored, except in such cases to abide by the ignition interlock installation requirements of G.S. 20-17.8. Upon receipt of notice of revocation of registration from the Division, the convicted person shall surrender the registration on all motor vehicles registered in the convicted person's name to the Division within 10 days of the date of the notice.

(a1) Upon receipt of notice of conviction of a felony speeding to elude arrest offense under G.S. 20-141.5(b) or (b1), the Division shall revoke the registration of all motor vehicles registered in the convicted person's name and shall not register a motor vehicle in the convicted person's name until the convicted person's license is restored. Upon receipt of notice of revocation of registration from the Division, the convicted person shall surrender the registration on all motor vehicles registered in the convicted person's name to the Division within 10 days of the date of the notice.

(b) Upon receipt of a notice of conviction under subsection (a) or (a1) of this section, the Division shall revoke the registration of the motor vehicle seized, and the owner shall not be allowed to register the motor vehicle seized until the convicted operator's drivers license has been restored. The Division shall not revoke the registration of the owner of the seized motor vehicle if the owner is determined to be an innocent owner. The Division shall revoke the owner's registration only after the owner is given an opportunity for a hearing to demonstrate that the owner is an innocent owner as defined in G.S. 20-28.2. Upon receipt of notice of revocation of registration from the Division, the owner shall surrender the registration on the motor vehicle seized to the Division within 10 days of the date of the notice. (1998-182, s. 10; 2007-164, s. 6; 2013-243, s. 5.)

§ 20-55. Examination of registration records and index of seized, stolen, and recovered vehicles.

The Division, upon receiving application for any transfer of registration or for original registration of a vehicle, other than a new vehicle sold by a North Carolina dealer, shall first check the engine and serial numbers shown in the application with its record of registered motor vehicles, and against the index of seized, stolen and recovered motor vehicles required to be maintained by this Article. (1937, c. 407, s. 20; 1971, c. 1070, s. 2; 1975, c. 716, s. 5; 1998-182, s. 11.)

§ 20-56. Registration indexes.

(a) The Division shall file each application received, and when satisfied as to the genuineness and regularity thereof, and that the applicant is entitled to register such vehicle and to the issuance of a certificate of title, shall register the vehicle therein described and keep a record thereof as follows:

(1) Under a distinctive registration number assigned to the vehicle;

(2) Alphabetically, under the name of the owner;

(3) Under the motor number or any other identifying number of the vehicle; and

(4) In the discretion of the Division, in any other manner it may deem advisable.

(b) Repealed by Session Laws 2001, c. 424, s. 6.14(g), effective September 26, 2001. (1937, c. 407, s. 201/2; 1949, c. 583, s. 5; 1971, c. 1070, s. 3; 1975, c. 716, s. 5; 1991, c. 53, s. 2; 2001-424, s. 6.14(g).)

§ 20-57. Division to issue certificate of title and registration card.

(a) The Division upon registering a vehicle shall issue a registration card and a certificate of title as separate documents.

(b) The registration card shall be delivered to the owner and shall contain upon the face thereof the name and address of the owner, space for the owner's signature, the registration number assigned to the vehicle, and a description of the vehicle as determined by the Commissioner, provided that if there are more than two owners the Division may show only two owners on the registration card and indicate that additional owners exist by placing after the names listed "et al."

An owner may obtain a copy of a registration card issued in the owner's name by applying to the Division for a copy and paying the fee set in G.S. 20-85.

(c) Every owner upon receipt of a registration card, shall write his signature thereon with pen and ink in the space provided. Every such registration card shall at all times be carried in the vehicle to which it refers or in the vehicle to which transfer is being effected, as provided by G.S. 20-64 at the time of its operation, and such registration card shall be displayed upon demand of any peace officer or any officer of the Division: Provided, however, any person charged with failing to so carry such registration card shall not be convicted if he produces in court a registration card theretofore issued to him and valid at the time of his arrest: Provided further, that in case of a transfer of a license plate from one vehicle to another under the provisions of G.S. 20-72, evidence of application for transfer shall be carried in the vehicle in lieu of the registration card.

(d) The certificate of title shall contain upon the face thereof the identical information required upon the face of the registration card except the abbreviation "et al." if such appears and in addition thereto the name of all owners, the date of issuance and all liens or encumbrances disclosed in the application for title. All such liens or encumbrances shall be shown in the order of their priority, according to the information contained in such application.

(e) The certificate of title shall contain upon the reverse side an assignment of title or interest and warranty by registered owner or registered dealer. The purchaser's application for North Carolina certificate of title shall be made on a form prescribed by the Commissioner and shall include a space for notation of liens and encumbrances on the vehicle at the time of transfer.

(f) Certificates of title upon which liens or encumbrances are shown shall be delivered or mailed by the Division to the holder of the first lien or encumbrance.

(g) Certificates of title shall bear thereon the seal of the Division.

(h) Certificates of title need not be renewed annually, but shall remain valid until canceled by the Division for cause or upon a transfer of any interest shown therein. (1937, c. 407, s. 21; 1943, c. 715; 1961, c. 360, s. 2; c. 835, s. 5; 1963, c. 552, s. 2; 1973, c. 72; c. 764, ss. 1-3; c. 1118; 1975, c. 716, s. 5; 1979, c. 139; 1981, c. 690, s. 20; 1983, c. 252; 1991, c. 193, s. 7.)

§ 20-58. Perfection by indication of security interest on certificate of title.

(a)　Except as provided in G.S. 20-58.8, a security interest in a vehicle of a type for which a certificate of title is required shall be perfected only as hereinafter provided.

(1)　If the vehicle is not registered in this State, the application for notation of a security interest shall be the application for certificate of title provided for in G.S. 20-52.

(2)　If the vehicle is registered in this State, the application for notation of a security interest shall be in the form prescribed by the Division, signed by the debtor, and contain the date of application of each security interest, and name and address of the secured party from whom information concerning the security interest may be obtained. The application must be accompanied by the existing certificate of title unless in the possession of a prior secured party. If there is an existing certificate of title issued by this or any other jurisdiction in the possession of a prior secured party, the application for notation of the security interest shall in addition contain the name and address of such prior secured party. An application for notation of a security interest may be signed by the secured party instead of the debtor when the application is accompanied by documentary evidence of the applicant's security interest in that motor vehicle signed by the debtor and by affidavit of the applicant stating the reason the debtor did not sign the application. In the event the certificate cannot be obtained for recordation of the security interest, when title remains in the name of the debtor, the Division shall cancel the certificate and issue a new certificate of title listing all the respective security interests.

(3)　If the application for notation of security interest is made in order to continue the perfection of a security interest perfected in another jurisdiction, it may be signed by the secured party instead of the debtor. Such application shall be accompanied by documentary evidence of a perfected security interest. No such application shall be valid unless an application for a certificate of title has been made in North Carolina. The security interest perfected herein shall be subject to the provisions set forth in G.S. 20-58.5.

(b)　When a manufacturer's statement of origin or an existing certificate of title on a motor vehicle is unavailable, a first lienholder who holds a valid license as a motor vehicle dealer issued by the Commissioner under Article 12 of this Chapter or his designee may file a notarized copy of an instrument creating and evidencing a security interest in the motor vehicle with the Division of Motor Vehicles. A filing pursuant to this subsection shall constitute constructive notice to all persons of the security interest in the motor vehicle described in the filing. The constructive notice shall be effective from the date of the filing if the filing is made within 20 days after the date of the security agreement. The constructive notice shall date from the date of the filing with the Division if it is made more than 20 days after the date of the security agreement. The notation of a security interest created under this subsection shall automatically expire 60 days after the date of the creation of the security interest, or upon perfection of the security interest as provided in subsection (a) of this section, whichever occurs first. A security interest notation made under this subsection and then later perfected under subsection (a) of this section shall be presumed to have been perfected on the date of the earlier filing. The Division may charge a fee not to exceed ten dollars ($10.00) for each notation of security interest filed pursuant to this subsection. The fee shall be credited to the Highway Fund. A false filing with the Division pursuant to this subsection shall constitute a Class H felony. (1937, c. 407, s. 22; 1955, c. 554, s. 2; 1961, c. 835, s. 6; 1969, c. 838, s. 1; 1975, c. 716, s. 5; 1979, c. 145, ss. 1, 2; c. 199; 2000-182, s. 2.)

§ 20-58.1. Duty of the Division upon receipt of application for notation of security interest.

(a) Upon receipt of an application for notation of security interest, the required fee and accompanying documents required by G.S. 20-58, the Division, if it finds the application and accompanying documents in order, shall either endorse upon the certificate of title or issue a new certificate of title containing, the name and address of each secured party, and the date of perfection of each security interest as determined by the Division. The Division shall deliver or mail the certificate to the first secured party named in it and shall also notify the new secured party that his security interest has been noted upon the certificate of title.

(b) If the certificate of title is in the possession of some prior secured party, the Division, when satisfied that the application is in order, shall procure the certificate of title from the secured party in whose possession it is being held, for the sole purpose of noting the new security interest. Upon request of the Division, a secured party in possession of a certificate of title shall forthwith deliver or mail the certificate of title to the Division. Such delivery of the certificate does not affect the rights of any secured party under his security agreement. (1961, c. 835, s. 6; 1969, c. 838, s. 1; 1975, c. 716, s. 5; 1979, c. 145, s. 3.)

§ 20-58.2. Date of perfection.

If the application for notation of security interest with the required fee is delivered to the Division within 20 days after the date of the security agreement, the security interest is perfected as of the date of the execution of the security agreement. Otherwise, the security interest is perfected as of the date of delivery of the application to the Division. (1961, c. 835, s. 6; 1969, c. 838, s. 1; 1975, c. 716, s. 5; 1991, c. 414, s. 1.)

§ 20-58.3. Notation of assignment of security interest on certificate of title.

An assignee of a security interest may have the certificate of title endorsed or issued with the assignee named as the secured party, upon delivering to the Division on a form prescribed by the Division, with the required fee, an assignment by the secured party named in the certificate together with the certificate of title. The assignment must contain the address of the assignee from which information concerning the security interest may be obtained. If the certificate of title is in the possession of some other secured party the procedure prescribed by G.S. 20-58.1(b) shall be followed. (1961, c. 835, s. 6; 1969, c. 838, s. 1; 1975, c. 716, s. 5.)

§ 20-58.4. Release of security interest.

(a) Upon the satisfaction or other discharge of a security interest in a vehicle for which the certificate of title is in the possession of the secured party, the secured party shall, within the earlier of 10 days after demand or 30 days from the date of satisfaction, execute a release of his security interest, in the space provided therefor on the certificate or as the Division prescribes, and mail or deliver the certificate and release to the next secured party named therein, or if none, to the owner or other person authorized to receive the certificate for the owner.

(b) Upon the satisfaction or other discharge of a security interest in a vehicle for which the certificate of title is in the possession of a prior secured party, the secured party whose security interest is satisfied shall within 10 days execute a release of his security interest in such form as the Division prescribes and mail or deliver the same to the owner or other person authorized to receive the same for the owner.

(c) An owner, upon securing the release of any security interest in a vehicle shown upon the certificate of title issued therefor, may exhibit the documents evidencing such release, signed by the person or persons making such release, and the certificate of title to the Division which shall, when satisfied as to the genuineness and regularity of the release, issue to the owner either a new certificate of title in proper form or an endorsement or rider attached thereto showing the release of the security interest.

(d) If an owner exhibits documents evidencing the release of a security interest as provided in subsection (c) of this section but is unable to furnish the certificate of title to the Division because it is in possession of a prior secured party, the Division, when satisfied as to the genuineness and regularity of the release, shall procure the certificate of title from the person in possession thereof for the sole purpose of noting thereon the release of the subsequent security interest, following which the Division shall return the certificate of title to the person from whom it was obtained and notify the owner that the release has been noted on the certificate of title.

(e) If it is impossible for the owner to secure from the secured party the release contemplated by this section, the owner may exhibit to the Division such evidence as may be available showing satisfaction or other discharge of the debt secured, together with a sworn affidavit by the owner that the debt has been satisfied, which the Division may treat as a proper release for purposes of this section when satisfied as to the genuineness, truth and sufficiency thereof. Prior to cancellation of a security interest under the provisions of this subsection, at least 15 days' notice of the pendency thereof shall be given to the secured party at his last known address by the Division by registered letter. (1961, c. 835, s. 6; 1969, c. 838, s. 1; 1975, c. 716, s. 5; 2011-318, s. 1.)

§ 20-58.4A. Electronic lien system.

(a) Implementation. - No later than July 1, 2014, the Division shall implement a statewide electronic lien system to process the notification, release, and maintenance of security interests and certificate of title data where a lien is notated, through electronic means instead of paper documents otherwise required by this Chapter. The Division may contract with a qualified vendor or vendors to develop and implement this statewide electronic lien system, or the Division may develop and make available to qualified service providers a well-defined set of information services that will enable secure access to the data and internal application components necessary to facilitate the creation of an electronic lien system.

(b) Minimum Standards for a Vendor Implemented System. - When contracting with a qualified vendor or vendors to implement the system required in subsection (a) of this section, the Division shall set the following minimum standards:

(1) The Division shall issue a competitive request for proposal to assess the qualifications of any vendor or vendors responsible for the establishment and ongoing support of the statewide electronic lien system. The Division may also reserve the right to receive input regarding specifications for the electronic lien system from parties that do not respond to a request for proposal to establish and operate an electronic lien system.

(2) Any contract entered into with a vendor or vendors shall include no costs or charges payable by the Division to the vendor or vendors. The vendor or vendors shall reimburse the Division for documented reasonable implementation costs directly associated with the establishment and ongoing support of the statewide electronic lien system.

(3) Upon implementation of the electronic lien system pursuant to subsection (a) of this section, the qualified vendor or vendors may charge participating lienholders or their agents a per-transaction fee for each lien notification. The per-transaction lien notification fee shall be consistent with market pricing in an amount not to exceed three dollars and fifty cents ($3.50) for costs associated with the development and ongoing administration of the electronic lien system. The qualified vendor or vendors shall not charge lienholders or their agents any additional fee for lien releases, assignments, or transfers. To recover their costs, participating lienholders or their agents may charge the borrower of a motor vehicle loan or the lessee of an automotive lease an amount equal to the transaction fee per lien notification plus a fee in an

amount not to exceed three dollars ($3.00) for each electronic transaction where a lien is notated.

(4) A qualified vendor or vendors may also serve as a service provider to lienholders, if all of the following conditions are met:

a. The contract with the vendor must include provisions specifically prohibiting the vendor from using information concerning vehicle titles for marketing or business solicitation purposes.

b. The contract with the vendor must include an acknowledgment by the vendor that it is required to enter into agreements to exchange electronic lien data with any service providers who offer electronic lien and title services in the State and who have been approved by the Division for participation in the system and with service providers who are not qualified vendors.

c. The Division must periodically monitor fees charged by a qualified vendor also serving as a service provider to lienholders and providing services as a qualified vendor to other service providers to ensure the vendor is not engaged in predatory pricing.

(c) Minimum Standards for Division-Developed System. - If the Division chooses to develop an interface to enable service provider access to data to facilitate the creation of an electronic lien system, then the Division shall do so for a cost not to exceed two hundred fifty thousand dollars ($250,000) and set the following minimum standards:

(1) The Division shall establish qualifications for third-party service providers offering electronic lien services and establish a qualification process that will vet applications developed by service providers for compliance with defined security and architecture standards as follows:

a. Qualifications shall be posted within 60 days of the effective date of this section.

b. Interested service providers shall respond by providing qualifications within 30 days of posting.

c. The Division shall notify service providers of their approval.

d. Within 30 days of approval, each qualified service provider shall remit payment in an amount equal to the development costs as a fraction of the number of qualified service providers participating in the electronic lien services.

e. If there is a service provider who later wishes to participate but did not apply or pay the initial development costs, then that provider may apply to participate if the provider meets all qualifications and pays the same amount in development costs as other participating service providers.

(2) Each qualified service provider shall remit to the Division an annual fee not to exceed three thousand dollars ($3,000) on a date prescribed by the Division to be used for the operation and maintenance of the electronic lien system.

(3) Any contract entered into with a service provider shall include no costs or charges payable by the Division to the service provider.

(4) Upon implementation of the electronic lien system pursuant to subsection (a) of this section, the service provider may charge participating lienholders or their agents a per-transaction fee consistent with market pricing.

(5) The contract with the service provider must include provisions specifically prohibiting the service provider from using information concerning vehicle titles for marketing or business solicitation purposes.

(d) Qualified vendors and service providers shall have experience in directly providing electronic solutions to State motor vehicle departments or agencies.

(e) Notwithstanding any requirement in this Chapter that a lien on a motor vehicle shall be noted on the face of the certificate of title, if there are one or more liens or encumbrances on the motor vehicle or mobile home, the Division may electronically transmit the lien to the first lienholder and notify the first lienholder of any additional liens. Subsequent lien satisfactions may be electronically transmitted to the Division and shall include the name and address of the person satisfying the lien.

(f) When electronic transmission of liens and lien satisfactions is used, a certificate of title need not be issued until the last lien is satisfied and a clear certificate of title is issued to the owner of the vehicle.

(g) When a vehicle is subject to an electronic lien, the certificate of title for the vehicle shall be considered to be physically held by the lienholder for purposes of compliance with State or federal odometer disclosure requirements.

(h) A duly certified copy of the Division's electronic record of the lien shall be admissible in any civil, criminal, or administrative proceeding in this State as evidence of the existence of the lien.

(i) Mandatory Participation. - Beginning July 1, 2015, all individuals and lienholders who are normally engaged in the business or practice of financing motor vehicles, and who conduct at least five transactions annually, shall utilize the electronic lien system implemented in subsection (a) of this section to record information concerning the perfection and release of a security interest in a vehicle.

(j) Effect of Electronic Notice or Release. - An electronic notice or release of a security interest made through the electronic system implemented pursuant to subsection (a) of this section shall have the same force and effect as a notice or release on a paper document provided under G.S. 20-58 through G.S. 20-58.8.

(k) Nothing in this section shall preclude the Division from collecting a title fee for the preparation and issuance of a title. (2013-341, s. 1.)

§ 20-58.5. Duration of security interest in favor of corporations which dissolve or become inactive.

Any security interest recorded in favor of a corporation which, since the recording of such security interest, has dissolved or become inactive for any reason, and which remains of record as a security interest of such corporation for a period of more than three years from the date of such dissolution or becoming inactive, shall become null and void and of no further force and effect. (1961, c. 835, s. 6; 1969, c. 838, s. 1; 1979, c. 145, s. 4.)

§ 20-58.6. Duty of secured party to disclose information.

A secured party named in a certificate of title shall, upon written request of the Division, the owner or another secured party named on the certificate, disclose information when called upon by such person, within 10 days after his lien shall have been paid and satisfied, and any person convicted under this section shall be fined not more than fifty dollars ($50.00) or imprisoned not more than 30 days. (1937, c. 407, s. 23; 1975, c. 716, s. 5.)

§ 20-58.7. Cancellation of certificate.

The cancellation of a certificate of title shall not, in and of itself, affect the validity of a security interest noted on it. (1961, c. 835, s. 6; 1969, c. 838, s. 1.)

§ 20-58.8. Applicability of §§ 20-58 to 20-58.8; use of term "lien".

(a) Repealed by Session Laws 2000, c. 169, s. 30.

(b) The provisions of G.S. 20-58 through 20-58.8 inclusive shall not apply to or affect:

(1) A lien given by statute or rule of law for storage of a motor vehicle or to a supplier of services or materials for a vehicle;

(2) A lien arising by virtue of a statute in favor of the United States, this State or any political subdivision of this State; or

(3) A security interest in a vehicle created by a manufacturer or by a dealer in new or used vehicles who holds the vehicle in his inventory.

(c) When the term "lien" is used in other sections of this Chapter, or has been used prior to October 1, 1969, with reference to transactions governed by G.S. 20-58 through 20-58.8, to describe contractual agreements creating security interests in personal property, the term "lien" shall be construed to refer to a "security interest" as the term is used in G.S. 20-58 through 20-58.8 and the Uniform Commercial Code. (1961, c. 835, s. 6; 1969, c. 838, s. 1; 2000-169, s. 30.)

§ 20-58.9. Repealed by Session Laws 1969, c. 838, s. 3.

§ 20-58.10. Effective date of §§ 20-58 to 20-58.9.

The provisions of G.S. 20-58 through 20-58.9 inclusive shall be effective and relate to the perfecting and giving notice of security interests entered into on and after January 1, 1962. (1961, c. 835, s. 6.)

§ 20-59. Unlawful for lienor who holds certificate of title not to surrender same when lien satisfied.

It shall be unlawful and constitute a Class 3 misdemeanor for a lienor who holds a certificate of title as provided in this Article to refuse or fail to surrender such certificate of title to the person legally entitled thereto, when called upon by such person, within 10 days after his lien shall have been paid and satisfied. (1937, c. 407, s. 23; 1993, c. 539, s. 332; 1994, Ex. Sess., c. 24, s. 14(c).)

§ 20-60. Owner after transfer not liable for negligent operation.

The owner of a motor vehicle who has made a bona fide sale or transfer of his title or interest, and who has delivered possession of such vehicle and the certificate of title thereto properly endorsed to the purchaser or transferee, shall not be liable for any damages thereafter resulting from negligent operation of such vehicle by another. (1937, c. 407, s. 24.)

§ 20-61. Owner dismantling or wrecking vehicle to return evidence of registration.

Except as permitted under G.S. 20-62.1, any owner dismantling or wrecking any vehicle shall forward to the Division the certificate of title, registration card and other proof of ownership, and the registration plates last issued for such vehicle, unless such plates are to be transferred to another vehicle of the same owner.

In that event, the plates shall be retained and preserved by the owner for transfer to such other vehicle. No person, firm or corporation shall dismantle or wreck any motor vehicle without first complying with the requirements of this section. The Commissioner upon receipt of certificate of title and notice from the owner thereof that a vehicle has been junked or dismantled may cancel and destroy such record of certificate of title. (1937, c. 407, s. 25; 1947, c. 219, s. 3; 1961, c. 360, s. 3; 1975, c. 716, s. 5; 2007-505, s. 2.)

§ 20-62: Repealed by Session Laws 1993, c. 533, s. 9.

§ 20-62.1. Purchase of vehicles for purposes of scrap or parts only.

(a)   Records for Scrap or Parts. - A secondary metals recycler, as defined in G.S. 66-420(8), and a salvage yard, as defined in G.S. 20-137.7(6), purchasing motor vehicles solely for the purposes of dismantling or wrecking such motor vehicles for the recovery of scrap metal or for the sale of parts only, shall comply with the provisions of G.S. 20-61 and subsection (a1) of this section, provided, however, that a secondary metals recycler or salvage yard may purchase a motor vehicle without a certificate of title, if the motor vehicle is 10 model years old or older and the secondary metals recycler or salvage yard comply with the following requirements:

(1)   Maintain a record on a form, or in a format, as approved by the Division of Motor Vehicles (DMV) of all purchase transactions of motor vehicles. The following information shall be maintained for transactions of motor vehicles:

a.   The name, address, and contact information of the secondary metals recycler or salvage yard.

b.   The name, initials, or other identification of the individual entering the information.

c.   The date of the transaction.

d.   A description of the motor vehicle, including the year, make, and model to the extent practicable.

e.   The vehicle identification number (VIN) of the vehicle.

f.   The amount of consideration given for the motor vehicle.

g.   A written statement signed by the seller or the seller's agent certifying that (i) the seller or the seller's agent has the lawful right to sell and dispose of the motor vehicle, (ii) the motor vehicle is at least 10 model years old, and (iii) the motor vehicle is not subject to any security interest or lien.

g1.   A written statement that the motor vehicle will be scrapped or crushed for disposal or dismantled for parts only.

h.   The name, address, and drivers license number of the person from whom the motor vehicle is being purchased.

i.   A photocopy or electronic scan of a valid drivers license or identification card issued by the DMV of the seller of the motor vehicle, or seller's agent, to the secondary metals recycler or salvage yard, or in lieu thereof, any other identification card containing a photograph of the seller as issued by any state or federal agency of the United States: provided, that if the buyer has a copy of the seller's photo identification on file, the buyer may reference the identification that is on file, without making a separate photocopy for each transaction. If seller has no identification as described in this sub-subdivision, the secondary metals recycler or salvage yard shall not complete the transaction.

(1a)   Verify with the DMV whether or not the motor vehicle has been reported stolen. The DMV shall develop a method to allow a person subject to this section to verify, at the time of the transaction, through the use of the Internet, that the vehicle has not been reported stolen, and that also allows for the DMV's response to be printed and retained by the person making the request. One of the following shall apply following the DMV response:

a.   If the Division of Motor Vehicles confirms that the motor vehicle has been reported stolen, the secondary metals recycler or salvage yard shall not complete the transaction and shall notify the DMV of the current location of the vehicle and the identifying information of the person attempting to transfer the vehicle.

b.   If the Division of Motor Vehicles confirms that the motor vehicle has not been stolen, the secondary metals recycler or salvage yard may proceed with the transaction and shall not be held criminally or civilly liable if the motor vehicle later turns out to be a stolen vehicle, unless the secondary metals recycler had knowledge that the motor vehicle was a stolen vehicle.

c. If the Division of Motor Vehicles has not received information from a federal, State, or local department or independent source that a vehicle has been stolen and reports pursuant to this section that a vehicle is not stolen, any person damaged does not have a cause of action against the Division.

(2) Maintain the information required under subdivision (1) of this subsection, and the record confirming that the vehicle was not stolen, required under subdivision (1a) of this subsection, for not less than two years from the date of the purchase of the motor vehicle.

(a1) Reporting Requirement. - Within 72 hours of each day's close of business, a secondary metals recycler or salvage yard purchasing a motor vehicle under this section shall submit to the National Motor Vehicle Title Information System (NMVTIS) such information contained in subdivision (1) of subsection (a) of this section, along with any other information or statement pertaining to the intended disposition of the motor vehicle, as may be required. The information shall be in a format that will satisfy the requirement for reporting information in accordance with rules adopted by the United States Department of Justice in 28 C.F.R. § 25.56. A secondary metals recycler or salvage yard may comply with this subsection by reporting the information required by this subsection to a third-party consolidator as long as the third-party consolidator reports the information to the NMVTIS in compliance with the provisions of this subsection.

(b) Inspection of Motor Vehicles and Records. - At any time it appears a secondary metals recycler, salvage yard, or any other person involved in secondary metals operations is open for business, a law enforcement officer shall have the right to inspect the following:

(1) Any and all motor vehicles in the possession of the secondary metals recycler, the salvage yard, or any other person involved in secondary metals operations.

(2) Any records required to be maintained under subsection (a) of this section.

(b1) Availability of Information. - The information obtained by the Division of Motor Vehicles pursuant to this section shall be made available to law enforcement agencies only. The information submitted pursuant to this section is confidential and shall not be considered a public record as that term is defined in G.S. 132-1.

(c) Violations. - Any person who knowingly and willfully violates any of the provisions of this section, or any person who falsifies the statement required under subsection (a)(1)g. of this section, shall be guilty of a Class I felony and shall pay a minimum fine of one thousand dollars ($1,000). The court may order a defendant seller under this subsection to make restitution to the secondary metals recycler or salvage yard or lien holder for any damage or loss caused by the defendant seller arising out of an offense committed by the defendant seller.

(d) Confiscation of Vehicle or Tools Used in Illegal Sale. - Any motor vehicle used to transport another motor vehicle illegally sold under this section may be seized by law enforcement and is subject to forfeiture by the court, provided, however, that no vehicle used by any person in the transaction of a sale of regulated metals is subject to forfeiture unless it appears that the owner or other person in charge of the motor vehicle is a consenting party or privy to the commission of a crime, and a forfeiture of the vehicle encumbered by a bona fide security interest is subject to the interest of the secured party who had no knowledge of or consented to the act.

Whenever property is forfeited under this subsection by order of the court, the law enforcement agency having custody of the property shall sell any forfeited property which is not required to be destroyed by law and which is not harmful to the public, provided that the proceeds are remitted to the Civil Fines and Forfeitures Fund established pursuant to G.S. 115C-457.1.

(e) Exemptions. - As used in this section, the term "motor vehicle" shall not include motor vehicles which have been mechanically flattened, crushed, baled, or logged and sold for purposes of scrap metal only.

(f) Preemption. - No local government shall enact any local law or ordinance with regards to the regulation of the sale of motor vehicles to secondary metals recyclers or salvage yards. (2007-505, s. 1; 2012-46, s. 30; 2013-323, s. 2; 2013-410, s. 28(a).)

§ 20-63. Registration plates furnished by Division; requirements; replacement of regular plates with First in Flight plates; surrender and reissuance; displaying;

preservation and cleaning; alteration or concealment of numbers; commission contracts for issuance.

(a) The Division upon registering a vehicle shall issue to the owner one registration plate for a motorcycle, trailer or semitrailer and for every other motor vehicle. Registration plates issued by the Division under this Article shall be and remain the property of the State, and it shall be lawful for the Commissioner or his duly authorized agents to summarily take possession of any plate or plates which he has reason to believe is being illegally used, and to keep in his possession such plate or plates pending investigation and legal disposition of the same. Whenever the Commissioner finds that any registration plate issued for any vehicle pursuant to the provisions of this Article has become illegible or is in such a condition that the numbers thereon may not be readily distinguished, he may require that such registration plate, and its companion when there are two registration plates, be surrendered to the Division. When said registration plate or plates are so surrendered to the Division, a new registration plate or plates shall be issued in lieu thereof without charge. The owner of any vehicle who receives notice to surrender illegible plate or plates on which the numbers are not readily distinguishable and who willfully refuses to surrender said plates to the Division shall be guilty of a Class 2 misdemeanor.

(b) Every license plate must display the registration number assigned to the vehicle for which it is issued, the name of the State of North Carolina, which may be abbreviated, and the year number for which it is issued or the date of expiration. A plate issued for a commercial vehicle, as defined in G.S. 20-4.2(1), and weighing 26,001 pounds or more, must bear the word "commercial," unless the plate is a special registration plate authorized in G.S. 20-79.4 or the commercial vehicle is a trailer or is licensed for 6,000 pounds or less. The plate issued for vehicles licensed for 7,000 pounds through 26,000 pounds must bear the word "weighted," unless the plate is a special registration plate authorized in G.S. 20-79.4.

A registration plate issued by the Division for a private passenger vehicle or for a private hauler vehicle licensed for 6,000 pounds or less shall be a "First in Flight" plate. A "First in Flight" plate shall have the words "First in Flight" printed at the top of the plate above all other letters and numerals. The background of the plate shall depict the Wright Brothers biplane flying over Kitty Hawk Beach, with the plane flying slightly upward and to the right.

(b1) The following special registration plates do not have to be a "First in Flight" plate as provided in subsection (b) of this section. The design of the plates that are not "First in Flight" plates must be developed in accordance with G.S. 20-79.4(a3). For special plates authorized in G.S. 20-79.7 on or after July 1, 2013, the Division may not issue the plate on a background under this subsection unless it receives at least 200 applications for the plate in addition to the applications required under G.S. 20-79.4 or G.S. 20-81.12.

(1) Friends of the Great Smoky Mountains National Park.

(2) Rocky Mountain Elk Foundation.

(3) Blue Ridge Parkway Foundation.

(4) Friends of the Appalachian Trail.

(5) NC Coastal Federation.

(6) In God We Trust.

(7) Stock Car Racing Theme.

(8) Buddy Pelletier Surfing Foundation.

(9) Guilford Battleground Company.

(10) National Wild Turkey Federation.

(11) North Carolina Aquarium Society.

(12) First in Forestry.

(13) North Carolina Wildlife Habitat Foundation.

(14) NC Trout Unlimited.

(15) Ducks Unlimited.

(16) Lung Cancer Research.

(17) NC State Parks.

(18) Support Our Troops.

(19) US Equine Rescue League.

(20) Fox Hunting.

(21) Back Country Horsemen of North Carolina.

(22) Hospice Care.

(23) Home Care and Hospice.

(24) NC Tennis Foundation.

(25) AIDS Awareness.

(26) Donate Life.

(27) Farmland Preservation.

(28) Travel and Tourism.

(29) Battle of Kings Mountain.

(30) NC Civil War.

(31) North Carolina Zoological Society.

(32) United States Service Academy.

(33) Carolina Raptor Center.

(34) Carolinas Credit Union Foundation.

(35) North Carolina State Flag.

(36) NC Mining.

(37) Coastal Land Trust.

(38) ARTS NC.

(39) Choose Life.

(40) North Carolina Green Industry Council.

(41) NC Horse Council.

(42) Core Sound Waterfowl Museum and Heritage Center.

(43) Mountains-to-Sea Trail, Inc.

(c) Such registration plate and the required numerals thereon, except the year number for which issued, shall be of sufficient size to be plainly readable from a distance of 100 feet during daylight.

(d) Registration plates issued for a motor vehicle other than a motorcycle, trailer, or semitrailer shall be attached thereto, one in the front and the other in the rear: Provided, that when only one registration plate is issued for a motor vehicle other than a truck-tractor, said registration plate shall be attached to the rear of the motor vehicle. The registration plate issued for a truck-tractor shall be attached to the front thereof. Provided further, that when only one registration plate is issued for a motor vehicle and this motor vehicle is transporting a substance that may adhere to the plate so as to cover or discolor the plate or if the motor vehicle has a mechanical loading device that may damage the plate, the registration plate may be attached to the front of the motor vehicle.

Any motor vehicle of the age of 35 years or more from the date of manufacture may bear the license plates of the year of manufacture instead of the current registration plates, if the current registration plates are maintained within the vehicle and produced upon the request of any person.

The Division shall provide registered owners of motorcycles and motorcycle trailers with suitably reduced size registration plates.

(e) Preservation and Cleaning of Registration Plates. - It shall be the duty of each and every registered owner of a motor vehicle to keep the registration plates assigned to such motor vehicle reasonably clean and free from dust and dirt, and such registered owner, or any person in his employ, or who operates such motor vehicle by his authority, shall, upon the request of any proper officer, immediately clean such registration plates so that the numbers thereon may be readily distinguished, and any person who shall neglect or refuse to so clean a registration plate, after having been requested to do so, shall be guilty of a Class 3 misdemeanor.

(f)   Operating with False Numbers. - Any person who shall willfully operate a motor vehicle with a registration plate which has been repainted or altered or forged shall be guilty of a Class 2 misdemeanor.

(g)   Alteration, Disguise, or Concealment of Numbers. - Any operator of a motor vehicle who shall willfully mutilate, bend, twist, cover or cause to be covered or partially covered by any bumper, light, spare tire, tire rack, strap, or other device, or who shall paint, enamel, emboss, stamp, print, perforate, or alter or add to or cut off any part or portion of a registration plate or the figures or letters thereon, or who shall place or deposit or cause to be placed or deposited any oil, grease, or other substance upon such registration plates for the purpose of making dust adhere thereto, or who shall deface, disfigure, change, or attempt to change any letter or figure thereon, or who shall display a number plate in other than a horizontal upright position, shall be guilty of a Class 2 misdemeanor. Any operator of a motor vehicle who shall willfully cover or cause to be covered any part or portion of a registration plate or the figures or letters thereon by any device designed or intended to prevent or interfere with the taking of a clear photograph of a registration plate by a traffic control or toll collection system using cameras commits an infraction and shall be penalized under G.S. 14-3.1. Any operator of a motor vehicle who shall otherwise intentionally cover any number or registration renewal sticker on a registration plate with any material that makes the number or registration renewal sticker illegible commits an infraction and shall be penalized under G.S. 14-3.1. Any operator of a motor vehicle who covers any registration plate with any frame or transparent, clear, or color-tinted cover that makes a number or letter included in the vehicle's registration, the State name on the plate, or a number or month on the registration renewal sticker on the plate illegible commits an infraction and shall be penalized under G.S. 14-3.1.

(h)   Commission Contracts for Issuance of Plates and Certificates. - All registration plates, registration certificates, and certificates of title issued by the Division, outside of those issued from the office of the Division located in Wake, Cumberland, or Mecklenburg Counties and those issued and handled through the United States mail, shall be issued insofar as practicable and possible through commission contracts entered into by the Division for the issuance of the plates and certificates in localities throughout North Carolina, including military installations within this State, with persons, firms, corporations or governmental subdivisions of the State of North Carolina. The Division shall make a reasonable effort in every locality, except as noted above, to enter into a commission contract for the issuance of the plates and certificates and a record of these efforts shall be maintained in the Division. In the event the Division is unsuccessful in making commission contracts, it shall issue the plates and certificates through the regular employees of the Division. Whenever registration plates, registration certificates, and certificates of title are issued by the Division through commission contract arrangements, the Division shall provide proper supervision of the distribution. Nothing contained in this subsection will allow or permit the operation of fewer outlets in any county in this State than are now being operated.

Commission contracts entered into by the Division under this subsection shall provide for the payment of compensation on a per transaction basis. The collection of the highway use tax is considered a separate transaction for which one dollar and twenty-seven cents ($1.27) compensation shall be paid. The issuance of a limited registration "T" sticker and the collection of property tax are each considered a separate transaction for which compensation at the rate of one dollar and twenty-seven cents ($1.27) and seventy-one cents ($0.71), respectively, shall be paid by counties and municipalities as a cost of the combined motor vehicle registration renewal and property tax collection system. The performance at the same time of one or more of the transactions below is considered a single transaction for which one dollar and forty-three cents ($1.43) compensation shall be paid:

(1)   Issuance of a registration plate, a registration card, a registration sticker, or a certificate of title.

(2)   Issuance of a handicapped placard or handicapped identification card.

(3)   Acceptance of an application for a personalized registration plate.

(4)   Acceptance of a surrendered registration plate, registration card, or registration renewal sticker, or acceptance of an affidavit stating why a person cannot surrender a registration plate, registration card, or registration renewal sticker.

(5)   Cancellation of a title because the vehicle has been junked.

(6)   Acceptance of an application for, or issuance of, a refund for a fee or a tax, other than the highway use tax.

(7)   Receipt of the civil penalty imposed by G.S. 20-311 for a lapse in financial responsibility or receipt of the restoration fee imposed by that statute.

(8)   Acceptance of a notice of failure to maintain financial responsibility for a motor vehicle.

(8a)   Collection of civil penalties imposed for violations of G.S. 20-183.8A.

(8b),   (9) Repealed by Session Laws 2013-372, s. 2(a), effective July 1, 2013.

(10)   Acceptance of a temporary lien filing.

(h1)   Commission contracts entered into by the Division under this subsection shall also provide for the payment of an additional one dollar ($1.00) of compensation to commission contract agents for any transaction assessed a fee under subdivision (a)(1), (a)(2), (a)(3), (a)(7), (a)(8), or (a)(9) of G.S. 20-85.

(h2)   Upon the closing of the only contract license plate agency in a county, the Division shall as soon as practicable designate a temporary location for the issuance of all registration plates, registration certificates, and certificates of title issued by the Division for that county. The designation shall be posted at the former agency location for not less than 30 days and shall include the street address and telephone number of the temporary location. A former contract agent shall allow the posting of this required notice at the former location for a period of not less than 30 days. A failure to comply with the posting requirements of this section by a former contract agent shall be a Class 3 misdemeanor.

(i)   Electronic Applications and Collections. - The Division shall accept electronic applications for the issuance of registration plates, registration certificates, and certificates of title, and is authorized to electronically collect fees from online motor vehicle registration vendors under contract with the Division.

(j)   The Division shall contract with at least two online motor vehicle registration vendors which may enter into contracts with motor vehicle dealers to complete and file Division required documents for the issuance of a certificate of title, registration plate, or registration card or a duplicate certificate of title, registration plate, or registration card for a motor vehicle, upon purchase or sale of a vehicle.

(k) Commission contract agents are authorized to enter into contracts with online motor vehicle registration vendors which are under contract with the Division to complete and file Division required documents for the issuance of a certificate of title, registration plate, or registration card or a duplicate certificate of title, registration plate, or registration card for a motor vehicle. (1937, c. 407, s. 27; 1943, c. 726; 1951, c. 102, ss. 1-3; 1955, c. 119, s. 1; 1961, c. 360, s. 4; c. 861, s. 2; 1963, c. 552, s. 6; c. 1071; 1965, c. 1088; 1969, c. 1140; 1971, c. 945; 1973, c. 629; 1975, c. 716, s. 5; 1979, c. 470, s. 1; c. 604, s. 1; c. 917, s. 4; 1981, c. 750; c. 859, s. 76; 1983, c. 253, ss. 1-3; 1985, c. 257; 1991 (Reg. Sess., 1992), c. 1007, s. 32; 1993, c. 539, ss. 333-336; 1994, Ex. Sess., c. 24, s. 14(c); 1997-36, s. 1; 1997-443, s. 32.7(a); 1997-461, s. 1; 1998-160, s. 3; 1998-212, ss. 15.4(a), 27.6(a); 1999-452, ss. 13, 14; 2000-182, s. 3; 2001-424, s. 27.21; 2001-487, s. 50(c); 2002-159, s. 31.1; 2003-424, s. 1; 2004-77, s. 1; 2004-79, s. 1; 2004-131, s. 1; 2004-185, s. 1; 2005-216, s. 1; 2006-209, s. 1; 2006-213, s. 4; 2007-243, s. 1; 2007-400, s. 1; 2007-483, s. 1; 2007-488, ss. 2-5; 2008-225, s. 8; 2009-445, s. 24(b1); 2009-456, s. 1; 2010-96, s. 40(a); 2010-132, ss. 2, 3; 2011-382, s. 4; 2011-392, ss. 1, 1.1; 2012-79, s. 1.12(a); 2013-87, s. 1; 2013-372, s. 2(a); 2013-376, s. 9(a), (b), (d).)

Vision Books Order Form

Fax Orders:	1-980-299-5965
Phone Orders:	1-704-898-0770
E-mail Orders:	www.visionbooks.org
Mail Orders:	Vision Books, LLC P.O. Box 42406 Charlotte, NC 28215

Shipp To:
Name_____
Address_____
City_____State_____Zip_____
Phone_____Fax_____
Email_____@_____

Bill To: We can bill a third party on your behalf.
Name_____
Address_____
City_____State_____Zip_____
Phone___(_____)_____Fax_____
Email_____@_____

Pamphlet Number ($15.00 Each)	Qty	Total Cost
_____	_____	_____
_____	_____	_____
_____	_____	_____
_____	_____	_____
_____	_____	_____
_____	_____	_____
_____	_____	_____
_____	_____	_____
<u>Full Volume Set 1-92</u>	<u>92 Pamphlets</u>	<u>1,380.00</u>

Free Shipping Shipping & Handling on Full Volume Orders
Add $1.00 Shipping & Handling per pamphlet $_____

Total Cost $_____

Thank You for Your Support. Management!

DID YOU ENJOY THIS BOOK?

Vision Books would like to hear from you! If you or someone you know has been falsely imprisoned, we would like to hear your story. If the 'North Carolina Criminal Law and Procedure' has had an effect in your life or if you have suggestions, we would like to hear from you. Send your letters to:

Vision Books, LLC
Attn: Staff Writers
P.O. Box 42406
Charlotte, NC 28215
Email: staff@visionbooks.org

Order Additional Copies:

Fax Orders:	1-980-299-5965
Phone Orders:	1-704-898-0770
E-mail Orders:	www.visionbooks.org
Mail Orders:	Vision Books, LLC P.O. Box 42406 Charlotte, NC 28215

www.ingramcontent.com/pod-product-compliance
Lightning Source LLC
Chambersburg PA
CBHW071401170526
45165CB00001B/140